D0462455

Nature's Operating Instructions

Also in the Bioneers Series

Ecological Medicine: Healing the Earth, Healing Ourselves,
edited by Kenny Ausubel with J. P. Harpignies

Nature's Operating Instructions

The True Biotechnologies

Edited by Kenny Ausubel
with J. P. Harpignies

Foreword by Paul Hawken

Sierra Club Books
San Francisco

MECHANICS' INSTITUTE LIBRARY
57 Post Street
San Francisco, CA 94104
(415) 393-0101

The Sierra Club, founded in 1892 by John Muir, has devoted itself to the study and protection of the earth's scenic and ecological resources—mountains, wetlands, woodlands, wild shores and rivers, deserts and plains. The publishing program of the Sierra Club offers books to the public as a nonprofit educational service in the hope that they may enlarge the public's understanding of the Club's basic concerns. The point of view expressed in each book, however, does not necessarily represent that of the Club. The Sierra Club has some sixty chapters throughout the United States and in Canada. For information about how you may participate in its programs to preserve wilderness and the quality of life, please address inquiries to Sierra Club, 85 Second Street, San Francisco, California 94105, or visit our website at www.sierraclub.org.

Copyright © 2004 Collective Heritage Institute

All rights reserved under International and Pan-American Copyright Conventions. No part of this book may be reproduced in any form or by any electronic or mechanical means, including information storage and retrieval systems, without permission in writing from the publisher.

Wade Davis, "A World Made of Stories: Saving the Web of Cultural Life," is adapted from text copyright © NPR® 2003. Any unauthorized duplication is strictly prohibited.

Published by Sierra Club Books
85 Second Street, San Francisco, CA 94105
www.sierraclub.org/books

Produced and distributed by University of California Press
Berkeley and Los Angeles, California
University of California Press, Ltd.
London, England
www.ucpress.edu

SIERRA CLUB, SIERRA CLUB BOOKS, and the Sierra Club design logos are registered trademarks of the Sierra Club.

Library of Congress Cataloging-in-Publication Data
    Nature's operating instructions : the true biotechnologies / edited by Kenny Ausubel with J. P. Harpignies : foreword by Paul Hawken.
        p.   cm.
    Includes bibliographical references.
    ISBN : 1-57805-099-5 (pbk. : alk. paper)
    1. Applied ecology.   2. Nature conservation.   3. Sustainable development.   4. Human ecology.
    I. Ausubel, Ken.   II. Harpignies, J. P.

QH541.29.N38   2004
333.95—dc22   2004045343

Book and cover design by Lynne O'Neil

Printed in the United States of America on New Leaf Ecobook 50 acid-free paper, which contains a minimum of 50 percent post-consumer waste, processed chlorine free. Of the balance, 25 percent is Forest Stewardship Council certified to contain no old-growth trees and to be pulped totally chlorine free.

07   06   05   04
10   9   8   7   6   5   4   3   2   1

333.95
N285

Contents

Foreword

Paul Hawken

WHEN I WAS A YOUNG ADULT living and studying in Japan, among the marvels that intrigued me about the Buddhist canon were its numerous lists. To me, a lapsed Catholic, they seemed more complicated than catechism: the eightfold path, the five *skandhas* (elements that sum up an individual's existence), and the six realms of reincarnation, to name but a few. One of the six realms is called the hungry ghost. It is depicted as a wretched figure with a huge protruding stomach, a pencil neck, and a tiny mouth, forever grasping for food, power, sex, or stimulation to feed an endless and insatiable appetite. It is, needless to say, one of the three hell realms.

The image of the hungry ghost is a useful metaphor today, for it has countless analogues in contemporary society: the compulsive shopper, the addict, the speculator, CEOs doing the perp walk, the global corporation privatizing the commons or commodifying life, the multinational enterprise doing everything it can to amass more capital, sales, and profits. We even have a science of voraciousness: economics. If you attend a university to get an economics degree, you must pay homage to the belief that consumption must grow for people to live well. In fact, constant growth is the conventional definition of a healthy economy. Economists like Herman Daly and Robert Costanza, who entertain the idea of steady-state consumption and production, are marginalized and ignored by most of their peers. The effects of ravenous desires are omnipresent. They are studied by police, psychiatrists, physicians, sociologists, environmentalists, and biologists, but not by economists.

The March 9, 2000, issue of *Nature* included an article about extinction, recovery, and biodiversity saying that it takes the earth ten million years to recover from a mass extinction of species, which is far longer than previously thought. The article cited a study by James Kirchner at the University of California at Berkeley and Anne Weil at Duke University predicting that up to half of all species could vanish over the next fifty to one hundred years and that human beings would be extinct long before any of the species returned.

Sustainability is about the relationship between the two most complex systems on earth—human social systems and living systems. In this book, people argue eloquently against corporate control of our living systems and for the adoption of a new ethos. We are losing our living systems either by overt destruction or, even more insidiously, by genetic pollution. The living systems that are being corporatized include our forests, oceans, coral reefs, and wetlands; they include our food, our seeds, our genome, the water, grasslands, and oceans. The interrelationship between human and living systems determines every person's existence and underlies the rise and fall of every civilization. While the word "sustainability" is relatively new, every culture has confronted this relationship for better or ill. Historically, no civilization has reversed its tracks with respect to the environment; rather, civilizations have declined and disappeared because they forfeited their own habitats. For the first time in history, meaningful numbers of people are trying to arrest this slide and understand how to live on earth. This is a watershed in human existence.

Sven Lindqvist, the author of A History of Bombing, wrote, "You already know enough. So do I. It is not knowledge we lack. What is missing is the courage to understand what we know and to draw conclusions." What is present in this volume is the courage to understand and draw conclusions. It is not hyperbole to say that the world is turning inside out, shedding its life, and dying. A once-familiar world is transforming into the unwanted and unimagined. As I write, European glaciers are melting like ice cream cones, London bakes like a pizza on 101-degree summer days, and thousands of people die in heat waves in France. Disturbing new forms of life are being created by corporations and released into the environment. Human clones are rumored. Food has been reduced to molecular nutrients and patented. Water rights are bought and sold like oil reserves. We go to war on the basis of a wink, a nod, and a smirk. All of these events, political and environmental, are the result of consuming life instead of considering it. In each instance, large corporations benefit hugely from the loss of ecological stability and living systems.

In this volume, an entirely new set of voices is heard speaking about a biological know-how that defies the conventional idea of what technology is. If industrial biotechnology is "graffiti in the book of life," these are the beginnings of illuminated manuscripts, biological strategies that carefully attend to the complexity of life. The inventors are pioneers like John Todd, Dan Dagget, and Paul Stamets. The sages include Janine Benyus, David Suzuki, and Dave Foreman. The beneficiaries are all the people on earth.

Martha Graham, the great dancer and choreographer, once described the creative process as "a queer, divine dissatisfaction, a blessed unrest that keeps us marching and makes us more alive." The authors herein are blessedly restless. This is a reader on social disturbance ecology. These are human edge species lodged between the end of industrialism/capitalism and the beginning of a regenerative era. We are talking about the future of life. These are some of the spores. Culture them well.

Sausalito, California
September 2003

I dedicate this book to ancestors, generations to come, and the three dearest women in my life:

My mother, Anne Ausubel, who enchanted me with her passion for story and language, and who with my father, Herman, had the great good sense to give my brother Jesse and me our glorious freedom for three months each joyous summer in the wilds of Cape Cod, where I merged irrevocably with the magic and mystery of nature.

My beloved wife and soulmate, Nina Simons, who is a gift beyond words and whose leadership in Bioneers since its inception has enriched the work and the experience with a spirit of celebration, fertility, and adventure.

My darling daughter, Mona, who melts my heart like a marshmallow over a bonfire; whose kindness, courage, and humor light my life; and whose dazzlingly original voice is a treasure now being written into the endless story.

Kenny Ausubel

Acknowledgments

FIRST AND FOREMOST, the Bioneers organization and I express our bottomless gratitude to the contributors to this book, who have so generously permitted us to feature their work here. They are some of the true heroes of our age. We thank them also for their thoughtful review and fruitful revision of the material.

I offer my profound thanks to Paul Hawken, who, with matchless vision and boundless energy, has forged the path to restoration for so many of us. It was Paul who first identified restoration as the grail, and he has fixed his keen eye unblinkingly on the horizon of positive possibility even in the darkest hours of environmental destruction. His dazzling originality and true-hearted inspiration have informed this movement, as well as the Bioneers Conference itself and me personally, at every turn. I am also deeply grateful to Paul for so generously contributing the foreword to this book.

I must honor two of the visionary elders and pathfinders of biomimicry who helped create and define the field itself. John Todd was a central inspiration to me in founding the Bioneers Conference. His revelatory work and generous spirit continue to guide me and countless others. And Janine Benyus, who gave this field a name, has brought her pure, compassionate heart and exceptional eloquence to cultivating the fertility of intellectual edge habitats. She has brought this work into the world with the loving and skillful hands of a true master.

The Bioneers organization and I are deeply grateful to Danny Moses, editor-in-chief of Sierra Club Books, who shared the vision of this book series and whose sure hand guided it to its full potential. Special thanks also to Helen Sweetland, publisher at Sierra Club Books, and editor Diana Landau, who seamlessly carried this book across the finish line. Diana's superlative eye vastly improved the book, while Jan Spauschus attended to the details of copy editing and helped make it sing.

The book could not have happened without the outstanding contributions of several of my Bioneers colleagues:

The incomparable J. P. Harpignies, my longtime collaborator and a central force in the Bioneers Conference since its inception, brought to a complex editing process his customary good humor, sage counsel, and humbling efficiency. To the introductions describing each contributor he added his sophisticated insight and singular capacity for cogently framing issues.

Celeste DiFelici, my personal assistant, has been an indefatigable associate. Her positive attitude consistently uplifted both the book and the process. Amy Theobald, publications manager for Bioneers, coordinated the final editing with acute intelligence, buoyant patience, and good humor.

Nina Simons, executive director of Bioneers (and my beloved wife), has been an indispensable partner in producing the conference since the beginning. She has helped envision and grow the organization and carry the vision with unwavering clarity and joy. She has also supported this book series and my intermittent writer's lifestyle with grace and love.

Bioneers managing director Ginny McGinn supported the project with a strong infrastructure and kept it on track from start to finish with good cheer and unflappable poise. Her deft management of the complexities of the conference and the Bioneers organization is truly breathtaking.

Kelli Webster, imperturbable Bioneers coordinator, and Celeste DiFelici navigated a seemingly endless blizzard of transcriptions. Cristina Mormorunni pulled together the resources section with intelligence and care.

To the Bioneers staff at large, I offer my genuine appreciation and thanks for their enthusiastic and professional ongoing work of producing the annual Bioneers Conference—which is, after all, the primary source for this book.

And last, many thanks to all the unsung heroes of restoration, who are doing this work on the ground every day and helping the earth heal.

Introduction

Kenny Ausubel

SPEAKING AT A BIONEERS conference, Paul Hawken reframed the defining image from the movie *Close Encounters of the Third Kind.* As you may recall, while the horizon fills with a flotilla of space ships, earthbound scientists feverishly fumble to make contact with the extraterrestrials. Awestruck, they send out a sequence of musical tones to try to establish communication. Meanwhile, unseen behind them rises the mother ship, dwarfing everything else, blotting out the entire horizon. The mother ship is the biology of our planet. The mother ship is Mother Earth. And, Paul said, it is bigger than anything we can imagine.

That's about the size of it. For all the chatter about the Age of Information, what we are really entering is the Age of Biology, and it is bigger than anything we can imagine.

It's worth remembering that until the 1960s, universities had no biology departments, only botany and zoology. This gaping omission reflects just how limited our perspective on the natural world has been. It also betrays our deep human cultural bias toward charismatic species such as plants and animals. Multicellular organisms like us are one very late-blooming tip on a single branch of the tree of life. It's a tree we know little about. Scientific estimates of life's diversity, including bacteria, lurch from 1.4 million to 200 million species. We don't know the number even to within an order of magnitude. If we had humility, we'd have everything.

We didn't invent nature. Nature invented us. Nature bats last, as the saying goes, but even more important, it's her playing field. We would be wise to learn the ground rules and how to play by them. That's in great part what this book is about.

When I founded the annual Bioneers Conference, from whose presentations this volume is largely drawn, in 1990, the impulse to do so originated from my exposure to the work of certain biological pioneers who were trying to find nature's own operating instructions. Their quest has been to glean what we might learn from four billion years of evolution and apply it in practical ways.

What bioneers are doing is mimicking nature in order to heal nature and serve human ends harmlessly—clearly, a case of imitation as the sincerest form of flattery. In many cases the knowledge they are employing is prefigured by ancient indigenous science from the First Peoples, the world's original bioneers. In contrast with corporate industrial "biotechnology," these ecologically based solutions are the true biotechnologies.

The great ecological play takes place in a food web that makes no waste, powered by a solar economy that neither mines the past nor mortgages the future. Some of the lead roles are played by diversity, kinship, symbiosis, reciprocity and community. It's all alive. It's all intelligent. It's all connected. It's all relatives.

One of the beauties of biology is that its facts become our metaphors. These underlying codes can serve as inspiring parables for how, as human beings, we might organize a more just, humane, and authentically sustainable society.

If there is a single story woven within the many stories in this book, it's the grand tale of interdependence. Life is intimately interconnected, and as a culture we've made a basic systems error in believing that we exist somehow separate from nature or from one another. That illusion could prove fatal at this momentous cusp, when our turbocharged technologies and overwhelming numbers have given us, for the first time in history, the capacity to blow it on a global scale.

The three central technologies of the twentieth century are proving disastrous. First, petrochemicals may well be the "greatest unintended weapons of mass destruction," as journalist and author Ross Gelbspan terms them in

his book *The Heat Is On*. Fossil fuel metabolism is a direct cause of global warming, whose potential is in itself sufficiently cataclysmic to topple human civilization as we know it and extinguish countless other life forms along the way.
The 80,000 or so toxic chemicals we've manufactured from hydrocarbons now
suffuse the most intimate tissues of our land, air, water, and bodies, precipi-
tating an emerging public health crisis of unprecedented proportions.

Second, nuclear energy has both concentrated and spread radioactivity
and virtually indestructible toxic waste into living systems worldwide. It's a
kind of technological terrorism that will haunt life on earth for tens of thousands of years to come.

Third, so-called genetic engineering is introducing an entirely new kind
of environmental threat: biological pollution. Now that the gene genie is out
of the bottle, it literally has a life of its own. The sorcerer's apprentice is self-
replicating. This approach to biotechnology is equivalent to splitting the atom
at the molecular level and is antithetical to the workings of biology described
by the bioneers. As Amory Lovins has pointed out, the very term "genetic
engineering" is a misnomer. Engineering presupposes an understanding of
causal mechanisms that yield precise, controllable, predictable results. In contrast, this genetic roulette is producing unintended, inherently uncontrollable,
menacing outcomes. It is fundamentally flawed, a simplified machine model
superimposed on the innate complexity and permeability of living systems.
It's more a product of market science than biological science, a genetic code
written in dollar signs. It is graffiti in the book of life.

Everywhere we turn today, we bear witness to the failure and harms of
the misconceived industrial paradigm we've come to rely on. Centralized com-
mand-and-control grids, top-down toxic high technologies, and globalized
monocultures characterize a dysfunctional civilization intrinsically at odds
with the decentralized intelligence of living systems.

As historian J. R. MacNeill has pointed out, the best survival strategy for
long-term biological success is to be very adaptable, pursue diverse sources
of subsistence, and optimize resilience. Our ways of living are suited only to
our current circumstances, which include a temperate climate, cheap fossil fuel,
and abundant fresh water. We have restricted our adaptability to such a de-

gree that we have created the very instability our brittle infrastructures cannot absorb.

. The good news is that for the most part, solutions exist. Brilliant innovators have tapped into models encoded in the ancient evolutionary intelligence
of the natural world. Biomimicry expert Janine Benyus observes with elegant
simplicity that life creates conditions conducive to life. That mission is perhaps the most essential work of the bioneers. They are illuminating a future
environment of hope by "wedding human ingenuity to the wisdom of the
wild," as John Todd puts it. Human beings are a keystone species essential to
the landscape, and we can make enormously positive contributions to ecological well-being.

Global society is beginning to reverse direction into an age of restoration.
Though this movement is relatively small today, it's growing by leaps and
bounds. It's a matter of when, not if, it will take hold and spread widely. But
we do not know how much time we have.

In 2002, a paradigm shift exploded a core tenet of conventional scientific
thinking. The assumption had been that ecosystems respond slowly and
steadily to degradation, that we will see the line coming before we cross it. A
new study concluded that humanity's assault on the environment has left many
ecosystems in such a fragile state that the slightest disturbance may push them,
without warning, into catastrophic collapse. Although they may appear viable, there comes a tipping point once their resilience has been sufficiently un-
dermined. Such changes may be irreversible, at least in a human time frame.

We simply do not know how close we are to the tipping point. Precau-
tion is the byword; we must move from managing harm to preventing it. The
precautionary principle being adopted around the world as a lens for evalu-
ating scientific, industrial, and commercial choices echoes Grandma's time-
tested maxims: "Better safe than sorry," "An ounce of prevention is worth a
pound of cure," "Look before you leap." Call it the "duh" principle.

As the pathfinding work of the bioneers represented in these pages consistently illustrates, we have a pretty good idea how to lighten our footfall by
90 percent or more. In economic terms, the enterprise of restoration promises
an unparalleled boom and vast global jobs creation, starting with a Marshall

Plan for clean energy. Sector by sector, from energy to agriculture to transportation, industrial production to land management, the true biotechnologies described in this book show how nature has already orchestrated a symphony of intelligent design that we can emulate and customize for human purposes.

The challenge we face is not ultimately a technical one. The real pivot will be the story we tell ourselves, the narrative by which we make sense of the world and that guides our lives. We need a new creation story.

Over a century ago, industrial robber barons hijacked Darwin's story of the evolutionary tree of life. They distorted Darwin's theory of natural selection into a parable of "survival of the fittest." They lionized "nature red in tooth and claw" and a violent, amoral struggle for existence where might makes right and the ruthless pursuit of self-interest automatically results in the greatest good for the whole. Though they were true believers, their social Darwinism was expedient political cover with which to justify economic monopoly and endemic social injustice. It was also bad science.

What Darwin was actually saying was that the fittest are those best adapted to existing conditions at a particular historical moment in a specific environmental context. (He was primarily addressing the relationship between food supply and population size.) Soon other biologists joined the fray, identifying group cohesion and solidarity to be equally crucial to survival. In other words, mutual aid is also the law of the jungle.

But the robber barons' compelling narrative and bottomless financing took science and society on a perilous detour. Their institutional support channeled scientific research into a reductionist machine model that has led to misbegotten mechanistic approaches to the life sciences, including single-action pharmaceutical drugs, toxic pesticides, and genetic modification. Mainstream science exalted the "selfish gene" and banished the study of relationships, ecosystems, and interdependence. Biologists proposing that any organism could live in partnership with others were relentlessly ridiculed. When the Swiss botanist Simon Schwendener correctly asserted that lichen were not a single organism but a symbiotic association of fungi and algae, he was viciously condemned. After the young biologist Beatrix Potter showed her meticulously detailed illustrations of symbiosis in nature at London's revered

Linnaean Society in 1896, the scientific establishment suppressed her conclusions entirely. Her biological insights would be vindicated by later generations of natural historians, but Potter was so repelled by what she described as the "grown-up world" of science that she abandoned biology and turned instead to writing *The Tale of Peter Rabbit* and her other famous children's books.

It took the contemporary genius of microbiologist Lynn Margulis to get symbiosis unstuck. She found what is very likely proof in DNA of an ancient evolutionary innovation between warring kinds of bacteria. After neither side could completely devour the other, they surrendered to the urge to merge, and multicellular life as we know it was born of cooperation.

Margulis calls earth a "symbiotic planet," one deeply informed by reciprocity and synergy. Hers is a radically different vision of ecology, as the art of interdependent relationships that navigate by the evolutionary North Star of symbiosis. Today, an ecological Darwinism is ascendant that tells that saga of symbiotic alliances in a far greater context of fitness: the survival of the whole. And the survival of the whole earth is staked on that evolution in our understanding.

The word "ecology" derives from the Greek word meaning "household." It's time to come home. We can then take our place, not as masters, servants, or even stewards, but as citizens in the democracy of all life. The new century invites a Declaration of Interdependence.

This transformation also demands a change of heart flowing from an empathic connection to the living earth. It's about a reverence for the sacredness of all life and its wondrous web. There are many deep wounds to heal, not least those of the human spirit. The bioneers' revolution from the heart of nature resonates in the human heart and will heal it. Life is endlessly dynamic, messy, and unpredictable. It develops on the fertile edge of creative chaos, which periodically shuffles the deck, introducing drastic changes. The behavior of complex living systems cannot be foreseen from a knowledge of its parts. The whole is always greater than the sum of the parts.

It's the innate wildness of life that stirs the chaotic cauldron of evolution. The complexity is beyond our comprehension. There's a quality to wildness

that some call unknowable and others call sacred. Whatever your perspective—
science or spirit—self-willed nature takes the same freedom she gives us: a
place to tell her own creation story.

This book is organized into five parts. Part I opens a window onto biomimicry
and the myriad imaginative technological applications drawn from nature that
have shown the capacity to decontaminate our polluted world. Part II looks
directly at the ways of the land and how people are using those to help the
land heal itself. Part III provides a cautionary glimpse into the basic conceptual flaws embedded in the design of current so-called biotechnologies and illustrates some of the consequent threats to the environment.

   Part IV applies nature's operating instructions to industry's central production processes and touches on some of the thorny political and economic
factors blocking their wider acceptance. (This section does not substantially
address energy, for reasons of space and because the topic is widely covered
in other sources.) Part V searches the human heart and spirit to invoke our
unique cultural facility to create an earth-honoring civilization. These many
realms comprise a journey through the multidimensional world of the bioneers.
They show that in great measure we know what to do to solve our environmental crises, and certainly that we know in which direction real and lasting
planetary restoration lies. As I hope this book poignantly shows, the largest
roadblocks facing us are not technological but political and economic.

   A few years ago, at a Bioneers Conference, I quoted a Paul Simon song
about these being "the days of miracle and wonder." John Mohawk sat me down
afterward, looked me deep in the eye, and in his jolly, Buddha-like fashion said
something like this: A miracle by definition is something that's impossible, that
contradicts natural law. If something happens, then it's not impossible, and
therefore it's not a miracle. Call it supernatural, but it's still natural. Maybe it's
magic, because that's what we call things we don't understand.

   I've come to see the work of the bioneers as magical realism. Again and
again we are finding that solutions residing in nature surpass our conception
of what's even possible. As we cross the transformational threshold into the
art and science of restoration, there's great hope in how little we know and in

the little we do know. Over and over, it's also the story of how great a difference just one person can make.

At this cathartic threshold in human and planetary evolution, the new
creation story is a cocreation story. Nature invented us, and the bioneers are
generously gifting us with a glimmer of how we might redeem that promise.
Beckoning us on is the reenchantment of the earth.

Santa Fe, New Mexico
September 2003

Part I

Biomimicry: Working with Nature to Heal Nature

Biomimicry:
What Would Nature Do Here?

Janine Benyus

If nonhuman nature could speak with a human voice, she'd sound a lot like Janine Benyus. Of course, human beings are a part of nature, not apart from it, and that has long been Janine's most essential message. Her work as an ardent naturalist eventually led her to get under nature's skin sufficiently to ask what is perhaps the most basic question people need to address to live sustainably on the land: What would nature do here? That deceptively simple query resulted in her momentous exploration of an emerging revolutionary approach to science and design chronicled in her landmark book, Biomimicry: Innovation Inspired by Nature.

Janine is an educator and life sciences writer who has degrees in forestry, natural resource management, and English literature. She combines a deep appreciation of science with an abiding love of the natural world. And she is no armchair naturalist: she has written three great regional field guides and a sly animal behavior guide, Beastly Behaviors. *She's been a backpacking guide and is active in protecting wildlands in her home state of Montana.*

Janine's love and respect for the "more than human" world vibrates through her words, conveying the magic, wonder, and humility she experiences through her work. An educator at heart, she believes that the better we understand the genius of nature, the more we will be moved to protect it. When she began to explore biomimicry— by interviewing biologists, engineers, designers, and inventors who study nature's own adaptations—she embarked on a quest to learn how we could design sustainable human technologies by adapting the genius of 3.8 billion years of evolutionary intelligence.

Janine's favorite role these days is as a "biologist at the design table." She serves on the Eco Dream Team at Interface, Inc., a biomimicking carpet company, and con-

ducts seminars for a wide range of people and institutions seeking more graceful ways to live on earth. She collaborated on a two-hour film on biomimicry that aired on the public television series The Nature of Things with David Suzuki. *Her advice to designers and engineers is to imitate life itself, because what life does is create conditions conducive to life, and that's a pretty lucid mission statement.*

IT HAS BEEN A WONDERFUL FALL in the Rockies, with cottonwoods and aspens more brilliant than I've seen them in years. When you duck into the groves, the air itself is golden. Quaking aspen has a great name: *Populus tremuloides.* It describes on the tongue what the aspen does, which is to tremble in the slightest breeze, with a sound like bones rattling.

My Native American friends say the trembling started because the Great Spirit asked all organisms to bow their heads in humility, and the aspen refused. "From now on," said the Great Spirit to the aspen, "you will quake whenever the wind blows."

My scientist friends have another explanation. The stalk of the aspen leaf is flat, so that when the wind hits it, the leaf tilts, spilling the wind like a sail. It doesn't build a rigid structure. It yields to the wind, and this yielding allows it to live on absurdly steep slopes where winds would pick other broad-leaved trees clean.

Both stories are about humility and adaptation, about yielding when it's good to yield.

There's something else going on in the Rockies these days, and it's similar to what happens here each year in October at the Bioneers Conference. It's called interspecies flocking. It's fall, and a tough winter is coming. Everybody needs to put on a nice layer of fat, so birds that normally would not associate with one another—different species, such as chickadees and warblers and woodpeckers—flock together and fly in ensemble through the canyons.

They lay down their arms and hook up in their diversity, in their difference. They hook up because they know that the berries are scattered and together they can spread out and find more than one bird could alone. If you think of berries as ideas, that's what we're like. Different people get together and say, "I've found an idea over here that may lead to sustainability," and we all go over to that idea. Then somebody else says, "Here's another idea," and we all go over to that idea. We're a mixed-species flock and winter is coming. One of the ideas in that mosaic is *biomimicry.*

Biomimicry is innovation inspired by nature, looking to nature as a teacher. One language caveat: Inherent in the phrase "looking to nature" is the lonely idea that we are not nature—that we're peering in from the outside. But that's not what I believe. I see us as biological organisms, and that means we *are* nature. There's no separation. So forgive the awkward rhetoric, but when I say "nature," I'm referring to what writer David Abrams calls "more-than-human" nature—our biological elders who have been here much longer than we have. Compared to them, we just arrived and have everything to learn about how to live gracefully on this planet. If the age of the earth were a calendar year beginning on January 1, and today were a breath before midnight on December 31, it would mean that *Homo sapiens sapiens* got here fifteen minutes ago and all of recorded history blinked by in the last sixty seconds. It's an eyelash on that timeline.

Bacteria bootstrapped themselves up out of the chaos in March of that theoretical year, and in the 3.8 billion years since, life has learned to do some amazing things—to fly, circumnavigate the globe, live at the top of mountains and the bottom of the ocean, lasso solar energy, light up the night, and make miracle materials like skin, horns, hair, and brains. In fact, organisms have done everything we humans want to do but without guzzling fossil fuels, polluting the planet, or mortgaging their future. So yes, we are part of nature, but we're a very young species still trying to get it right. When I look at technology these days, I don't say "yes" or "no." I ask how well adapted a particular technology is. How well adapted is that product, that process, that policy to life on earth over the long haul? That's the key question. Ninety-nine percent of species that have been on earth are now extinct because their products or their processes were not well adapted.

Together, life's adaptations spell out a pattern language for survival. Think of the wood frog that can freeze solid in winter and hop away unharmed in the spring. Or the much maligned garden snail that builds its own highway of slime, a lubricant that absorbs 1,500 times its weight in water almost instantly, allowing the snail to climb up and over a thorny branch without hurting itself. Banana slugs can do the same thing. We humans don't have anything close to that in terms of an effective lubricant. Rhino horn surprises us by healing when cracked, even though the horn has no living cells in it. We don't know how it manages to do that, but what a great model for self-healing materials that wouldn't have to be thrown away.

Up on the northern California coast is the western hemlock, a denizen of our northwestern rain forests, each tree with sixty million needles that tilt like Venetian blinds to catch the sun and then comb moisture out of the fog, so that 30 percent more moisture lands on the ground around a western hemlock than anywhere else in the forest. The breathing pores of those needles are deeply embedded, tucked away in the wax, so the wind can't wick their water vapor away.

Now why is it that a tree that receives up to a hundred inches of rainfall a year has all those adaptations for drought? It's because there are two glorious rain-free months in summer, and that's a long, dry time if you're a tree. So well-adapted species have done the obvious—they've acknowledged the limits and evolved adaptations for drought, even though they're in a rain forest.

Another of my favorite examples is the hummingbird, an organism about the size of my thumb. It flies up to 35 miles an hour (faster than you can get around most cities in a cab) and migrates about 2,000 miles a year. Those journeying down the eastern flyway reach the lip of the Gulf of Mexico and then pause for a while, fueling up on 1,000 blossoms a day. Finally, they burst across 600 miles of open water without stopping, on a whopping 2.1 grams of fuel. And that's not jet fuel: it's nectar.

But here's what amazes me even more. In the process of fueling up, the hummingbird manages to pollinate its energy source, ensuring that there will be nectar next year—for itself, for its offspring, or for completely unrelated species of nectar feeders. Imagine doing that at your gas station. And of course, when it dies, its body decays and nurtures the roots not only of flowers, but of mushrooms, grasses, trees, and shrubs. There's nothing special about it; no government regulations are behind it, it's simply part of the system that keeps us all alive. In the process of meeting their needs, organisms manage to fertilize the soil, clean the air, clean the water, and mix the right cocktail of atmospheric gases that life needs to live.

What life in ensemble has learned to do is to *create conditions conducive to life*. And that's what we have to learn. Luckily, we don't need to make it up. We need only step outside and ask the local geniuses that surround us. The key question for a biomimic is "What would nature do here?" And that's a rare question, even for ecological designers. We tend to puzzle instead over how to tweak our conventional solutions. For instance, when we want to clean a surface, we get hung up on questions such as "What's the least toxic detergent to use?" or "How can I reduce the energy involved in sandblasting?" A more helpful question might be "How does nature stay clean?" Other organisms don't use detergent or sandblasters at all, and yet many of them depend on staying clean for their survival.

A leaf, for instance, has to stay dirt-free so it can breathe and gather sunlight. Botanists in Germany looked to the lotus, a symbol of purity in Asia because it rises from muddy swamps yet remains dry and pristine. Under a microscope, they saw that instead of being smooth, for easy cleaning, the leaf surface is incredibly mountainous. Dirt particles teeter on the peaks instead of adhering strongly, and raindrops ball up instead of spreading out. As the drops roll, they lift the loose dirt particles, like a snowball lifting leaves from your lawn. And it's not just lotus; many leaves are like this, it turns out. The question then becomes not which detergent to use but how to keep things from getting dirty in the first place. A German company called ispo makes a building façade paint called Lotusan based on the lotus effect. The dried paint has the structure of the lotus leaf, and rainwater cleans the building. The deep design principle is that life surfs for free. Plants use the kinetic or motion energy in falling rain to keep themselves clean. Simple. Wondrous.

And how does nature power itself? Obviously, not the way we do. Of course we all rely on photosynthesis, on sunlight captured by plants. But in our case, it's ancient sunlight trapped 65 million years ago by plants that we now dig up and ignite in a huge bonfire. We burn 100,000 years of ancient plant growth every year. That's not a normal decay pattern. It's like taking all the furniture in your house, piling it up, closing your windows, and lighting a match. We're fueling our bonfire with ancient sunlight. What we need to do is learn how to tap into the current sunlight streaming down all day long. So at last we're turning to the masters of sunlight capture—green plants—and asking them, "How are you powering yourself?"

A leaf has tens of thousands of tiny photosynthetic reaction centers. They're like molecular-scale solar batteries operating at 93 percent quantum efficiency, which means that for every hundred particles of light that strike the leaf, ninety-three are turned into sugars. That's stellar in terms of effectiveness. The best part is that these solar cells are manufactured silently, in water, and without toxins. So plant biologists and engineers are finally looking to leaves to help them make a smaller, better solar cell.

One of the many gifts of biomimicry is that you enter into deep conversation with organisms, and this student-elder dialogue absolutely fills you with awe. Seeing nature as model, measure, and mentor changes the very way you view and value the natural world. Instead of seeing nature as warehouse, you begin to see her as teacher. Instead of valuing what you can extract from her, you value what you can learn from her. And this changes everything. As Land Institute founder Wes Jackson says, "When we begin to see nature as mentor, gratitude tempers greed and the notion of resources becomes obscene." My fondest hope is that this gratitude will blossom into an ardent desire to protect the wellsprings of locally evolved wisdom. When we finally realize that unencumbered evolution is more precious than any vein of oil, the rationale for protecting wild places will become self-evident.

A lot of the research in biomimicry is years and years from fruition, but it is a path, an approach. It requires us to visit wild places and keep asking, How does nature teach? How does nature learn? How does nature heal? How does nature communicate? Quieting human cleverness is the first step in biomimicry. Next comes listening, then trying to echo what we hear. This emulating is hard and humbling work. When what we learn improves how we live, we grow grateful, and that leads to the last step in the path: stewardship and caretaking, a practical thanksgiving for what we've learned.

The practice of biomimicry requires community, not just with other organisms, but with people in other disciplines. We need to bring together fields of study that have been kept separate. As it stands now, we educate biologists to learn how life lives, how life has managed to find out what works and what lasts here on the earth. We educate a different set of people to find out how we should feed ourselves, power ourselves, make our materials, and run our businesses. I'll call these people the engineers, for want of a better word: people who design human systems. So we have the biologists and the engineers, and, very sadly, few people get to work in the fertile crescent between those two intellectual habitats. Yet the rest of nature revels in these in-between places. In fact, abrupt boundaries are rare in nature, and some of the most fertile habitats are commingled edges—like estuaries, where freshwater and salt water come together. I've been on a quest to find people who are living in that fertile commingling place, the estuary between biology and human systems design.

I've long had fantasies of gathering experts from many fields who rarely interact to see what they could learn from one another. An agricultural engineer might put forth the first problem: "With our industrial agriculture, we grow annuals in a monoculture, but we have to dig up the soils each year. When we do that they lose fertility and bleed off into the rivers, so we have to feed them with nitrogen fertilizers, a petroleum product. And because we have one species for miles, it's sort of an all-you-can-eat restaurant for pests, so we have to use pesticides (also a petroleum product), and it's gotten to the point where we're using ten kilocalories of oil to grow one kilocalorie of food on our industrial farms." A prairie ecologist might chime in, "Let me tell you how the prairie did it in the Midwest. The original pre-Columbian prairie was composed of 99.9 percent perennial plants, hundreds of species in four categories: cool-season grasses, warm-season grasses, legumes, and composites. They held the soil, so not only didn't it bleed away, it was actually enriched over the years, and because the prairie was a mixture of species, it resisted pest attacks." And the agricultural engineer might then think, "Wouldn't it be wild if we could redesign our agriculture in the prairie's image in this part of the world, and then look at other parts of the world and see what grows there naturally and follow that wisdom?"

In another scenario a materials scientist might complain, "We make ma-

terials the 'heat, beat, and treat' way. For instance, we take petroleum products, heat them at high temperatures, subject them to high pressures, and then
treat them in chemical baths—a very toxic and expensive way to do things.
It's also excessive: after using a plastic fork for fifteen minutes, we toss it in a
landfill, where it endures for thousands of years." An arachnologist might offer
some help: "A spider makes silk (they make six kinds, and I'm talking about
drag-line silk that frames the web) that is five times stronger, ounce for ounce,
than steel. It's resilient and tough—a true miracle fiber. Even more incredible,
a spider uses flies and crickets as raw material and creates the fiber at body temperature (a life-friendly temperature), because the manufacturing plant is the
spider's body. Furthermore, the fiber is biodegradable so the spider can eat the
web to make more web." This gets the materials engineer thinking: "We make
Kevlar, our strongest material, by taking petroleum, boiling it in sulfuric acid
at 1,400 degrees Fahrenheit, and drawing it out under enormous pressure, and
when we're done, we have flak jackets that will repel bullets and microbes for
thousands of years. What if we could emulate spiders and figure out how to
take carbon-based, abundant raw materials and allow them to self-assemble in
a silent manufacturing process that operates in water at room temperature and
produces a biodegradable fiber?"

In another of my fantasy meetings of the minds, an engineer from the energy industry could sit down with a plant biologist and admit, "We've been
burning a finite fossil resource, and we know we can't go on." His compan-
ion replies, "Every fern frond, grass blade, and leaf out there right now is producing energy more effectively than we do, with benign solar collectors, and
we're beginning to understand how the process works. Within each leaf, a
wishbone-shaped reaction center absorbs the sun's energy, sending a negative
charge to one side of a membrane and a positive charge to the other side; it's
essentially a tiny battery. Wouldn't it be great if we could mimic that molecular battery to split water and make storable hydrogen?"

A pharmaceutical researcher knows that plants are chock-full of medically
important compounds and worries that by conservative estimates, four species
go extinct with each passing hour. She wonders if there's a more sensible way
to screen plants for potentially useful medicines or foods. A primate re-

searcher might tell her about animals that are thought to self-medicate in sophisticated ways. For instance, chimpanzees with intestinal problems will leave
the troop and travel to find a particular plant, swallow a few choice leaves,
and recover within twenty-four hours. It turns out that animals are selecting
plants to treat illness, influence their own fertility, and even prevent illnesses.
Plants chemists find secondary compounds in these plants that have antibacterial and antiparasitic qualities, and some even show activity against human
cancer tumors. So what if we actually followed animals and took notes about
what they have found to be useful in the pharmacies of the jungle?

Well, here's the surprise. The hypothetical cross-disciplinary encounters
I just described have already occurred, and more are happening every day in
field after field. Cell biologists, for example, now realize that every cell in our
body is, in a sense, a sophisticated computer, responding appropriately to
signals and information from enzymes, antibodies, antigens, and so on, that
attract or repel one another, that scan one another and then hook together and
self-assemble. Computer scientists are starting to take note of this, and it may
lead to a whole new paradigm for computing, because what our computers
can't do very well right now is pattern recognition, and what three-dimensional
molecules do so well is pattern recognition, adapting, and learning.

On the broader, macroeconomic level, some leading-edge planners, indus-
trialists, and entrepreneurs, concerned about the prodigious waste generated
by our economy, are starting to look at ecosystems where densely interconnected species fill every niche you can possibly imagine and eat every crumb
before it even falls off the table. They are trying to envision how we could
shift our economy from a linear, throughput kind of model to a closed-loop,
diverse, highly interconnected system in which only solar energy is coming
in, all the "nutrients" are juggled forever in a loop, and very little waste results.
The discipline has a name that I hope will someday not be such an oxymoron:
industrial ecology.

It's important news that this type of work is actually happening, that some
bench scientists are starting to move into that estuary between biology and engineering. I've traveled and gone to their labs and spent time with them. They're
trying to pulp wood like a fungus, adhere like a gecko, create color like a pea-

cock, grow ceramics like an abalone, cool a building like a termite, make green plastics like a bacterium, and wick water from air like a desert beetle. It's very exciting to see the fruits of these cross-pollinations.

It's also gratifying to see metaphors from biology flowing in the direction of human technology, instead of the other way around. For too long we've been trying to understand our bodies and our world as if they were machines and studying them in a reductionist way, as if the parts could tell us everything about the whole. Several centuries later, we're discovering that cogs and gears aren't adequate to explain the real world. Lo and behold, industrial PCBs somehow wound up in the Antarctic because it's not Newton's mechanical machine world—it's a web. In order to deal with that kind of complexity, we need to start paying attention to how organisms live in context. We need to throw a party where people who are asking, "How does life operate in a way that enhances place?" can get together with people who are asking, "How shall we live?"

In writing books about adaptive organisms, I often ask myself what adaptive traits humans have. One thing that seems to make us different from other creatures, as far as we know, is our ability to act collectively—as a whole species—on our understanding. We can decide as a culture to listen to life, to echo what we hear, to not be a cancer on the earth. Having this will and the inventive brain to back it up, we can make the conscious choice to follow nature's lead in living our lives. The good news is that we have plenty of help. We're surrounded by geniuses. They are everywhere with us, breathing the same air, drinking the same water, moving on limbs built from blood and bone. Learning from them will take some stillness on our part, so we can hear their symphony of good sense. What biomimicry offers us, in learning *from* nature instead of just *about* nature, is the opportunity to feel a part of, rather than apart from, this genius that surrounds us.

I do want to sound a note of caution. Biomimicry can't just be about clever design. We are extremely aware now that we are a single species on a single planet, watershed earth. The earth is abundant and resilient, but she is not endlessly abundant nor endlessly resilient. Our most important work right now is to figure out how to share our global commons equitably, and how to treat it with infinite justice and care. We must learn to lighten our footfall. We in the United States take up about thirty acres of bioproductive land and sea per capita right now, and there are only five acres per person available globally. Our ecological footprint is a clown's shoe compared to that of the rest of humankind. I believe that by consciously emulating life's genius, we can start to reduce that footprint and live in better-adapted ways.

So mimicking natural form is only the first part of becoming better adapted. We can mimic the self-opening and -closing hooks on an owl feather, say, to get a backpack that opens anywhere without the need for a metal zipper. But if we make that backpack out of petroleum-based nylon, and we make it in a sweatshop, and we put it on a cross-continental truck spewing diesel fumes, what's the point? Mimicking natural form is a start, but really learning from nature means remembering that the feather is part of an owl that self-assembles on that owl through nature's chemistry. A deeper mimicry has to do with mimicking not just form, but also nature's processes and ecosystem strategies.

That owl is fit *because* it fits its context. It's part of the forest, which is part of a watershed, which is part of a biome, and it follows rules that are consistent at each level of that nested system. Until we create products that, in their manufacturing, use, disposal, and marketing, are part of an economy that mimics a living system rather than a machine, we haven't reached the full extent of biomimicry.

I'm going to end with a biomimicry story, an episode that brought some of my most exciting fantasies of cross-disciplinary explorations to life. After attending a workshop I gave at the 2000 Bioneers Conference, a woman named Mary Hansel, who works for a conventional wastewater treatment and water purification firm, proposed that we take the company's lead engineers to the Galapagos Islands to see if biomimicry could stimulate them to think in new ways. A boat trip to Darwin's islands was a dream come true for me as a biologist—they were at the top of my life list of places to go. And the Galapagos *are* extraordinary. This series of islands came up out of the sea 600 miles west of Ecuador as completely uninhabited lava cones, until critters started to raft in on the twelve ocean currents that converge there. Critters who showed up exhausted on the shore woke up the next morning to a whole new world.

The landmass was smaller than many of these animals were used to, there was different food, if food at all, and most important, there were many different critters there that they weren't used to. But eventually, over a long period of evolution, they knitted together a society. They tuned themselves to place and placed themselves in community. And most amazingly, they built soil, cleaned the water, filtered the air, and sweetened the Galapagos; they created conditions conducive to life, as life does.

When we got there on the boat, I asked the engineers, "Why don't you tell me what it is that's keeping you from purifying water in a sustainable way, and then we'll go snorkeling to find organisms that are solving those same problems." Initially, I got blank stares and an arms-folded-across-the-chest kind of resistance. The first day was a cacophony of whirring cameras, because they were attempting to take nature's face home; nature was scenery. But then there was a shift, and after that we could hardly get them to come back to the boat. They stayed underwater for hours and crawled through the mud on their hands and knees, cameras forgotten. They kept calling me over, marveling at how creatures were doing what they, the engineers, had been trying to do for years.

Here we were, surrounded by filter-feeding organisms with membrane gills, barnacles and mussels secreting underwater glues, and mangroves desalinating water with the sun as their only energy source. Every fish that swam by had the kind of streamlined fluid dynamics they dream of in pipe design. We looked at leaves that were cleaning themselves with microscopic bumps the way the lotus does, and the engineers thought about how that would improve the inside of pipes, where sewage buildups now require flushing with toxins.

Another problem these engineers deal with is scaling, the buildup of minerals like calcium carbonate, which they remove with harsh chemicals. To find a better way, we went walking on a beach with thousands of calcium-carbonate shells. I described the intricate shell-making process: "Organisms release proteins into seawater. These proteins self-assemble into scaffolds that attract floating minerals, which land in particular spots on the scaffold and crystallize into shells." Then they asked the obvious question: "But why aren't shells huge—

why don't they just keep mineralizing?" You could have heard a pin drop. I told them that shelled organisms know how to release "stop proteins" that adhere to the surfaces of the growing crystal and stop the growth. They actually stop the scaling without toxic chemicals. Now that got their attention.

Suddenly they realized that these organisms were no different than they are—engineers trying to solve problems in ways that are life-friendly. The only difference is that these organisms have had about 400 million years of R & D. Could a mimicked version of such stop proteins be used to end calcium accumulation in pipes without toxic chemicals or excessive energy use? they wondered. That's when I told them about the shell biologist and the engineer who have already created a bio-inspired product that will do what they hoped.

This was a whole new way for them to think about living things. For once, they weren't thinking about how they could use the organisms—they wouldn't be farming bacteria, or harvesting the barnacles for their glues, or planting the mangroves to filter water. Instead they would be borrowing the barnacle's recipe and trying to mimic the mangrove's root membrane design to make a solar desalination device. The change came when they realized that their design challenges—things like better filters, membranes, sealants, and adhesives—had already been solved, in ingenious ways, by other life forms. In a few short days, their stance toward nature changed from that of voyeuristic conqueror to that of admiring, respectful student.

Once they got the hang of it, they were positively exuberant and at the same time increasingly respectful of the organisms around them. The change of heart that I saw take place on that boat is what's really important about this work, even more important than the eco-friendly technologies that might come from it.

When they went home, the engineers starting hiring biologists to join their design teams. We are seeing this more and more—companies and local governments inviting biologists to the design table when creating buildings, transportation systems, products, manufacturing processes, and so on. If you are involved in any kind of design, whether of a product, a process, or a policy, go to your university or your natural history museum and ask for a biologist, someone who has broad knowledge of the natural world, amoeba through zebra. (If you think this whole discussion is simply an advertisement for the importance of fusty, old-fashioned natural historians and zoologists— you're right. Folks with this breadth of knowledge are usually driving taxis nowadays and would love to come to the design table and talk about the smartest problem-solvers they know, which are plants and animals, fungi and microbes.)

One project we've been working on is creating a huge web-based database of nature's solutions that will be catalogued by engineering and design search terms, so that people can type in questions such as "How does nature thermoregulate?" or "How does nature package?" and find thousands of biological research papers, pictures, and experts. We want to put this out in the public domain, so that nature's ideas are never patented. We also hope to create university courses in which people can study biology functionally. Right now, many engineering, architecture, and design students take no biology classes, so this would be a welcome change.

Of course, don't forget that the wellspring of good ideas is readily available to all of us. We're all designers and we all have an innate knowledge of the biological world. So when you are designing something and you want to ask, "How would nature do this?" go right ahead: Turn the doorknob, step outside, and enjoy the quaking golden light of the aspen grove.

After all, it's not a new gadget that's going to make us more sustainable as a culture; it's a change of heart and a new set of eyes, a new way of viewing and valuing the world in which we are embedded and on which we depend. We're a young species, but we're very adaptable, and we're uncanny mimics. With the help of our ten to thirty million planet-mates, I believe we can learn to do what other organisms have done, which is to make of this place an Eden, a home that is ours but not ours alone.

Living Technologies:
Wedding Human Ingenuity
to the Wisdom of the Wild

John Todd

John Todd is a bard of biology, one of the truly visionary architects of the ecological design revolution and an elder in the burgeoning field of biomimicry. His work reveals that we can create benign technologies that imitate and adapt nature's evolutionary wisdom and enlist its extraordinary regenerative capacities to restore the world's waters. He has shown how we can redesign our production practices to eliminate waste and pollution, and in turn stop wasting the environment.

John studied agriculture, and parasitology, and tropical medicine before getting a doctorate in fisheries and spending several years at the famed Woods Hole Oceanographic Institute. He then started to invent new fields because none of the existing ones could contain his brilliance. Around 1971, John, his wife, Nancy Jack Todd, and their compatriot Bill McLarney founded the New Alchemy Institute to explore a "new alchemy of earth stewardship." It was the perilous state of the world's waters that spoke to John most poignantly. His early work building solar greenhouses for fish farming serendipitously led him to observe a basic bioneer principle: waste equals food. In nature the concept of waste simply doesn't exist.

When young friends began dying prematurely from cancer near his home on Cape Cod, John suspected that the culprit was careless dumping of sewage and other so-called wastes in pits just twenty-five feet above the shallow water table. This personal loss set him on a journey of discovery to design solar-driven, simulated ecosystems for treating waste and restoring the world's waters to health. Ultimately he was able to build systems that are cost-effective and treat an impressive range of wastes, from sewage to industrial poisons.

17

John has coauthored several seminal classics on ecological design, including The Village as Solar Economy, Tomorrow Is Our Permanent Address, *and* From Eco-Cities to Living Machines. *Nancy Jack Todd is his coauthor and unfailing partner in his projects and edits the* Annals of Earth *journal of their nonprofit organization,* Ocean Arks International. *Their latest effort is the formation of a global* Water Stewards Network.

John is currently a research professor and distinguished lecturer at the University of Vermont, where he continues to dream the future. He is systematically designing and implementing, in locations from Lake Champlain to China, model systems of living technologies that will serve as lighthouses for the ecological design revolution that is destined to transform all aspects of the human enterprise over the coming decades.

WE ARE DISCOVERING principles of ecological design in the language of nature—guidelines that will allow us to change how we live and help us create a technological and social framework that supports humanity while healing the earth. By learning this language and applying ecological knowledge of the natural world to the restoration of the planet's ills, we will cultivate a new generation of earth stewards.

In my work I seek to link a variety of natural ecological subsystems, with the help of hundreds or even thousands of species of organisms, to create a new kind of meta-intelligence out of living systems. I call these human-directed linkages eco-machines, and they have the potential to carry out work previously considered difficult or even impossible. Eco-machines can be used to generate fuels, grow foods, transform wastes into clean and usable products, regulate climate in buildings, and even restore degraded environments. The work involves bringing together different ecologies and designing them using human ecological engineering.

To get our instructions for this design revolution, we need to turn to the three-and-a-half-billion-year experiment called life. For years I have explored many of the planet's great ecological realms: coral reefs, coastal marine environments, lakes, rain forests, northern forests, and even deserts. Each of these places has had a tale to tell. Among my favorites are the eelgrass communities found in shallow waters along the edge of the sea. Dominated by dense stands of eelgrass hosting exquisitely complex biotic communities that purify water and create sediments that build food chains, they are one of the ocean's finest and most productive nurseries. To study an eelgrass community along the East Coast of the United States is to observe ecological design at its finest.

As much as I love the coastal communities, practicing ecological engineering successfully requires a working knowledge of a wide variety of ecosystems. From the study of lakes one learns about nutrients, energy flows, chemistry, and the dynamics of liquids. From the rain forest one can learn about diversity, the portioning of light, and the way many different life forms can efficiently share a complex, quickly changing environment. There is nowhere better than the tropical rain forest to study nature's pathways of decay and transformation. From the northern forests I have gathered an appreciation of the exquisite relationship of geology and bedrock to soils, and the ways in which higher plants negotiate these interactions. Two entirely different ecologies and their radical variations may exist within a short distance of each other because of subtle differences in the minerals of the soil. In deserts, which are environments of extremes, ecological processes are easier to read because plants and animals are more spread out. Various forms of life are starkly etched on the landscape, and sometimes this starkness clearly reveals patterns and illuminates the mechanisms of ecological organization.

The more I learned of various ecosystems, the more I perceived their ability to self-design, self-organize, self-repair, and self-replicate. If you were to take a chainsaw and cut down a patch of trees in the woods, for example, then come in with a bulldozer and push the woody debris aside, years later you would begin to see weedy plants appear, then shrubs, and eventually trees. You would see a phenomenal organizing ability on that piece of land. You can observe this succession in quick time if you fill a big glass jar with water, mud, and life forms from a local pond or lake. Within a matter of days you will observe nature rapidly organizing itself out of chaos inside the bottle exposed to sunlight. This is ecological design.

Coral reefs, for example, are ecosystems living under bright sunlight, swept by a sea almost devoid of nutrients. For all intents and purposes, this is an impoverished environment, yet it contains so much richness and diversity. The delicate creatures that reside on the reef have the extraordinary ability to withstand pounding waves and violent storms, even hurricanes. When you look carefully at them, you begin to see how the architectures of the coral break up the brute force of the waves. Or you observe the way plants and animals are so coordinated that they exchange minuscule amounts of nutrients in a sort of cosmic dance. You begin to understand that these systems, powered mainly by the sun, are self-designed with exquisite simplicity, elegance, and diversity.

Studying these processes, I began to realize the forces behind them could be harnessed technologically. Human beings, I suspected, might be able to use the same forces to carry out the work needed for us to live, and more important, to live without destroying ecosystems and the environment. It is now possible to envision symbiotic technologies between humans and the natural world in which the boundaries barely show—like the intricate, invisible symbiosis of plants and animals in a coral reef.

Eco-machines are in many ways like ordinary machines. Like all machines, they are intended to do work. But the difference between the eco-machine and the inert machine is that the living one is made up of hundreds, occasionally thousands, of species of life forms ranging from microorganisms to mollusks and fish to higher plants, including trees. All these species work together symphonically as part of a dynamic integrated system. As a consequence, eco-machines have attributes most machines do not. They have limits, but like natural ecosystems they also have the ability to self-design, self-organize, and self-repair. If the human guide is clever enough, they can even self-replicate. A living technology can, in theory, last for hundreds, possibly thousands, of years. It can behave like a forest.

I have found that in order for a living eco-machine to do what you ask of it, it must be made up of at least three different types of interacting ecosystem. In other words, if we base a living technology solely on a pond, it won't work. If we base it just on a marsh, it won't work for long. If we base it on a stream, it won't work either. However, if we combine the pond, the marsh, and the stream in one integrated system, it will work. When the three ecological types are brought together, they acquire a phenomenal degree of organizational intelligence.

My first foray into ecological design for the treatment of wastes was in a community not far from where I'm based on Cape Cod, Massachusetts. Around this community were septic lagoons into which were pumped wastes from the septic tanks of households and small businesses, including restaurants. When I investigated the lagoons, I discovered that they contained most of the priority toxic pollutants on the Environmental Protection Agency's hit list. And because they were just unlined excavations in the sand, the wastes quickly leached into the water table below—the town's source of drinking water. My response to this horror was to design and build an eco-machine at the site of the lagoons. I placed twenty clear-sided solar tanks on the side of a hill, connecting them to create a "river" into which the septic waste was pumped. Between tanks ten and eleven, mimicking its approximate stage in the process nature uses, I designed a marsh-based raceway. Then into the tanks went hundreds of different forms of aquatic life gathered from half a dozen local aquatic environments, including nearby salt marshes. My hope was that the life forms would organize themselves in the solar "river" and transform wastes into pure water.

After a journey through the system that took twelve days, the water was indeed transformed, and 100 percent of the priority pollutants had been removed. Only one toxin, toluene, was left, in trace amounts (it was 99.99 percent gone). The heavy metals in the wastewater were sequestered by the algae in the first few tanks, where the process began. (Theoretically, the metals could have been recycled.) Human pathogens, as measured by fecal coliform bacteria, had numbered in the tens of millions in the first tank; by the end of the process they were almost gone and the water met federal swimming water standards. Sunlight and a diversity of organisms, which had never occurred in these combinations or communities before, coevolved with the waste to provide a solution.

An elected official from Chattanooga, Tennessee, heard about that project and invited me to look at the notorious Chattanooga Creek, which flows for five and a half miles through the center of the city. So polluted was the stream by the industrial production of pesticides, creosote, and other toxic coal tar—based hydrocarbon materials that it was mostly devoid of life, the bottom sediments thick with poisons. Many people in the predominantly African American neighborhoods along the creek were sick, children with leukemia and adults with cancer. They had been told there was no solution short of dredging the whole creek at prohibitive cost.

On my first visit, when I put my arm in the creek, it quickly turned bright red from the toxic chemicals in the creek. I took a sample of sediments back to my laboratory and designed a small eco-machine to see if these compounds— known as polynuclear aromatic hydrocarbons, or PAHs (they included pesticides such as the banned DDT and aldrin)—could be destroyed. Most of the animals in the eco-machine, including the fish, died upon exposure to minute amounts of the material, but the snails, aquatic plants, and microbes survived. The snails became my indicator organisms, determining the rate at which I introduced the toxic sediments into the eco-machine. As long as the snails laid eggs, I would continue to introduce toxic water and sediments, and when they stopped, I would stop. When the snails began to lay again, I would add more material. After sixty-seven days the majority of the compounds, including the DDT and aldrin, had been converted to less harmful compounds by this wonderful little process. It was a remarkable example of the power of a living ecology to help heal even the most damaged places.

I went on to design a full-scale eco-machine that I hoped would clean about a half mile of creek a year, at a cost I estimated at the time to be about $15 million. Unfortunately, the EPA was not sufficiently impressed by the work. My plans were shelved and replaced with a much more expensive conventional dredge-and-incinerate-the-waste solution.

This bureaucratic mentality highlights why it's important that we redefine the meaning of waste and waste treatment. Our current approach is wrong in that it uses too much energy and too many dubious additives and generates little or no secondary economic activity. In sewage treatment, for example, the waste-conversion industry uses potentially harmful chemicals such as polymers (some of which are still not regulated) to alter wastewater so that it meets discharge standards. Further, the waste is often incompletely treated, and many dubious compounds, including endocrine-disrupting chemicals harmful to wildlife and humans, are discharged into streams, lakes, and estuaries.

From an engineering point of view, modern sewage treatment is expensive and fairly sophisticated. It is also symptomatic of a disconnected culture. Why not instead view wastes as resources out of place? Why couldn't they be used to enhance our environments and even become economic engines? The models I've demonstrated indicate that one day the waste treatment plants of the world could become economic assets rather than burdens to communities.

Since my first trials and demonstration projects in the 1980s and early 1990s, we've created a great variety of ecological technologies that exemplify this principle of transforming wastes into resources—in all sizes and in many places. One of them is along the shores of Lake Champlain in South Burlington, Vermont. There, with EPA support, we built a greenhouse structure that contains an unusual and magnificent garden. Inside the 7,800-square-foot structure are eighteen tanks, each fifteen feet wide and fifteen feet deep, sunk into the ground so that only the top five feet of tank show. The tanks are connected to make two parallel "rivers" in the greenhouse. Using two systems provides redundancy, so that if one "river" is damaged by a toxin, organisms and water from the other can bring it quickly back to life. In addition, using two parallel systems allows a researcher to hold one line steady while varying elements in the other to learn new management techniques or identify underlying ecological mechanisms.

Visually, what dominates the scene are the flowers and trees being grown in the tanks on special racks on the surface of the water, many rising up to the greenhouse roof. We have studied several hundred plant species for their ability to help purify water, and this garden within the greenhouse is actually a sewage treatment plant. It employs ecological strategies to transform raw sewage from the city of South Burlington into clean water, a process that takes less than two and a half days. The tanks that make up the treatment trains are filled with plant roots, microbial communities, and diverse animal life that includes snails, freshwater clams, and fish. But the plants are the primary workhorses. Some help grow and feed bacteria with compounds secreted into the water by their roots. Others, such as the bulrush, are known to break down carcinogens and other hazardous chemicals. Still others sequester heavy metals. It's this symphonic action of many life forms that allows the rapid transformation of sewage into clean water.

Part of the ecological designer's journey is to look for allies in nature, to find those creatures that can be of maximum use for specific functions. The plants we use in most of our eco-machines are usually native to the site or at the very least well established in the area. But in the far northern climate of Vermont, where most natives are dormant for a large part of the year, we also use tropical plants that continue to hang on to their leaves and grow in winter. Tiny snails help keep these systems clean, eating accumulated sludge on the walls of the tanks and the roots of the plants. Fish downstream in the system eat the dead and dying bacteria to help reduce the volume of sludge produced. (Sludge accumulation, to an ecological designer, is a symptom of incomplete design.)

Fish in the system also can play a secondary economic role. Japanese koi and baitfish, which grow by eating detritus and sludge, can be sold as ornamental pond fish or as bait for fishermen. The plants can serve an economic function as well. They spend their first year or so growing on special racks in the water, after which many species are removed, separated, potted, and sold in the horticultural market. In the early parts of their lives, our plants purify water. Later, as houseplants, many of these same species purify air. This is the beginning of a new economic paradigm, the conversion of waste into wealth via ecological pathways. The koi, for example, grow to a much larger fish in a period of eight or nine months and go from being worth less than $1 to being worth close to $10. There's a new economy evolving here, one made possible by building viable economic elements into the restoration process.

Similar ideas and models can be employed in very difficult environments. At Ethel M Chocolates, a company based on the outskirts of Las Vegas, an eco-machine is used to treat high-strength organic wastes from chocolate manufacturing. It's difficult to treat such wastes because they contain fats, oils, and greases that most organisms (except, apparently, human beings) have a hard time digesting. We designed the Ethel M eco-machine to be absolutely odorfree, to recycle the treated water, and to be built within an existing desert botanical garden. It's now one of the most visited non-gambling sites in Nevada. As you walk through the garden, below it you see interconnected tanks in parallel rows inside a sunken structure. You can observe the dark chocolaty water becoming gradually cleaner as it passes from tank to tank, through differing ecologies. The containment structure has a sliding roof that is closed at night to keep daily warmth from being lost to the clear desert sky, particularly in the winter. What emerges from the eco-machine is clear, clean water, pumped to a nearby pond and reused for nonpotable purposes, including maintaining the desert garden.

Natural systems can also be used to repair damaged and polluted aquatic environments. More than a decade ago we started a project to clean up a badly polluted thirteen-acre pond on Cape Cod that was being assaulted with thirty million gallons a year of toxic leachate from a landfill on its northern shoreline. When we started work, the pond was "comatose," or close to it. There was no oxygen near the bottom, and some zones were devoid of bottom-dwelling animals. We started the restoration process using windmills that floated on the surface of the water, turning an underwater rotor that brought oxygen-deprived water from the bottom to the surface and exposed it to light and oxygen. The pond as patient soon began to "resuscitate," but the windmills alone could not help it cope with the huge incoming pollution load. So we designed a new living technology, also floating on the water, that we called the Restorer.

A combination of marshes, mangroves, and ponds inspired the Restorer's design; a windmill and a bank of photovoltaic panels fulfilled its electrical requirements. It was capable of pumping up to 100,000 gallons of pond water a day through its nine physically distinct cells. Cells one through three—the "marsh" component—were filled with host media, including a mixture of pumice rock and clamshells that harbored freshwater clams, algae, bottom-dwelling organisms, and aquatic plants. Cells four and five—the "pond"—transitioned to higher plants and their roots but remained hydraulically isolated from the real pond, to allow a longer period of contact between the plant roots and the dirty water flowing through the Restorer. In cells six through nine, shrubs, flowers, and trees grew on racks on the water's surface, in direct contact with the pond. In this "mangrove" component, the plant roots dangled down into the pond and cleaned the water, and the root zones became favorite haunts of native pond fish.

Within months the pond began to improve. Oxygen became present all the way down to the sediments. Within two years, the volume of sediments on the bottom was reduced by two feet and the biological diversity of bottom-dwellers increased severalfold. Fish began to reappear in significant numbers and after several years, analysis found them free of contamination. Organic toxic compounds, though still prevalent in the landfill leachate, disappeared from the water. Gone too were earlier signs of human sewage contamination. Despite the fact that the pond still was receiving the leachate from the landfill, the Restorer continued to do its job for a decade. The town reopened the pond to fishing, boating, and swimming, and the Restorer became a model for eco-machine designs that treat wastes and polluted waters around the world.

One of our biggest Restorer projects took place in Berlin, Maryland, on a watershed that drains into Chesapeake Bay. This Restorer is situated on a large lagoon into which 1.3 million gallons of high-strength waste flow each day from a poultry processing plant that handles a million chickens a week. The Restorer is built of rafts and underwater baffles that create a serpentine flow through the lagoon. It was designed to reduce the chicken processing plant's energy requirement by over 70 percent and to reduce sludge volumes dramatically. It has done both. The company has been in compliance with its discharge standards.

In 2002 we got a chance to start a canal restoration project in Fuzhou, in southern China, a city of over a million people known for its approximately eighty kilometers of canals. Unfortunately, untreated sewage flows directly into the canals. In places the stench is unbearable, and the surface water is a mess of floating debris and sewage. We built a prototype Restorer right on the Baima canal. Just under a kilometer in length, it features a floating walkway down the center, flanked by rows of higher plants growing in floating racks on the water surface. Underneath are an artificial support medium and an air diffusion system comparable to those in the Maryland Restorer. When it became operational in 2002, the stench disappeared, the water cleared, and we were able to introduce Chinese carp into the canal. Flowers bloom on the canal as far as the eye can see, and residents said they have seen butterflies and birds that had been missing from the area for decades.

Ecological design can be integrated with architecture and inform it. One such example is the Lewis Center for Environmental Studies at Oberlin College in Ohio. It's the brainchild of David Orr, a formidable thinker and the father of ecological literacy in North American education. David's goal was to create a building that would both embody an ecological sensibility and evolve into a carbon-neutral building that does not need petrochemical fuel. He wanted the rhetoric of his teaching of ecological stewardship to match the reality of the physical educational environment; he wanted to walk his talk. The building had to be made of materials that did not produce toxic pollution during manufacture and could one day be recycled into new buildings. He wanted a building that would connect to the grid but produce its own power from solar cells. The longer-term goal was to have the building produce more power than it uses.

Hydrologic cycles were also important in the design, which is where my team came in. Our plan called for treating the building's sewage in an eco-machine and recycling the water after ultraviolet sterilization (to kill viruses). It was equally important to connect the interior system to rainfall collection and stormwater management, and to an outside pond/wetlands complex that was the brainchild of the landscape designer John Lyle. The building has other links with the land around it: an orchard and food garden shelter the building on the north and west, and to the northeast is a small example of restored prairie lowland. It in turn is linked to wetlands and pond communities on the southeast. The building, designed by green architect William McDonough, was completed in 2000, and in the intervening years its performance has continued to improve to the point where it may be the most energy-efficient institutional structure in the country. The Lewis Center has become a living symbol for ecological design as well as an inspiration to the Oberlin campus and campuses throughout the country. Inspired by the center, my own school, the University of Vermont, has begun the process of retrofitting an existing natural resources building.

A recent project—growing foods in urban and rural areas through integrated ecological design—involves making still more new connections. This project has given a second life to the South Burlington eco-machine; after the EPA-sponsored sewage treatment demonstration ended in the winter of 2000, we began to plan a new future for it. About a thousand yards from the facility stood the Magic Hat Brewery, whose waste products included high-strength liquids and spent grains. Why not adapt South Burlington, after the system had time to decontaminate itself, to serve as an agricultural waste-to-food facility? Our objective was to develop integrated food production systems that derive their initial input from brewery wastes. Using them, we would create ecological food webs that we hoped would demonstrate the potential of integrating different kinds of processes and provide an economic model for local food production. We were already proficient in raising warm-water fish and in the aquaponic culture of food plants linked to fish culture. But other parts of the plan, like growing mushrooms, were totally new to us. We were evolving a new concept: organic wastes could be ecologically magnified and transformed into distinct and valuable products.

Waste in the form of spent grains from the brewery was the starting point for the design, which aimed to transform this material through the activities of vastly different kinds of organisms. We began by blending the spent grains with straw and pasteurizing the material in a hot water bath. Inoculating the material with oyster mushroom spawn, *Pleurotus ostreatus*, initiated the first biological process. We then packed the material in clear plastic bags with holes punched in them and placed them in special chambers in the greenhouse where light, humidity, and temperature could be controlled.

The mushroom mycelia, fine white hair-like structures, began to grow throughout the bags and break down and transform the waste material. The by-products included essential amino acids like lysine. After the mycelia had fully colonized the bags, fruiting bodies, or mushrooms, started to develop and grow out of the holes. Every ten pounds of dry straw and brewery waste yielded about six pounds of fresh mushrooms as tasty as any I have experienced, and they are commercially valuable. (Paul Stamets, the leading American authority on mushroom cultivation, has written that oyster mushrooms not only are nutritious but contain compounds that help reduce blood pressure, stress, and cholesterol, as well as fight cancer and viruses.)

The oyster mushrooms were the first product of the waste transformation. The second was the mycelia-filled material that produced them, which can be used in a number of pathways and processes. It's a nutritious animal feed, which the team successfully fed to beef cattle. It also can be used to break down various environmental pollutants.

By this point we had developed three products from the brewery wastes and straw. Next we put a very different kind of organism to work on the material. After harvesting the last crop of mushrooms we deposited the contents of the plastic bags into large boxes. Earthworms were introduced to transform the mushroom waste into yet another valuable medium: in several weeks the worms converted the material in the greenhouse bins into dark, rich compost, from which we obtained three more products. The first was the worms themselves, which we used for protein in the diet of the tilapia and yellow perch we were raising (although the worms themselves have a high resale value). The second product was horticultural; we put the worm compost, ideally suited to raising plants, in shallow growing benches, and during the winter, when local farm lettuce was not available, we grew lettuce and mesclun crops, creating high demand and good prices for our salad greens. The third product was the compost itself, which we bagged and sold as a soil amendment.

The final agricultural food web we developed at South Burlington was based on combining aquaculture and aquaponics. We raised fish and also grew plant crops in the recycled water, which was loaded with nutrients and wastes from the fish. We focused on warm-water species of tilapia, which are fast-growing, easy to breed, resistant to diseases, and capable of feeding low on the food chain. We designed an aquaculture facility for tilapia that includes the internal production of foods like algae, zooplankton, and small aquatic plants that comprise over 50 percent of the fish diets. By virtue of integrating internal purification with the food webs that fed the fish, our aquaculture facility was remarkably efficient, needing less than one pound dry weight of external feeds, including earthworms, to produce one pound of fish. The tilapia and tilapia burgers were a big hit locally, and we also experimented with yellow perch culture with modest success.

The water in the recirculating aquaculture/aquaponics facility was puri-fied with ecological processes that included filtration by the roots of plants. When we grew tomatoes, we found that not only did the roots remove par-ticulate matter from the water, but the plants were also fertilized by fish-waste nutrients.

The major handicap to our aquaculture and aquaponic culture lay in the amount of heating, aeration, and water-circulating energy required to grow foods in our systems in a northern climate. In spite of this challenge, by the end of 2002 we had successfully demonstrated on a pilot scale in the South Burlington greenhouse the value of our waste-to-product strategy and the po-tential for integrating the functions among the components of a food-producing system.

At this point we moved from the South Burlington facility to a project on the other side of town, where an eco-park based on agriculture is being de-veloped on the Intervale, a seven-hundred-acre floodplain along the banks of the Winooski River. The project will help us tackle the energy issues head-on and test our food-growing systems on a commercial scale.

The site on the Burlington side of the river is an agricultural incubator managed by the Intervale Foundation. The eco-industrial park is being de-veloped by the foundation in cooperation with the City of Burlington and Burlington Electric Utility. Its focus is to produce foods and food products, with the goal of providing an infrastructure for year-round food production. The plan is to use waste heat from a nearby generating station to provide in-expensive heating for the core structure, a greenhouse and building complex. As the park develops, there will be access to heating and adequate space to demonstrate our techniques, designs, and processes on a commercial scale.

The path I have traveled has led me to conclude that humanity can reduce its negative footprint on the planet by 90 percent. I also believe it's possible to create a culture where vibrant wilderness permeates nearly every locale, even urban settings. It would be an extraordinary world if we could give the

90 percent of it that we've damaged back to the wild. To release this wildness should be the challenge and the opportunity of the twenty-first century. I don't know if we can rapidly overcome the inertia of the dominant culture, but, at the very least, we must hope to be like the small mammals of the late dinosaur age, scurrying around the doomed behemoths and creating a new world without their even noticing.

Ultimately, of course, behind the technologies and the economies, we need to forge a culture of stewardship where the highest calling is restoring the lands, protecting the seas, and informing the earth's stewards. Perhaps no one got it better than J. R. R. Tolkien when he said, speaking through the wizard Gandalf, "The rule of no realm is mine. But all worthy things that are in peril as the world now stands, those are my care. And for my part, I shall not wholly fail in my task if anything that passes through this night can still grow fairer or bear fruit and flower again in days to come. For I too am a steward. Did you not know?"

Magic Mushrooms:
Planetary Healing with Deep Biology

Paul Stamets

Paul Stamets, mycologist extraordinaire, may at last have answered the ancient philosophical question, "If a tree falls in the forest and no one is there to hear it, does it make a sound?" Paul knows that the fungi are there to hear it, and they communicate news of this new food source almost instantaneously for miles around. He believes that the mycelial web infiltrating all the world's landmasses is central to our survival as a species, and no one has done more to bring the wondrous capacity of this vast fungal network to our attention.

Paul has extensively explored the remarkable nutritional, medicinal, and psychedelic value of mushrooms. His recent experiments on the potential of certain mushroom species to clean up even lethal toxins in the environment represent some of the most brilliant and hopeful work to be found in any field. In this case, the solution may literally be under our feet.

Paul is a kind of bio-ambassador on behalf of the fungal realm. He is a dedicated teacher and has authored five books, including the classics The Mushroom Cultivator *and* Growing Gourmet and Medicinal Mushrooms. *His company, Fungi Perfecti, is the top educational and technological resource for cultivators of medicinal and gourmet mushrooms. A dedicated hiker, he is a staunch defender of old-growth forests and their biodiversity and has discovered several new mushroom species. He also has a powerful social vision that honors indigenous knowledge and opposes biopiracy, and he is preparing to bring his work to some communities in the Amazon via a new research initiative,* The Rainforest Mushroom Genome Project. *He works closely on all these projects with his partner and wife, Dusty Yao.*

Paul personifies a practical visionary who has looked to the natural world for joy, inspiration, sustenance, healing, revelation, and guidance. His transformational

*explorations of new "myco-technologies" offer some of the most promising strategies
for healing damaged ecologies.*

IT IS MY CONTENTION that mushrooms and fungi are far more crucial
to the planet's ecological health than we previously thought. We know that
many mushrooms have powerful healing capabilities for humans, but what
I've learned is that these organisms also appear to serve as primary healing
agents for land and ecosystems. My study of fungi and mushrooms has led
me to demonstrate powerful new ways of rehabilitating degraded and polluted
landscapes and enhancing soil fertility.

In some ways, we know less about the fungal domain today than our distant ancestors did. Ten thousand years ago we were all forest people, and there
are many indications that our practical knowledge of mushrooms was far
greater then. For example, the famous prehistoric iceman whose frozen remains
were discovered high in the Alps on the border of Italy and Austria in 1991
had three wood conk mushrooms tethered to his right side. He probably used
them for multiple purposes.

The mushrooms he prized sufficiently to carry with him on a long solo
journey included a fragment of a birch polypore, which has very strong antibiotic properties. It's likely that he was using it to treat an infection or stomach disorder. He also carried some *Fomes fomentarius*, which can be hollowed
out and used to carry fire because it burns only very slowly. This function
would have been a matter of life and death in that era, allowing people and
nomadic groups to travel without losing their ability to make fire. We've recently discovered that *Fomes fomentarius* seems to be effective against *E. coli*
0157, a potentially deadly bacterium often found in spoiled food. Although
we've rediscovered this fact only in the past several years, it seems proba-
ble that the iceman's culture knew about *Fomes fomentarius*'s antibacterial
properties 5,300 years ago. That's speculation, but we do know that the
Greek physician and herbalist Dioscorides described a related species, *Fomitopsis officinalis*, in his *Materia medica* in 65 AD as a treatment for the disease
we now call tuberculosis. On the opposite side of the world, the Haida people

of the Northwest also considered this particular mushroom supremely important.

Sadly, the species is now on the brink of extinction in Europe. Many fungal species around the world today are under threat. To help ensure *Fomitopsis*'s survival, my partner, Dusty Yao, and I have gathered strains of *Fomitopsis officinalis* from specimens found deep in the forest in Washington State.

Mushrooms are widely represented in ancient art and sculpture throughout the world, and many species are still highly sought after as foods and medicines in a wide range of cultures. Our own culture in the United States may be the world's least mycophilic (mushroom friendly). Fortunately, however, we have become an increasingly multiethnic society; African, Asian, South American, and Eastern and Western European immigrants, all much more mycophilic than Anglo-Americans, have brought their mushroom knowledge with them, to the great benefit of us all.

To understand the wondrous properties of many mushroom species, it's helpful to know some of the basics of how they grow. When we see a mushroom, we are seeing just the tip of the iceberg, so to speak. That mushroom is merely the fruiting body of a much more extensive organism, the mycelium, growing in the ground. Overlapping mosaics of mycelial mats actually permeate all the landmasses on the planet in the first two to four inches of soil. Such a mycelium may reside in the ground for years, and may, after many years, produce mushrooms.

The mushroom's emergence above ground is a major event in the life cycle of the mycelium, which otherwise grows invisibly in the soil. As with a fruit, the mushroom's function is reproductive: after mushrooms are formed, specialized cells on the gills or the pores produce spores that are jettisoned into space. When these spores are triggered into germination, they form a new mycelial mat.

Mycelia are remarkable phenomena. We have fossil records of mushrooms going back over ninety million years, to the earliest onset of the dinosaurs and vastly predating humans. Clearly they are highly successful life forms. Mycelia are everywhere, and they grow very quickly: they can travel from one edge of a room to the other in two to four weeks. A single cubic inch of soil can contain more than a mile of overlapping and interpenetrating cell networks, just one cell wide but extremely pervasive. In fact, mycelial mats constitute the largest organisms on the planet. The biggest one found to date extends over 2,200 acres. It's 165 football fields long, 3 feet deep, and 2,400 years old.

Along with bacteria, fungi are the primary recyclers and digesters of life. We now know that the complexity of the fungal kingdom gives soils the ability to respond to catastrophes, whether from a tornado, a hurricane, or somebody chipping wood or building a house. My research shows that the saprophytic fungi (those that promote decay) in particular seem to be running after human beings as quickly as they can, repairing the damage we cause to ecosystems—which appears to be one of their ecological functions. Until very recently, this capacity of mycelia for ecological repair has not been sufficiently understood or appreciated.

Scientists are increasingly realizing that species they considered to be parasitic fungi are not blights on the forest, as was once thought. Such fungi actually build soil so the landscape can become a pedestal for greater ecological diversity. Many mushrooms play an absolutely critical role in maintaining forest biodiversity. For example, mycorrhizal species such as chanterelles, matsutake, and porcini, which are symbiotic, grow in association with the root zones of higher plants. With very few exceptions, virtually all deciduous trees and shrubs have mycorrhizal mushroom hosts that sheathe their roots, increase their capacity to absorb water, extend their root zones, and protect them from disease vectors. Today this is basic forestry science, although just twenty years ago only people on the extreme fringe of forestry science understood it.

The absence of mycelia in soils indicates an imperiled habitat; conversely, mushrooms in your garden are a sign of a healthy ecosystem. The mycelium produces enzymes and acids and compounds with antibiotic properties that break down large organic complexes of molecules into simpler forms that plants can absorb. Mycelia are the great soil builders of our planet: they create habitats in which vegetables and other plants can grow. This characteristic of fungi is also what makes them so useful in ecological restoration, where the need often is to break down wastes and toxics.

I find fascinating structural similarities among mushroom mycelia, the brain's neural networks, and the Internet. Mushroom mycelia seem to form a sort of planet-wide biological Internet that transmits information. If a twig falls in the forest, to the mycelia it's like a pebble being thrown into a pond. When trees or plant materials fall and die, mycelial networks sense it almost instantaneously. This process has been proven in the laboratory; for instance, if a dead beetle is put into a petri dish, mycelial mats growing on the opposite edge of the dish will move quickly toward that nutritional source, through means we don't understand. The mats are geographically separated from the food source by what for them is a great distance—hundreds of thousands of microns—yet are able to sense it, target it, and stream mycelium to it rapidly. In Japan, scientists recently showed that a slime mold can repeatedly navigate a maze in the most efficient manner to capture nutrient sources with the least amount of cellular production, suggesting a form of cellular intelligence.

About 465 million years ago, humans shared a common ancestry with fungi. We share about 30 percent of our genes with fungi, giving us more in common genetically with them than with any other kingdom. So perhaps it's not such a leap to speculate that mycelial networks might display a form of natural intelligence. It's certainly compelling that human neural structures, mushroom mycelia, and the model of the Internet all share a very similar de-centralized, networked architecture. There is no point-specific central location on the Internet or in a mycelial mass where you can fatally harm the entire organism.

Whatever one may think about the prospect of fungal intelligence, the practical uses of mushrooms are indisputable. Dusty and I have been working in three main areas: preserving potentially useful mushroom species and fungal biodiversity in general, which above all entails protecting habitats, especially forests; doing research on the medicinal uses of mushrooms; and devising new technologies that use some of the remarkable properties of the fungal realm to clean up pollution, enrich agricultural soils, and create environmentally benign pesticides.

We live in the Pacific Northwest, an ideal place to work on biodiversity. Our home and laboratories are located at the base of the Olympic Peninsula of Washington State, south of Seattle, and we go into the rain forest frequently to find new mushroom species and ancestral strains of fungi with interesting properties. The forest is in a sense our church, and we're passionate about protecting it. I feel I have a karmic debt to repay because I was a logger at one time (although I must say that some of the best environmentalists I've ever met were loggers).

Because mushrooms can be cloned just from their spores, the "wildcrafting" we do requires only a minuscule amount of physical material. (Cloning a mushroom is a natural process that does not involve genetic modification but simply takes tissue that will regrow in its natural expression.) We can walk into a grove of old-growth forest where there may be hundreds of mushrooms of one species, and our impact on the environment is minimal because we can select just one specimen, even just a small portion of one specimen. This procedure stands in direct contrast to the wild harvesting of mushrooms for profit, where people descend on chanterelle patches and harvest everything in sight because they see dollar bills growing on the ground.

We have four laboratories where our culture collection now houses several hundred species that are specific to our interests. After cloning specimens in the laboratory, we capture the phenotype—its genetic expression—and grow its mycelium, preserving the identical genetic individual. This way the strain is conserved, we hope forever, even if the habitat from which it came is tragically destroyed. The mycelium can be expanded into tons of mycomass. We grow about 250 strains in our culture library and have commercialized about 25 species.

In the area of medicine, mounting research is confirming the enormous potential for new curative compounds waiting to be found in the fungal realm, including entirely new classes of medicines. In light of the fact that penicillin comes from a mold, it's surprising that the pharmaceutical industry has not paid more attention to this field. What I want to focus on here, however, is the capacity of fungi to heal polluted sites and ecosystems, and how they can be used for insect control. Fungi can be great allies for rehabilitating environments and re-creating sustainable biotic communities.

We've begun several such projects. One involves helping habitat recovery where people are cutting trees. We're demonstrating a technique of putting spore mass into chainsaw oil, so that when trees are cut, the oil—which mushroom mycelia love—will inoculate the stumps and accelerate the processes of decomposition and restoration. When the stumps are inoculated, the mycelium propagates rapidly. Its water-transporting properties increase resident moisture and attract all sorts of other microorganisms, so that when the stumps and the trees are cut, they become an oasis of life instead of just drying out.

Another of our remediation projects using fungal technologies took place after a diesel fuel spill near Bellingham, Washington. We entered a state-sponsored pilot project with other bioremediation companies that were using standard bacterial and enzymatic processes to try to decontaminate the soil, which was saturated with oil and mounded up in piles about three feet high, forty feet long, and six to eight feet wide. Each company was given a soil module to work on. We inoculated ours with the mycelium of oyster mushrooms, and like the other companies, we then covered it with a tarp and came back about six weeks later.

As the tarps were lifted from the other companies' modules, the odor of oil was overwhelming. Their piles remained starkly devoid of any life. When the tarp came off ours, the mound was literally blanketed with oyster mushrooms, some as big as twelve inches in diameter. Hundreds of pounds of oyster mushrooms ultimately arose from this diesel pile. Subsequent laboratory tests found virtually no toxic oil residue in either the soil or the mushrooms, the result of enzymes and acids that the fungi release that break down such molecular complexes. This finding is especially significant because hydrocarbons are the basis for many other toxic industrial products, including most pesticides and herbicides. (None of the other companies' methods destroyed a significant amount of the oil, by the way.)

But the really exciting part of the story is what happened next. After the mushrooms matured, flies came in and laid eggs in them. Maggots appeared, birds flew in, and other small mammals began to eat the mushrooms and the maggots. The birds and animals carried in seeds, and plants started growing. The mushrooms initiated a process that led to rapid habitat recovery. The polluted pile of dirt was transformed into an ecosphere of life. That's what these mushrooms are: keystone species that precipitate a catalytic, downstream reaction that invites other life forms. This is what nature can do, but she needs a little help from us.

Oyster mushrooms are one of the prime candidates for breaking down petroleum-based and hydrocarbon-based contaminants and pesticides. They are by far the easiest of any mushrooms to grow, and they'll grow on almost anything: old chairs, soggy money, or coffee grounds. (They're also delicious and contain lovastatin, a cholesterol-lowering agent.)

For several years I've been working with Battelle Laboratories to test some of my strains for bioremediation. We've discovered that at least one strain was able to break down highly toxic materials, including VX, the notorious nerve-gas agent. VX contains a recalcitrant molecule that's very difficult to degrade and is the core constituent of other chemical warfare agents, which poses a huge problem because the U.S. government has them in storage in great quantities. The only other method of disposal currently used is incineration, which of course disperses it into the air and could be quite dangerous. A laboratory experiment we conducted for the Department of Defense, reported in the British military-affairs magazine *Jane's Defence Weekly*, showed that by using mushrooms we were able to break down the VX in an unprecedented manner, and its transformation into a harmless substance occurred very quickly. Since this mushroom is native to old-growth forest, I see a strong argument for saving our primeval forests as a matter of national defense.

Benign insect control is another area of key interest. The mushroom *Termitomyces* is well known to native peoples in Africa as a delicious edible fungus cultivated by "white ants," or termites. They live in its mycelium, where they produce a beautiful honeycomb-like structure from which mushrooms later pop out. The termites are absolutely dependent on these fungi and have developed a close collaboration with them, an interspecies symbiosis. Insects and mushrooms share a close and ancient relationship, which we can adapt for human ends.

How we began experimenting with insect-targeting species is a funny story. Despite putting great care and resources into creating our state-of-the-art laboratories, Dusty and I hadn't much attended to our house, which was being seriously damaged by carpenter ants. It was already in really bad shape, and after the Olympia earthquake in 2001, the roof tilted another two or three inches. A friend of mine said, "If all the carpenter ants stopped holding hands in your house, it would fall down."

I had to do something, but I didn't want to use toxic pesticides, especially in my home. Instead I started researching whether there might be fungi that are nontoxic to humans and other mammals but would target specific insects such as carpenter ants. I learned that big corporations, including Monsanto and Dow, had spent millions to develop biological controls using fungi spores to kill termites and other insect pests. Their thinking was that fungi use spores to infect insects, which then become launching pads for dispersing more spores. But the corporate entomologists and mycologists had used a different paradigm and missed something that we found.

The problem with the conventional spore-delivery systems these corporations devised is that insects aren't stupid. Millennia of evolution have taught them to avoid danger when they sense it. Commercially designed bait traps house lethal spores that would kill insects coming into contact with them. But the insects sense this peril, and instead of going into the bait traps, they head in the other direction.

I felt that the key was to find the precise fungal species that has evolved as a parasite to a specific insect (and therefore has developed chemical compounds that attract that insect), and, crucially, to entice the insects into eating its mycelium in its pre-sporulating phase. So I focused on selecting strains that delay sporulation. My goal was to grow mycelium rather than spores. Experimenting in my house, I put out a dish with about fifty kernels of rice that contained mycelium prior to sporulation, which I wanted to occur later as a delayed reaction. The ants took away all the kernels of rice, and one week later we had no more carpenter ants in the house. Our house was thereafter free of carpenter ants because the moldy carcasses repelled future invasions.

It turns out that prior to sporulation some fungi develop attractant properties specific to an insect species they have evolved to parasitize. The fungi entice the insects to ingest and carry them away, thus spreading the infection.

The insects are beguiled into coming closer, whereupon they gorge themselves with mycelium and take some back into the nest, breaking it up to feed their queen and brood. Thus the workers effectively spread mycelium throughout the nest, which it then colonizes. When sporulation does occur, the entire insect colony is wiped out.

We have a series of patent-pending technologies that have been tested at Texas A&M University over the past four years. The tests have shown that our techniques are 100 percent effective against Formosan termites and eastern subterranean termites, and 98 percent effective against fire ants.

If these techniques pan out, we might be able to replace many pesticides with totally benign myco-insecticides. But let me be clear about my own philosophy as a biologist and ecologist. The point is not to wage a war of annihilation against whole insect species. I seek to restore balance and equilibrium; it's absolutely crucial to protect the insect genome, which is essential to the web of life. The point of such a myco-technology is that it be highly targeted and localized. Insects, fungi, and microbes have coevolved successfully over great periods of time without wiping each other out, and all have much to teach us. The more we study these relationships, the more likely we are to find other highly practical applications.

We're trying to apply our approaches to a variety of other uses. For example, logging roads cause siltation in salmon beds, posing a major threat to salmon. We're working on a strategy of putting wood chips infused with myco-pesticidal species of fungi onto logging roads. As the fungi grow, they provide myco-filtration, catching the silt before it gets to streams and helping accelerate regeneration of the landscape. And eventually the logging roads would become perimeter barriers preventing insect plagues, such as beetle blights, from sweeping across the forest.

By partnering with fungi and harnessing their extraordinary powers, we are entering a new frontier of knowledge. I believe that the future of our planet and our health will increasingly depend on our working synergistically with other organisms. Fungi can provide us with a powerful array of tools for living in harmony within our ecosystems.

Bioremediation:
Waste Equals Food

Randall von Wedel

Randall von Wedel is one of those rare scientists able to combine a sophisticated technical grasp of living systems with the social strategies that usher their applications into the real world. A biochemist, he has been one of the world's leading innovators in practical bioremediation and has developed new techniques for cleaning up a grisly range of oil-contaminated sites.

CytoCulture International, the California-based company he founded and directs, employs its own bioreactor technology and laboratory-selected strains of aerobic bacteria (which need oxygen to live) to biodegrade an impressive set of hydrocarbon pollutants, including diesel fuel, crude oil, and waste oil, in soil and groundwater. In 1987, Randall served as a consultant to California's first groundwater bioremediation project, and he subsequently went on to meet a remarkable series of escalating challenges using innovative practices he evolved. Recently, Randall achieved astonishing success in Berkeley, California, where he ran an eighteen-month trial program resulting in the City of Berkeley's becoming the first municipality in the world to commit to complete conversion of its entire fleet of 192 trucks, school buses, street sweepers, and garbage and recycling trucks from petroleum diesel to 100 percent biodiesel fuel. Randall's company is expanding biodiesel cooperatives in the San Francisco Bay Area and opening new biodiesel stations.

Randall's successes give us confidence that ecological technologies—whether the adaptation of acclimated bacteria to break down petroleum or the utilization of plant oils to produce a clean-burning, sustainable fuel for diesel engines—are the keys to solving our environmental pollution problems. It's further evidence of just how great a difference one person and a few trillion microbes can make.

MOST OF MY EARLY RESEARCH was in medicine, but I became discouraged about the deterioration of the environment, the way our planet was being mistreated, and the careless behavior of corporate America. When I reached my thirties, I decided I had more opportunity to make an impact by putting my energy into environmental technologies than by staying with electron microscopy and basic medical research (i.e., killing mice in basements of laboratories). My day-to-day research now is focused on trying to use relatively simple approaches to solve fairly complicated real-world pollution and public health problems.

There are three areas of research I have been working on in the past decade to employ biological methods to reduce pollution: *bioremediation* (the use of natural bacteria selected to biodegrade specific contaminants under aerobic or anaerobic conditions, depending on the pollutant), *biosolvents* (effective solvents chemically derived from vegetable oils instead of petroleum distillates and used, for example, in oil spill cleanups), and *biodiesel* (a clean-burning fuel made from nontoxic renewable vegetable oils and recycled cooking oils). I'm primarily addressing the first two topics here.

Bioremediation is a natural process, a technology based on using laboratory-selected bacteria and bioreactor systems to eat or biodegrade pollutants. It has a wide range of applications. Although it is hardly a new technology, what is relatively new is making it commercially viable on a small scale and making it available to important community institutions we often overlook or disdain: gas stations, oil companies, truck and UPS terminals—facilities that make our day-to-day life possible in the internal-combustion age. It's part of our role as scientists to help industries solve problems that affect everyone. We all have connections to the earth and we all contribute to polluting it. Bioremediation can be a way to provide cheap, practical, and reliable ways for many industries to start solving pollution problems in their own groundwater and soil, so that in the long run we all have a cleaner and healthier environment.

Industrial biotreatment plants are basically bioremediation systems using living bacteria to process polluted water in ponds and tanks. Biological processes are a very efficient way to break down all kinds of contaminants, and bioremediation can be applied to all kinds of industrial toxins, even to oil spills. The target compounds range from all the petroleum products to many of the chlorinated solvents once considered "recalcitrant" (nonbiodegradable). Today we know that many of them are, in fact, biodegradable; we just had to learn what conditions would foster the growth of naturally occurring bacteria or fungi that can break down these complicated materials.

It's not just carbon compounds that can be bioremediated. We can even break down nitrates, which are a big pollution problem in the Central Valley in California due to agricultural runoff. We can also treat certain minerals such as selenium, which is threatening to wildlife in large enough doses. Ammonia, a by-product of a lot of chemical and biological processes—including the waste generated by the digestive processes of living creatures—is very easily assimilated by bacteria.

We always start in a laboratory. I have a small lab where we conduct studies in tiny bioreactors about the size of a milkshake blender. I recently did a lot of work on phenol, a highly toxic material that is abundant in refineries. Phenol turns out to be relatively biodegradable, but you really have to work at it. As with any bioremediation effort, you need to acclimate bacteria to the point that they will use the toxic material as a source of food, as energy, and as a source of carbon to make their own little cells. The goal is to convert toxic compounds into carbon dioxide and water. That's really the basic principle of all biodegradation involving carbon compounds, including sewage.

Once we've achieved success with the small model, we scale up to five-gallon tanks and then to larger drums. Later, in the field, we work our way up to big tanks that basically serve as miniature wastewater treatment systems. Each of these tanks is, in a sense, a bacterial aquarium, to which we add oxygen. All biological processes require oxygen, just as we do. The right bacteria will consume the oil and other pollutants, but you need to provide them with oxygen. I wish we could use solar and wind power to provide the oxygen, but we're operating on a very high-density scale that requires more oxygen than these sources currently can deliver. So we pump oxygen in, aerating the tanks just as you would aerate an aquarium—but instead of growing fish that eat food, we're growing bacteria that eat oil.

The conditions are very bad at a lot of the sites where we have to clean up oil. Our first step is to install a tank to preprocess the water and separate out what we call the "free-phase" oil. In many places, such as Emeryville, California (on San Francisco Bay, just west of Berkeley), you can pull a sample container out of a well, and the first couple of inches are oil. We have to process off that oil, but the good news is that we can recycle it. It goes back to a refinery.

How do you clean groundwater under an old gas station? Our bigger projects involve working under acres of land: entire shopping centers or truck terminals, for instance. The task is pretty straightforward: We try to intercept the flow of the water where the oil and gasoline or diesel concentrates. Then we process the water in our aboveground reactors, treating it over a period of about twelve to fifteen hours until the water comes out clean. This process is not aimed at industrial chemicals but rather at more conventional fuel—the slightly more benign pollutants—but the concept of all bioremediation is the same: you're letting bacteria eat something that has energy. They use the energy to grow and we get back clean water.

A typical example of the kind of site we deal with is one in downtown Redwood City, where a new shopping center called Sequoia Station was to be built. To prepare the site and begin restoring Mother Earth underneath, we had to dismantle five gas stations and a dry cleaner. We start with big machines, excavating tanks and pulling out hydraulic lines. They come out oozing hydraulic fluid; you can imagine the condition of the water underneath. A couple of inches of oil—actually degraded diesel that's been sitting on the ground for years—usually lies on top of the water table. We excavate around the site, create a gradient using pumps, and install trenches that allow us to capture the water flowing downhill; then we pump water out of these trenches. Through pipes in a French drain (a fabric-lined gravel pit), we pull up the water, separate out the oil, and biotreat the water by adding what we call acclimated bacteria—organisms that have learned how to survive on these pollutants. We also add oxygen and nutrients to the water to stimulate the bacteria. All we're doing is helping them to expand and be as effective as possible in the ground. This is in situ remediation (it occurs in place).

Through processing water, returning it to the ground, monitoring the system, and adding oxygen, we achieve a very effective cleanup of the whole site over a period of about seven or eight months. Construction typically starts before we finish.

People often ask me what difference our work makes since these are urban sites and no one is going to drink the water anyway. But it does make a difference. In most of the country more than 50 percent of the drinking water comes from groundwater. Whatever finds its way into water eventually goes back into the water table. And the standards are very rigorous. In order for a site to be approved for a construction project, the level of benzene, for example, must be reduced to less than one part per billion. The remediation technologies have to be very effective because benzene is highly carcinogenic. So a cleanup that reduces benzene levels to parts per million isn't good enough—the more threatening aromatic compounds in petroleum fuels must get down to parts per billion.

Another technology we use to detoxify soil—one that doesn't require nearly the kind of strenuous activity we have to put into water remediation—is bioremediation with solar-enhanced "land farming." This is done to convert industrial sites, such as old oil fields, to other uses, turning them into farms, wineries, and housing developments. Typically, we treat 4,000-8,000 cubic yards of soil at a time. The technique is to build heaps and insert pipes between three-foot layers of soil to provide oxygen. The benefits of biodegradation in this scenario are pretty apparent. Most important, it works and is cost-effective compared to older methods. Remediation companies used to haul soil off and bury it in a landfill, just transferring the problem from one place to another. We're trying to avoid transporting and dumping contaminated soil; instead we work to renew the soil and use it on-site. In effect what we're doing is recycling: we recycle groundwater and soil at their original sites.

One of the things that got me excited when we started developing these technologies was the prospect of applying them to big oil spills, such as the *Exxon Valdez* spill. What could we do biologically to remove oil from contaminated beaches, and how could we hasten biodegradation after these terrible spills? We've all seen how pathetic the current types of cleanup are; sometimes they consist of little more than men in white suits using rakes. After the *Valdez* spill, fishermen were paid a lot of money to scoop up oil with buckets or suck it up with pumps. Neither worked very well. Some years ago our team came up with a plan to use a biosolvent, chemically very similar to biodiesel. Both are made from recycled cooking oil and, usually, recycled soybean oil. The biosolvent we developed can be used to extract oil from beaches, sandbars, or marshes.

We have put a lot of energy into figuring out how to restore marshes. In some parts of the United States—Maine, for example—when there's a spill, the marsh vegetation is mowed and it and the oil are burned, because it's too much work to clean it up. Going in there with the mowing machinery pretty much destroys the whole marsh area, however. We wanted to find a way to remove the oil gently, in a more natural fashion. Rather than putting the oil in a dump and calling it hazardous waste, we wanted to collect it and recycle it back into the economy. That's exactly what we're able to do with our solvent.

With the help of grants from the federal government, we developed a biosolvent, a vegetable-based oil that has been chemically processed to remove glycerin. Natural oils—including the oils in our bodies and those we eat, such as olive oil and butter—are all triglycerides. But if we cut the individual hydrocarbon chains, the fatty-acid chains, off the triglyceride, those chains have remarkable properties as solvents. They're like snakes with big heads: the head contains oxygen and the long body is pure hydrocarbon. So it's a molecule with two personalities: an aggressive "head" that interacts with water, but a hydrocarbon body that, just like any other oil or wax, can dissolve crude oil.

A biosolvent based on this hydrocarbon chain can therefore interact with both oil and water—much like a detergent, but with one major difference. A detergent disperses oils into water, whereas this biosolvent can actually separate the dissolved oils from water, making it possible to recover them. We can use cold water to flush treated oil off a beach or out of a marsh, collect it with special machines and recycle it back into oil at a refinery. It took us about two years to explain this to the state of California, but now the state is a big advocate of the technique. The federal government has also come on board, and we are starting to work in Germany as well.

Ours is a technique the EPA likes to refer to as "lift and float." Here's how it works: the biosolvent is sprayed on the oiled sand and it dissolves the crude oil into itself. Then the crude oil and solvent mixture floats on the water. It's the exact opposite of what the usual detergents/dispersants do, which is to make the oil disperse into very fine droplets. Some claim it "disappears" into the ocean, but actually, it stays right in the few centimeters near the surface, damaging all the phyto- and zooplankton. With our method, little globules of oil coalesce as they ooze out of the sand, and then are easily collected off the water with skimmers. The oil can be reused: in a demonstration at a fuel oil spill in Puerto Rico, the recovered oil-biosolvent mixture served as an excellent burner fuel for the local power plant.

We had to document laboratory tests for the EPA, showing what kind of extraction efficiencies we could get. We showed that in just one pass we could get fairly remarkable rates: 89–90 percent recovery of oil from the collected medium. When we used California beach sand, we had even better recoveries; the remaining oil was almost undetectable. We published a paper with the California Fish and Game Department and got its approval; our biosolvent is now the only chemical product in California licensed for use in ocean spills.

It's a very effective way of removing oil with, besides our biosolvents, just plain water. There's no soap involved and no need for heat. You may remember that in the *Valdez* "cleanup," a lot of hot water and steam were used. When you talk to biologists, you find out that not only the rocks were sterilized, but also a lot of the local ecosystems, because the temperature was too high. In some places, this technique only drove the oil deeper; you can still dig down a foot or so and hit areas with pockets of oil. If the oil had just been left cold and floating, it eventually would have degraded on the surface and washed away. What we're trying to do is come up with a way to respond quickly, prevent birds and wildlife from getting soaked in the oil, and most important, recover that oil and get it back in the refinery, rather than leaving it in the environment.

This is a practical, commercial process, and I take care not to be too far "out there," so I can still walk into Chevron and say, "Let's work on a project together. Fund me to do this research so we can help you avoid a problem." I'm trying to span two worlds, the environmental community and the corporate and bureaucratic realms, and I'm not embarrassed by it; it's my reality. Meanwhile, we are part of the community, trying to control environmental damage that affects all of us.

On the west coast of Japan in 1998, 10,000 villagers worked to clean an oil spill manually, even though the authorities had access to machines and people like us saying, "We'll help you." The Japanese, said in effect, "We're going to take the money from the International Monetary Fund and use it to employ our people." It was winter, and I have pictures of women wading into the oil with buckets and pots and pans, scooping it up. Five people died, not from toxicity but from exposure to the cold. As a global community, we need to use technology in a responsible way for the benefit of humans and the earth, and to take advantage of nature's own methods, such as bioremediation. We can be resourceful and reuse waste materials, just as we now make biodiesel and biosolvents from recycled cooking oil. We have many opportunities to use nature's ways to solve human-caused problems. But we have to be diligent and intelligent about it.

Heavy Metal Blues:
Botanical Detox Centers

Rufus L. Chaney

Behind those red suspenders, Rufus L. Chaney is an improbable revolutionary em-bedded in the arcane and usually retrograde bureaucracy of the U.S. Department of Agriculture. An award-winning research agronomist, he has been one of the genuine trailblazers in the field of phytoremediation—the use of specific types of plants to de-contaminate toxified land. Because of him, there are farmers growing crops of nickel.

Rufus's specialty is the study and breeding of super-strains of "hyperaccumu-lator" plants that can suck heavy metals out of the soil. The nation and world are riddled with abandoned mine sites saturated with toxic metals, for which no one now has legal responsibility. Aware of this ticking time bomb, Rufus began searching for plants that have an affinity for these metals. From the Agricultural Research Ser-vice at the USDA's Beltsville, Maryland, station, he set out on one of the most re-markable recycling projects ever conceived, using the improbable agency of plants. He has become the preeminent specialist in the phytoextraction of cadmium, nickel, cobalt, zinc, and other metals from soils, as well as the developer of "tailor-made" composts and biosolids used to remediate metal contamination and protect food safety and soil fertility.

Since beginning his career in 1969, Rufus has written 367 papers and 180 published extracts on these topics. He has consulted with the EPA, Food and Drug Administration, Office of Management and Budget, and many states in preparing plans and regulations for utilizing phytoremediation and biosolids. His work first came to public attention a decade or so ago when he collaborated with artist Mel Chin on a controversial project, "Revival Field," which combined landscape art and phytoremediation and was turned down for a grant from the National Endowment for the Arts.

This humble public servant has devised a true biotechnology that optimizes the plant-human partnership. The phytoremediation methods Rufus has helped find and refine hold out hope for contaminated areas of the world where no government-funded cleanup is in sight. Thanks to his vision, one day citizen gardeners in many places will be able to provide inexpensive botanical solutions to help restore otherwise orphaned toxic landscapes.

FOR MOST OF MY CAREER I've worked on mitigating heavy metal contamination from one source or another, to protect the food chain and restore ecosystems, decontaminate systems so we can have cleaner food, and help solve some of the problems of poor folks living in communities around the world that were harmed by one hundred years of extraction metallurgy. When smelters started operating more than a century ago, they were very inefficient and badly contaminated the areas around them. Such contamination exists everywhere there were mines and smelters—from small areas to many square miles of dead earth. Nothing is being done about most of these contaminated places.

We have worked at one site in Palmerton, Pennsylvania, where a company began smelting zinc in 1898. It was closed in 1980, mostly because of economics but also because of pressure to stop polluting the environment. The land around the smelter site was virtually dead, because excessive zinc in the soil kills plants. Kentucky bluegrass was the major grass, and it just couldn't live. Imagine living in a town where the soil is so polluted you simply give up trying to grow a lawn.

One way to remediate such soils, which we used at Palmerton, is to apply a mixture of biosolids or composts, as well as alkaline fly ash, limestone, and/or wood ash. We mix alkaline fly ash or wood ash with biosolids and apply it on the soil surface to provide neutral pH, nutrients, and organic matter, and the remediation mixture doesn't run off with the rain. The ingredients create a reaction that makes them bond together, and as soon as vegetation is established, the amendments and soil are held in place by the vegetation. This "persistent revegetation technology" is appropriate for extensive sites that are so dead from metals that one can't afford to remove soil. It can solve the toxicity and infertility of the contaminated site and support a diverse vegetation that's safe for wildlife and humans.

Treating soil with biosolids and alkaline by-products in this way (called phytostabilization) has been one of my two main approaches to phytoremediation. The other is phytoextraction, a technology that uses rare plants that are able to accumulate remarkable quantities of metals because they evolved over millennia on naturally mineralized soils. We collect such plants, test them, and breed and farm them for use in decontaminating and restoring ecosystems. The hyperaccumulation of metals by plant species occurs in nature. Now there's actually an industry that can recycle these metals in the biomass and recover part or all of the cost of the remediation.

Back in 1980, when I first introduced the phytoremediation idea, it was dismissed entirely. Then Reagan took over and no work was done in the field for a decade. The engineers had that decade to show us how they were going to remediate toxic sites cost- effectively. But at $1 million an acre-foot for their preferred method of soil removal and replacement, the estimated cleanup bill for several thousand acres at Palmerton alone was $3 billion. It's just too expensive using conventional methods, yet it remains desperately necessary to remediate such areas. The engineers' alternatives are to dig and haul soil away to a landfill or hazardous waste disposal site; to "solidify" the soil with cement and put it in a landfill; or to try using acid to wash the metals out, then treat the acid to remove the metals and find some use for the ruined soil. These methods work poorly and are very costly.

Using the biosolids/wood ash mixture, however, brings the cost of restoring an ecosystem down to $1,000 to $3,000 an acre. This alternative in situ remediation technology is a much wiser choice on several levels. Phytoextraction is straightforward, simple, and less expensive for society.

The idea of phytoremediation began to spread quickly in 1990. Part of the reason was that I was approached by artist Mel Chin, who wanted to create an art installation for Earth Day's twentieth anniversary in 1992. He had seen an article in the *Whole Earth Review* about using plants to restore and remediate contaminated soils and had the idea of doing something related to this.

Although that particular slant did not prove workable, phytoextraction was waiting to be developed.

Chin applied for a National Endowment for the Arts grant for a piece called *Revival Field*. It was supported by all the committees but turned down at NEA headquarters for political reasons. The art community joined up in force, and word spread around the United States and the world, even garnering a half-page article in *Science* magazine. I could have worked a decade publishing papers about phytoextraction and not attracted the attention of one-tenth as many people. The NEA's rejection actually spread the idea of phytoextraction widely; I thank them for that.

Here's how the process works. We breed and then grow the new metal hyperaccumulator crops. (We have identified accumulators for zinc, copper, nickel, cobalt, arsenic, and selenium, although not, to date, for lead, chromium, and most other elements.) We farm the crops and make hay from them, burn the hay for biomass energy, and recover the metals from the ash for dollar value.

Some plants accumulate metals at extraordinary levels; some comprise about 3 to 4 percent zinc in their hay form. Normal plants are severely harmed at 0.05 percent zinc, so this is about 100 times higher than any crop plant can tolerate. Our farming with hyperaccumulator plants is already taking up 25,000 parts per million of zinc. We're removing 125 kilograms per hectare, and the ash produced from burning the hay is on the order of 40 percent zinc. That's a high-grade ore that can be recycled to offset the cost of the phytoextraction.

Wherever there was a zinc industry, there was also cadmium contamination, which can build up in the food chain and harm humans. People accumulate cadmium in their kidneys over a lifetime. *Thlaspi caerulescens* (alpine pennycress) is the plant we've worked with that is extremely effective at removing cadmium. *Thlaspi* cultivars can accumulate a thousand times more cadmium per year than crop plants, so cadmium risk from these soils can be remediated in a few years of phytoextraction.

We're starting a project in Bulgaria in a place where tobacco is grown around a zinc smelter. Tobacco accumulates cadmium, people smoke the tobacco, and cadmium moves into their lungs and kidneys. The Bulgarians can't sell this cadmium-loaded tobacco anywhere else, so they consume it within the country. Our project aims to grow *Thlaspi* to remove the cadmium and make this a viable income-producing alternative to growing tobacco, and to decontaminate the soil for any crop they want to grow. In developing countries they don't have a Superfund to do the job. In Japan and China there are many villages where people suffer from cadmium poisoning from homegrown rice. Phytoextraction is the only cost-effective alternative for these rice soils.

In contrast to *Thlaspi*, a Philippine tree, *Dichapetalum*, doesn't take up cadmium at all, but it takes up zinc in huge quantity. Plants that have evolved on polluted sites demonstrate a remarkable range of responses and genetic adaptations for taking up one or more of the heavy metals.

To use phytoextraction technology, the metals must be at rooting depth, otherwise you can't get enough out in any one year to make it worthwhile. That's an engineering limitation of the hyperaccumulator plants. In the United States, the plant shoots grown to remove metals must be big enough to be handled mechanically. But in some developing countries even hand-harvesting could be cost-effective if people can make as much money growing metal as they can growing a food crop. And if metals must be removed in any case to make the soil safe for growing food, phytoextraction appears to be the lowest-cost method available, far less expensive than soil removal and replacement.

Our farming and nickel phytoextraction methods are already being used commercially on mineralized soils in the northwestern United States and on smelter-contaminated soils in Canada. Twenty-two companies in the United States now offer some kind of phytoremediation service. Our work on cadmium and zinc is cost-effective in developing countries but not yet in the United States. There are also many situations in which you can use plants to biodegrade toxic organic compounds in soil and prevent erosion during the remediation period.

The hardest part is finding the plants in the first place. Perhaps 2 to 5 percent of all metal-tolerant species hyperaccumulate. So we go to places where the earth was killed a long time ago or where there is naturally contaminated soil, sort among the species that thrive there, and almost always find some hyperaccumulator plants.

Soil contaminated with radioactive material is a tougher challenge, although we're now collecting or identifying radionuclide accumulators to use to decontaminate radioactive soils. People have happened onto things like a desert weed that accumulates strontium, or red-root pigweed, which accumulates cesium, but otherwise we still need to conduct a lot of testing to find useful radionuclide-accumulator plants.

In addition to our work on hyperaccumulator plants and phytoextraction, we continue to use treatment with biosolids plus alkaline by-products wherever it's appropriate. We brought the technology we developed in Palmerton to the Silesia region of Poland, where people live close to smelter-contaminated soils. The site had been barren for fifty years. We used a waste limestone product and other inexpensive local resources to make remediation mixtures for the phytotoxic soils. (Each possible amendment must be analyzed to make sure it is safe when applied to soils.) Then we added biosolids from some of the local towns that actually had sewage treatment. We created scientifically controlled field plots with different treatments. Our remediation approach completely allowed the return and survival of grasses and herbs. I've since conducted, with my Polish colleague, a feeding study of calves showing that the grass is perfectly safe for ruminant livestock.

At Bunker Hill, Idaho, one of the real bad-boy U.S. Superfund sites, we worked with the EPA and many local parties, including the Coeur d'Alene Tribe, that were interested in remediating dead or wildlife-injuring soils resulting from metal poisoning. We installed plots using a tailor-made approach to cure zinc toxicity, prevent cadmium risk, and deactivate lead so it is not bioavailable even if the soil is eaten by wildlife. We were able to apply our mixture even on a 30 percent slope using a machine called an aero-spreader. The biosolids/wood ash mixture that we made at Bunker Hill is about 40 percent solids; it can literally be thrown on the mountain. We worked out practical ways to mix and apply it to revegetate the area. Our large test plots at Bunker Hill are the only steep hillsides at this site that have been effectively revegetated.

The bottom line is that we've been able to show viable approaches for remediating some of the most toxic metal-contaminated sites I've been able to find to study. I don't want easy sites. I want the tough sites, because once we've solved those, the technologies we've developed can be applied elsewhere. The technologies now emerging will be useful in nearly every community that has a metal toxic site.

Nature's Filters:
From Cattails to Bureaucrats

Doug Kepler

*Though a native Pennsylvanian, Doug Kepler could only imagine what the once fa-
bled trout streams in that state's mountains must have been like before coal strip mining suffocated them. Most of the mining companies had cut and run. Those outfits
left said they couldn't afford to do much about cleaning up the mess, and their chem-
ical-based methods often just compounded the problem. With a degree in resource
management from Penn State University and graduate work in aquatic ecology at
Clarion University of Pennsylvania, Doug started to look to nature's own purification systems, such as marshlands, and became part of an early wave of innovators
who found that wetlands plants are remarkable living filters. He set out to bring back
the dead, and in 1991 started a company called Damariscotta, an old New England
Indian word for "the gathering place of many fish."*

*Since that time Doug and his partner Eric McCleary have worked wonders.
Damariscotta's accomplishments have included many watershed restorations and
groundbreaking work in ecological design to repair lands and waters severely damaged by acid mine drainage. Most recently the company developed the Aluminator,
a system for treating aluminum-contaminated water and recovering the metal for subsequent sale. The Aluminator facility is the first and only regional collection and processing installation of its kind for this highly toxic metal. Damariscotta has also become a leader in the field of constructed wetlands for waste treatment.*

*But the cleanups have proved to be easy compared to dealing with the profitable
high-tech industrial-waste complex and inert government bureaucracies. Their response to Damariscotta's empirical success was, "Sure, it works in practice, but
what about in theory?" In the process of answering that question, Doug has shown
how to work successfully with industry leaders, watershed organizations, and gov-*

ernments on projects involving coal, oil, and gas cleanups in thirteen states and seven countries.

Doug has made formidable scientific and environmental contributions, but his greatest gift might be his tact. He has managed to navigate through some of the most entrenched bureaucracies and bring elegant natural treatment systems into being. At the same time, he has been a pied piper galvanizing communities to bring back their clear running waters so that once again the fish may gather.

I HAVE TAKEN A ROAD of trying to restore polluted watersheds, and our work has succeeded by using constructed wetlands treatment systems. We construct wetlands primarily to treat the effects of coal-mine drainage—mostly from abandoned mines that no individual or company has taken responsibility for—and waters associated with old abandoned gas and oil wells. As long as the coal industry in Pennsylvania was good, people here didn't care about the environment. They cared about the economy. The coal industry is now dead. People are out of work, they don't have clean water to drink, and they're starting to realize the problems they created.

A typical "kill area" from a coal-mine operation is devoid of vegetation, its waters and streambeds stained orange with iron. The polluted water trickles down into the receiving stream and the stream dies, along with all the fish and other creatures that live there. The conventional way to remediate such areas is to treat the water with caustic soda and chemicals dispensed from tanks. What we're trying to do instead, based on extensive scientific research, is to establish natural ecologies of cattails, rushes, and sedges that will restore the watershed to life. Wetlands are nature's living filters and perform this purifying function in the natural environment.

A constructed wetland is a technology specifically designed to remediate a particular contaminated site or type of waste. It's actually not the plants themselves that do the cleansing, but the microbes on their roots. The principles of wetlands treatment can be applied all over the world, but each system has to be very site-specific and in tune with the community's particular goals.

Getting our constructed wetlands to work effectively is not our greatest challenge, however. Anytime we're at the crossroads of an innovative technology, we have to face skeptical regulators, scientific experts, elected officials, and a public that have been raised on the "trust me" formula. Overcoming their resistance is really tough to do if you have all the facts and figures and tables to prove your method works; it's even tougher without them. That's what we have to face and it can get very frustrating on a day-to-day basis. But we see a public that wants a solution to water treatment needs, and economically there's no way to do it with the costly concrete-and-steel engineering and chemical treatment alternatives for most places.

For example, bioremediation just might meet certain regulatory discharge limits, and it might improve water quality by 99.99 percent, but it can be hard to show that on paper with absolute mathematical precision. I have tables showing how a lot of our cleanup efforts improved water quality by ranges of 88 to 98 percent. In one case, we removed iron and changed the water's lethal acidity, raising the pH to the middle range that is crucial to supporting life. We designed the constructed wetlands to cover a certain acreage at a specific depth, and retention times for the wastewater were carefully modulated. We conducted extensive research to select the substrate materials and plants. But when I sat down and looked closely at the numbers, I couldn't correlate them with the removal of the constituents. I was actually able to remove 98 percent of the iron, but I could account for only about 94 percent of it. I didn't know where that other 4 percent was going, and I didn't know if the scientific community could accept those numbers.

The story of another project illustrates what we're up against. In the late 1980s, we did a pilot project that was up for review by Pennsylvania's environmental regulatory agency to become a permanent installation. We wanted to use a constructed wetlands technology developed by Don Hammer at the Tennessee Valley Authority that employs limestone drains to help treat contaminated water. These are simple trenches or holes in the ground filled with limestone and maintained in an unoxygenated condition so that the limestone doesn't coat with metals. Water that is undesirably low in pH is run through this system, and the physical contact with the limestone increases the pH. The regulator would not accept this process, however. He wanted something based on "more extensive research." He didn't like the idea of a hole filled with lime-stone because it would coat with iron, he said.

We tried to explain that an unoxygenated condition prevents the coating from occurring, but he insisted we go back and give him something based on more scientific research. We thought about it for a while, and knowing that the agency really liked acronyms, we resubmitted the plans using an "RFH system." The regulator liked it a lot. He never asked what the acronym stood for, but said, "This is the kind of science that we're looking for." The RFH is a "rock-filled hole."

Having successfully overcome this major regulatory hurdle, I next went to one of our local elected officials, who are also somewhat resistant to change. We asked this individual for help, through legislative support and funding, to implement some of our other proposed bioremediation projects on a com-munity-wide volunteer basis. He said that such support wouldn't be consis-tent with the goals of some of his major campaign contributors (such as in-dustrial polluters), because as long as the water remained somewhat polluted, they had a better chance of getting their permits to continue discharging con-taminants into the environment. We argued, "If you don't help us, people aren't going to vote for you." He just laughed, because he knew that coming from a rural part of the state as we did, our small voting bloc didn't matter that much.

Our response to this kind of resistance has been to develop a community-wide strategy. We targeted an area known as the Mill Creek Watershed, in Clarion County, a beautiful part of western Pennsylvania. The northern half of this watershed is pristine, covered with big tumbling mountain streams with brook trout. It looks like a Coors commercial. But the southern half of the wa-tershed was completely dead, devastated because it lies on top of a deep un-derground coal mine that had spewed forth biologically dead waters for ap-proximately the past seventy years.

Mill Creek had been a beautiful hemlock-rhododendron type of stream, and people now in their seventies and eighties had known it as a clear stream. They had fished and swum in it. During high water people still kayaked it. But when I went walking there with my kids, all we saw was a dead, red stream. The kids wanted to know where the fish were. That was a pretty simple question. I knew where they had gone, but at that time I didn't know how to put them back.

We knew there was strong public feeling about cleaning up this place, so we went directly to the public, who first asked us, "What did the regulators, experts, and elected officials have to say about this? Are they supporting you?" We said that they were less than enthusiastic. People seemed to like that. Then they wanted to know if we had tables and extensive scientific research to back what we were saying. I said, "No, I don't have any tables either." And then they asked, "Should we trust you?" I was ready for that one: "The check is in the mail." Then they all laughed and inquired, "Well, what is it you really want?" I answered, "That's what I'm here to ask *you*. What do you really hope to accomplish through this bioremediation project? You have to define a goal and why you want to accomplish it. Then determine whether the goal is obtainable and how you can reach it."

The reality is that to implement projects on such abandoned sites, everything has to be done on a volunteer basis, for obvious financial reasons. No private company or individual any longer has legal responsibility for them; they are orphan sites whose harms are foisted back into the public domain. At the time I was living near the Mill Creek area and working for an engineering firm whose main concern was to generate billable hours, so I couldn't volunteer a lot of my time. As a result, one of my coworkers and I eventually left to form a company called Damariscotta, a New England Indian word that means "a gathering place of many fish"—and that was the symbolic goal we held. Clearly we had to generate some billable hours on our own so that we could eat, but now we had a lot more leeway to do volunteer community work as well.

We decided to form a coalition of people interested in the Mill Creek Watershed cleanup. It was composed mostly of faculty from the biology department at Clarion University, plus local chapters of environmental groups such as the Audubon Society, Ducks Unlimited, and the Sierra Club, and a lot of regular people interested in returning the area to what it used to look like.

We faced a lot of challenges getting this first coalition project off the ground. Even though the pollution discharges had gone on unabated for sixty or seventy years, the regulators demanded strict compliance with often arbitrary water quality standards before we could take any action. They wanted us to work far to the right side of the decimal point—in the fine tuning—not on the big overall pollution issue where the major qualitative problem was. We had to cut through a lot of red tape to get them to accept our first goal, which was to put fish back into the stream. Since no one else was dealing with these cleanup problems at the time, anything we did would be beneficial. But the experts simply said, "It won't work"—and just in case it did work, the elected official wanted credit.

One thing we learned was that elected officials and people in the regulatory community were concerned that, in raising public awareness of these problems, we were in some way implying that they weren't doing their job. We had to make them feel as though they were a part of the solution rather than part of the problem, and we did that by involving them. As our success grew, more and more people jumped on board and the elected officials even helped get funding. It's very important early on in the process that these people understand that you're not attacking them, that you're not saying it's something they created, but that they can help you clean it up.

The general public simply wanted to know what they could do to help. We made the goal very obtainable. We had done some pilot projects showing that we could clean up the waters, and the public just wanted to bring the streams back to some form of life. People understood very clearly that the fish don't read the regulatory permit statistical tables. They wanted real results.

Ultimately we were able to stock one of the wetlands treatment ponds with fish, which was the goal. We aren't quite meeting all of the regulatory constituent numbers, but we did put fish back in that pond, which discharges into Mill Creek.

Another installation we did was an old abandoned gas well called the Howe Bridge project. The waters there had a low pH, a very high iron content, and a very high flow that for years had run directly into the nearby stream. We knew we had the technology to improve the water, but we didn't have any funds to do it. So we enlisted the volunteer help of our local National Guard unit. Rather than have the guardsmen push dirt piles back and forth at their base, we asked them to come help us as a training exercise. For two weeks they brought in their bulldozers, backhoes, and other equipment. The project was so successful that our local Guard unit received several national awards, and they wanted to come back again and again. Through their contribution and the volunteer efforts of the rest of the group, we were able to obtain grants for matching funds to get materials, such as rock and compost, to help build the wetlands.

The real measure of success that we're hoping to obtain is to restore a diverse flora and fauna native to these watersheds and streams, not some kind of compliance with regulations. You know you're not going to clean up these watersheds overnight. In the Mill Creek Watershed, we are dealing with around 30 miles of the main stream and roughly 125 to 150 tributaries. Perhaps half those tributaries are polluted, and on each of those tributaries there might be from one to ten point sources of pollution. You can't fix this in a summer or two, or even five. You must have the perseverance to stick with it over time.

One of the most satisfying stories from our early cleanup efforts is about a farmer now in his early seventies. He grew up on the same farm where he still lives, and he remembers as a child that the stream going through his property was very pristine. It died around forty years ago from the effects of coal mining, and since then his cows would not drink from it.

Because it had only one point source of pollution, at the headwaters, we put a wetlands treatment system at that spot. Within two years the stream had come back to life, and the cows now drink out of it again. To the farmer, this was everything. This was his goal. It proved to be an obtainable goal, and that man did more good for our coalition than I or anyone else ever could have done, because he was a member of the grassroots public who knew the other farmers and residents in the watershed. After that we had people knocking at our door asking, "Can you come to my property and do the same thing for us?"

The goals are usually very simple, but the vehicle for obtaining them is seldom simple. Inevitably these projects need some level of funding. It's very clear that the chemical types of treatments are simply cost-prohibitive, especially on abandoned sites. Even a lot of wetlands treatment systems can be cost-prohibitive for a volunteer coalition, because you still have to pay for raw materials, including the plants, limestone, compost, and construction materials. Then you need to build consensus and obtain official cooperation. For the more expensive, large-scale projects, you have to convince officials to allocate public funding as well.

Setting clear goals is paramount. In setting goals for cleaning up watersheds, communities need to realize that some of the really bad discharges may get cleaned up by only 60 or 70 percent. These streams were destroyed over many, many years and can't be fixed up right here and now. Pollution usually took a lot of time to happen and the cleanup may take as much. But over time wetlands treatment systems do work to return fisheries.

It's also essential to set priorities. It's crucial that the first system people undertake works. If you go out and convince the public and everyone else to help and then that first system doesn't work, it's all over. My advice to communities is to pick a discharge that is relatively small and relatively easy to address. Then go a little overboard: develop a Cadillac system instead of the Volkswagen model and make sure it works. It might even be prudent to do that first system with a very small group, rather than involving a lot of the community. Once it does work, then bring the community on board and play the PR game. Get the newspapers in there. Let the politicians take the credit. Do whatever is necessary to get people excited and get more funds freed up. Make sure everyone understands that they ultimately need to view such cleanup efforts on a watershed basis.

Other than cost-effectiveness, one crucial reason to go with biological over chemical treatment—even though chemical treatment may be 100 percent effective most of the time—is that just one chemical mistreatment can wipe out an entire stream. That's not consistent with the goal of returning a fishery. With the biological treatment, even if every project on a watershed is only 75 percent successful, some type of recovery within the watershed will occur.

I work every day with officials and regulators to make a living, but my higher goal is to restore watersheds. I once overheard a conversation that crystallized the difference for me. My home phone rang one day not long after I had left my other company. My three-year-old son answered, and the caller was trying to find out if his daddy was the same person who used to work for the other company. He said, "No, my daddy works for the environment." A three-year-old could grasp the reality of what we were doing, and that made me feel really good.

MECHANICS' INSTITUTE LIBRARY
57 Post Street
San Francisco, CA 94104
(415) 393-0101

Listening to the Land: Ecology as the Art of Restoring Relationships

The Human-Nature Dance:
People as a Keystone Species

Malcolm Margolin

Malcolm Margolin is a sixty-something, very smart, nice Jewish guy with a distinct Boston accent and an awesome beard who falls in love with cultures. When he moved to the San Francisco Bay Area in the early 1970s, he founded Heyday Books to publish works about California. The company has become a vital small press with an expanding list of titles covering the Golden State's natural history, ecology, literature, and, above all, Native American peoples, perhaps Malcolm's greatest passion.

One of the first books he published (and wrote), The Ohlone Way, *became an instant classic. He has become one of the most important publishers of works on Native American topics and one of those most respected by indigenous peoples. He also operates the Clapperstick Institute, a nonprofit wing of Heyday Books that publishes the magazines* News from Native California *and* Bay Nature.

When Malcolm arrived out west, he thought he might write a pamphlet on the Native Americans who inhabited San Francisco before the arrival of Europeans. Having imagined a simple people living off the abundant land with slight impact, he was curious about what it had been like before Europeans so drastically altered the landscape. But his extensive research revealed that the Bay Area had not been a wilderness at all when indigenous peoples lived there. Firsthand accounts instead revealed a superbly managed coevolutionary landscape in which humans were a keystone species consciously affecting the health and well-being of the greater biotic community.

Malcolm's work has helped transform our understanding of pre-Columbian land management methods. With unwavering dedication, he has been instrumental in preserving and resurrecting that knowledge, reviving ancient guideposts from indigenous science and culture whose practical and spiritual wisdom are invaluable today.

THE FIRST EUROPEANS to arrive in California in the late eighteenth and early nineteenth centuries had a wonderful vision of the land. Ship captains have given us marvelous descriptions of coming through the Golden Gate past enormous pods of spouting whales, huge waves of smelt, and tremendous runs of king salmon. As they commonly described the experience, it looked as though you could walk across the straits on the backs of the salmon. Geese and ducks blackened the sky with their numbers. Inland, the Europeans found massive herds of tule elk and pronghorn antelope, as well as giant condors, eagles, and grizzly bears. It was an astoundingly fertile area.

Besides the extraordinary wealth of wildlife, early travelers remarked on the paradisiacal character of the landscape itself. One description came from George Vancouver, a British sea captain who had sailed with Captain Cook in the 1780s and later formed his own expedition, which explored a lot of Alaska and what's now Vancouver Island and Vancouver Straits. In November 1792, he sailed into San Francisco Bay, stopped at the Presidio, then headed down the peninsula to the Santa Clara Valley by boat and horse. In *A Voyage of Discovery to the North Pacific Ocean*, Vancouver crowed about the luxuriant fertility of the verdant open spaces enriched with stately trees of many varieties:

> About noon, having been advanced about 23 miles, we arrived at a very pleasant and enchanting lawn situated amid a grove of trees at the foot of a small hill by which flowed a very fine stream of excellent water.
>
> We had not proceeded far from this delightful spot when we entered a country I didn't expect to find in these regions. For about twenty miles, it could only be compared to a park, which had originally been closely planted with true old English oak. The underwood that had probably attended its early growth had the appearance of having been cleared away, and had left the stately lords of the forest in complete possession of the soil, which was covered with luxuriant herbage, grasses, and beautifully diversified with pleasing eminences and valleys.

Traveler after traveler would come through and find big bold oak trees and a wonderful clear understory of open land. Most observers described it as looking like an old English park—meaning an open woodland with well-established trees, such as aristocrats maintained on their estates to hunt in. In 1833, the fur trapper George Yount settled in the Napa Valley in what's now Yountville, not far from Napa. In a chronicle of his adventures (published by the California Historical Society in 1923), Yount wrote:

It was nothing more than a wide and extended lawn, exuberant in wild oats and the place for wild beasts to lie down in. The deer, antelope, and noble elk held quiet and undisturbed possession of all that wide domain. The above-named animals were numerous beyond all parallel, and herds of many hundreds . . . might be met so tame that they would hardly move to open the way for the traveler to pass. They were seen lying or grazing in immense herds on the sunny side of every hill, and their young like lambs frolicking in all directions. The wild geese and every species of water fowl darkened the surface of every bay and firth, and upon the land in flocks of millions they wandered in quest of insects and cropping the wild oats which grew there in the richest abundance. When disturbed, they arose to fly. The sound of their wings was like that of distant thunder. The rivers were literally crowded with salmon. It was a land of plenty, and such a climate that no other land can boast of.

Here's a description from *Indian Summer* by a man named Thomas Jefferson Mayfield, who came to California as a child in 1850. He traveled into the San Joaquin Valley, where he described the profusion of different kinds of flowers:

As we passed below the hills, the whole plain was covered with great patches of rose, yellow, scarlet, orange and blue. The colors did not seem to mix to any great extent. Each kind of flower liked a certain kind of soil best, and some of the patches of one color were a mile or more across. I believe that we were more excited out there on the plains among the wild flowers than we had been when we saw the valley for the first time from the mountain the day before. Several times we stopped to pick the different kinds of flowers, and soon we had our horses and packs decorated with masses of all colors.

The California these travelers observed was an extraordinarily lovely land of bursting fecundity, abundant wildlife, and dazzling flowers. They considered it a "wilderness," and believed that what they saw was the land in its natural state. Indians were living there, of course, but they were viewed as environmentally inconsequential, merely living off the fat of the land. When a few acorns fell off a tree, they ate them, and they would hunt a few deer and gather some seeds.

According to the Europeans' naïve view, Indians had lived in California for thousands of years without altering the land. But the landscape discovered by the newcomers was not what natural California looks like. If you leave the land alone, you do not get forests that look like parks. You do not get meadows that grow in this way. Of course, it wasn't as though the native people cultivated every square inch, but to a large extent "primeval" California was a landscape managed by human beings in a very particular and conscious way.

For California natives, managing the land began with a deeply detailed knowledge of place—climate, seasons, soil, plants, and animals—around which their own lives were organized. Encoded in their intricate and eminently practical relationships with the land was a conscious ecological ethos, a living land ethic that recognized people as playing a central environmental and spiritual role in the web of life.

I remember once walking with Ben Lucas, a wonderful old Pomo Indian gentleman from the Stewart's Point Reservation, on the hills above Stewart's Point near Mendocino. It was springtime and the elderberry was flowering. I said, "Ah, Ben, isn't that elderberry just beautiful?" He replied, "It's beautiful, but it makes me sad, because when the elderberry flowers, it means that we can't go down to the bay anymore and collect shellfish, because the shellfish have become poisonous. When the berry ripens in the fall, that's the signal that you can go down and start collecting shellfish again."

Another time, on a Hupa reservation, a fellow named Ray Baldy was walking around when a wren began to tweet, singing its little heart out. Ray said, "Oh, good. That means the salmon will be here in another four days."

I started to collect some of this information, because it fades away rather rapidly when the elders die. I found that all of these people had a phenomenological calendar of some sort, specific to cycles and to particular places. It was wonderfully supple and flexible, reflecting a world in which natural events were keyed to one another with great subtlety and nuance. According to this kind of calendar, people knew that when the strawberry ripened, you would have a festival, and then so many days later you'd know you could go up to certain hills and collect *Brodiaea* bulbs to eat. All these events were linked, one to the next. Every community had an intense and highly localized relationship to a place and a very precise knowledge of the land.

One common method of managing land and resources was to control animal populations. For example, everyone in California had rabbit drives at certain times of the year, often in the spring. Whole villages would get together and either burn the rabbits out or run them into nets, using special rabbit sticks, like boomerangs, to fling at their legs. Afterward there was feasting on rabbit, and the skins were used to make warm blankets and very strong ropes.

Viewed from the standpoint of land management, this activity has very interesting implications. People tended to do it in the spring, when new plants were growing. A big population of rabbits would compete directly with humans and other herbivores for the plants, so the rabbit drives were a deliberate strategy to keep their numbers down while gaining multiple other benefits, including food and tools.

The California natives ate lower on the food chain than we do today. They consumed foods that white settlers had contempt for, such as squirrels, mice, gophers, and grasshoppers, which everybody said tasted like shrimp. They also ate oak moths and moth larvae, which everybody said tasted like shrimp. And they ate shrimp, which everybody said tasted like moth larvae. But, of course, eating certain animals at certain times of year was a powerful land management tool, controlling populations that could otherwise compete too successfully for the food supply or harm the land's productivity.

Food was shared communally—a marvelous social device that prevents overconsumption and uses resources very efficiently. When people hunt and gather food individually, they have to stockpile because the next week they might be sick or have bad luck in their hunting. When it's shared among people, there is less need to stockpile. Sharing becomes an amazingly efficient way of using resources.

Perhaps the most powerful of the natives' land management practices was to burn the land. When the first Europeans came, they were horrified at what they called the Indians' "addiction" to burning the land. At certain seasons smoke rose everywhere, looking like Los Angeles smog. Among the earliest laws of every county in California was a regulation forbidding the burning of public land. It was specifically aimed at Indians, providing a basis to arrest them for burning.

But the natives knew exactly why they burned. It cleared the understory, removed undesirable trees, and fostered the growth of large trees. Whole parts of the Klamath River area that today are choked with Douglas fir and other coniferous trees were open meadows with sugar pine when the first Europeans came. Those forests Vancouver was talking about—those large English-style parks the explorers admired—were not a natural environment. They arose from continual burning and clearing.

The Indians burned because it cleared out the brush and fostered certain kinds of grasses with large seeds that were used for food. It improved the game habitat. People who relied on acorns for food would burn at certain times of year to get rid of oak moths, which could create terrible infestations. They knew that if they burned at the stage when the oak moth lives underground, they could eliminate the moths for that year.

Another cultural technique was to repeatedly clip and coppice plants used for basketry. Certain plants, like willows, hazel, and redbud, were continually trimmed down to a nub, because this causes them to grow up the next year with tall, straight shoots that are great for basketry. If you don't trim them, they get kinky and are no good for weaving. Basket-weaving provided yet another reason to burn, because bear grass and other kinds of basketry grasses come up as straight shoots after they're burned.

The glorious meadows of flowers that Europeans exclaimed over were in some cases created or enhanced by Indians for practical purposes. In a poignant irony, the whites who first came to California—many of them to dig for gold—contemptuously called the natives "digger" Indians because they were out digging for roots a lot of the time. The term was intended as a slur.

One of the plants they dug for most often was the *Brodiaea* bulb, a little lily that people liked to eat. Feasts were held when people came home with huge baskets full of the bulbs. When I read a description of this, I wondered how they could possibly harvest such quantities of bulbs with just a digging stick.

Kat Anderson, who worked at Yosemite and was a student of California native culture, began to listen to some of the older Indians talking about how they went out to gather *Brodiaea*. She asked them, "How did you gather these bulbs? When was the right time to go out? You didn't just go out anytime, did you?"

She learned that they went at a very precise time, and they dug the plants in a special way. They would push the digging stick in and pry it up. If you do this at the right time of the year, not only do you find a bulb, but all around each bulb are nearly fifty tiny bulbettes just beginning to form. Part of the gathering is to rip the top off, rub the bulbettes off the bulb, throw it in the basket, and collect another one.

Kat tried this technique. The second year she did it, she went back to the same place and discovered not just a few *Brodiaea* bulbs, but many. She realized that this digging technique loosened the soil and scattered the bulbettes. When she went back the third year, there were incredibly many more *Brodiaea* bulbs. And after five years, it began to look like those old descriptions of California's abundance.

In truth, it was a reflection of a cultivated landscape. The indigenous knowledge was that by gathering something, you increased the productivity of the land. Rather than collecting plants in a predatory way and depleting the *Brodiaea* bulbs, by gathering you propagated the plant.

In modern times, we don't eat this kind of food, and people say we don't need a primitive digging stick. But if we want these bulbs to be there, we should go out and gather them anyway, in a knowledgeable way.

An example of this are the huge clam beds that once existed in the Bay Area, which were actually created by people. The Bay Area was widely known for years for its rich clam and oyster beds. Over time, much of this resource was destroyed within San Francisco Bay itself, but it endured for much longer in Tomales Bay, just north of San Francisco. Until the 1920s, Tomales Bay had eleven major clam and oyster beds that were used by the Coast Miwok people, who were living much where they'd always lived, near the present town of Marshall. They would collect clams in fairly large numbers from the bay and sell them.

In the 1920s the state parks and wildlife people took over the management of this area and began to set controls on what could be hunted, fished, and collected. The Miwok protested, saying, "Our harvesting these things is what's keeping these clam beds alive." The government asked what they meant, and the Indians said, "It's because the clams know that we're coming that they're growing; we've had this long relationship with them." Of course, that kind of reasoning doesn't hold water with parks and wildlife bureaucrats, who declared that the beds were a wild resource that the Indians were depleting. Officials banned the collecting, and soon nearly all the Miwok moved away from Marshall. Four or five years after their leaving, only one of the eleven original clam beds was still viable. The government then did a scientific study that found that the act of taking clams out was aerating the beds. Removing the larger ones was creating room for others, like weeding. The harvesting also served to build up the walls and banks of the clam beds against erosion from the incoming tides. The scientists wrote a very interesting paper that essentially concluded, "Well, we thought this was a wild resource, but it wasn't. It was a cultivated farm that was kept by human beings."

These were not wild systems, and the Indians had their own regulations—for example, on salmon fishing and on game taking. There were prescribed techniques by which you could hunt certain animals and not others. There were nuanced practices for game management. There was a very foggy line between domestic and wild and an altogether much more porous relationship with the animal world than we have.

Another aspect of food gathering has to do with local ownership, or access to resources based on local wisdom. Despite a misperception that Indians didn't own land, the fact is they did own rights in some places. In California, some things were owned, such as fishing places, trees, gathering rights, and even land itself in some cases. Different families had collecting rights in certain places, and people would go back to the same place year after year.

Property ownership was one of the greatest tools of land management. Ownership of this kind was, I believe, a thoughtful way of allocating scarce resources. It entailed not only a right to gather but a responsibility to the land. The idea was that when you owned something, it created an incentive for moderation. You might have responsibilities to a particular tree, for example, and you would show restraint because you knew you would have to come back to it next year. We have a lot to learn from such systems of ownership, which gave rights but also demanded responsibilities.

Some lands were held in common and some were not owned by anyone, but access to certain other lands was strictly limited. If your family wanted access to such a place, you had to ask for it, and there would be a trade-off of some sort. (When warfare broke out in California, which it did on a fairly localized level, it was usually over somebody invading a resource that belonged to another family or tribe.) California Indians had very conscious systems of conservation and control, and private property was indeed one of them.

A beautiful example of conservation was a rock quarry near Oroville that was a source of chert, a hard rock used for making scrapers, arrowheads, and the like. This area doesn't have a lot of obsidian or other minerals, so the chert was extremely valuable. The Indians had been quarrying this spot for who knows how long. In a sense it was owned in common. Any local male could go into the quarry, which was dug into the hill like a cave, once each year and take out as much as he could get with the single blow of a hammer. He had to leave an offering of money beads on the way out. These laws were encoded in religion, and if a person broke them, there were grave repercussions. That the rules were strictly observed was a tribute to the power of this place, and in part clearly reflected a conservation ethic. Limiting access to the quarry and making certain that nobody took more than his share assured that the chert would last for several generations.

Another example of cooperative conservation concerned fishing rights. People living on northern California rivers would build a dam or a fish weir that was, to an extent, common property. However, religious officials were allowed to go first and get whatever fish they could use; then the common people came and got their share. The weir could not be built more than a third of the way across the river, and even then all the fishing had to be done in the morning, after which the weir was opened so that the fish could get through.

The entire fishing season was regulated and ended after about three weeks. Again, there was a conscious purpose to this: people living upstream from the weir could get their fish, and the fish would be able to spawn, reproduce, and replenish their numbers. All the way up and down the Klamath River drainage, among the Yurok, the Karok, and the Shasta peoples, up the Trinity River, among the Hupa and the Wintun—among all these peoples speaking different languages there existed, in effect, a whole series of international fishing treaties.

California Indians also observed different kinds of hunting territories, and who could and could not use them, who could use them in exchange for gifts, and so on. The penalties were ferocious for anyone who broke these laws. The values that people have held in complex, traditional societies that have lived in the same place for thousands of years are encoded in language, religion, customs, and intricate clan relationships. It's a marvelously deep knowledge. We love to think that we live in a complicated world and Indians lived in a simple world, but it's not necessarily true.

To be a human being in this way, to learn such practices, required more than one generation. Among California's Native Americans, this knowledge was learned and transmitted over many generations, and a lot of it is still around. Perhaps above all, it gives us a view of humanity as not living apart from nature and being destructive to the natural world. These traditions and peoples show us splendidly how, by our way of living, we can actually be a blessing to the world.

Indigenous Science:
The Cultivated Landscape
of Native America

Dennis Martinez

Dennis Martinez can usually be found foraging in the wilderness or repairing a damaged landscape. A Native American restoration ecologist, he has an encyclopedic knowledge of Turtle Island—now known as North America—that stands on the shoulders of his indigenous ancestors. He has studied their practices closely, and his mastery of their varied, complex, and highly sophisticated land management techniques has given him a singular depth and scope of expertise.

Of Chicano and O'odham descent, Dennis is founder of the Indigenous Peoples' Restoration Network. He has worked with the InterTribal Sinkyone Wilderness Council, the Takelma Intertribal Project, and the Kaho'olawe Island Reserve Commission of Hawaii, among many others, as a contract seed collector, vegetation surveyor, eco-forester, and restoration contractor and consultant.

Part of the story that Dennis tells and lives is how the First Peoples successfully managed Turtle Island as a vast coevolutionary landscape of exceptional fertility and endurance. His work reviving a treasure trove of indigenous know-how shows how people can live in a beneficial reciprocal relationship with the land. There are few endeavors more important and relevant today than regaining this practical knowledge. As we face a host of unnatural disasters caused by centuries of land mismanagement and the absence of a land ethic, one of our best hopes is someone like Dennis, patiently and lovingly heeding the heartbeat of the land, teaching us anew the ancient ways of humans on earth.

FIRST I WANT TO ACKNOWLEDGE all the traditional elders, my ancestors, because without them we wouldn't be here. I acknowledge their contributions, not only to our lives and our learning, but also to the very land-scape that in North America became the breadbasket of the world. It wasn't by accident that this is a fertile country. It wasn't by accident that tremendous numbers of old-growth trees have gone into the building of city after city.

The spacing of those trees, their ability to reach their full genetic poten-tial, and all the qualities that have inspired so many activists to protect the an-cient forests were not the product of chance. For at least 12,000 years, since the last ice age and probably well before that, fertility was continuously main-tained in most North American ecosystems by fire: the intentional fire of in-digenous people, augmented by random lightning fires. Every account of pi-oneer settlers recognized the continent's tremendous biodiversity: flowers and their pollinators, seed carriers such as ants, and the incredible numbers of birds and other wildlife, including the large predators at the top of the food chain. Native America was truly a paradise, an amazingly fertile place that did not require any input of petrochemicals. This fertility and diversity disappeared in a relatively short time. When you look around at the landscape now, it's not so easy to see how it used to be.

Although I'm speaking from a Native American perspective, I want to make it clear that my viewpoint does not invalidate other perspectives. I'm not saying that the way the Indian people conducted agroecology is the only way to do things. A lot of things have changed and we have many new tools at our disposal, as well as environmental problems we've never faced before. Restoration must be adaptive, balancing fidelity to a historical reference ecosystem (as an initial guide to basic features of forest structure and compo-sition) with ecological functionality, which may fall short of our historical model but which strives to achieve as much integrity as possible under changed modern conditions. Why are past Indian burning regimes and se-lective harvesting, for example, important? Because the millennia-long co-evolution of Indians and their environment built a relationship that un-doubtedly affected the abundance and distribution—and probably the very DNA—of many species favored by Indian management. To ignore this fact is to risk doing poor ecological science.

Nor can we ignore the fact that many indigenous people made serious mistakes in how they treated the environment. The evidence on the extinctions of megafauna (large mammals) is ambiguous, but it's entirely possible that people in Hawaii and in other parts of the world, including North America, made serious miscalculations. For example, one environmental modeler in the United Kingdom calculated that just a 2 percent annual take of mastodons, if other environmental factors were also contributing to their decline, was all that was necessary to make them extinct.

Mistakes aside, the evidence of thousands of years of human presence on the continent demonstrates overall a deep understanding of how the land could be shaped and sustained to the benefit of all life forms. And it demonstrates that, contrary to what Europeans may have believed, they found in North America a well-populated land. This contradicts the prevalent image that there were just a handful of native people, more or less living in a Garden of Eden, enjoying the bounty of nature without really doing much. (Over the past century, estimates of North American Indian populations have been consistently revised upward, from 2 million, estimated by James Mooney in the early 1900s, to Henry Dobyns's current estimate of 18 million, and 112 million for the hemisphere.)

In the sixteenth century, Pope Leo X called the New World *terra nullius*, empty land, and his papal doctrine justified the ensuing genocide of native people. Because, in the eyes of Europeans, native peoples were not doing anything to enhance the productivity of the land, the immigrants claimed the God-given right to exploit and develop it. The British philosopher John Locke, building on Saint Thomas Aquinas's labor theory of value, asserted that lands stolen from Indians could be made legal and legitimate by the labor of settlers. As we shall see, Indians were in fact doing a lot to enhance the productive capacity of Turtle Island. *Terra nullius* was a self-serving myth for stealing Indian lands. (In Australia the doctrine of *terra nullius* held sway for over two hundred years, until it was successfully challenged in 1992 by the Australian High Court, which ruled that native land title had not necessarily been extinguished.)

The great myth of the pioneers is that they came to a land of deep dark forest and took down the trees, then worked this virgin land and made it bloom. This idea could not be farther from the truth. If it had not been for Indian fires on the Great Plains, there would have been no breadbasket to feed the world, because over time, trees encroach on grassland, especially tallgrass prairie. American cities could be built with old-growth trees because Indians had conducted complex agroforestry practices that included regularly thinning trees and burning the understory, including tree seedlings and saplings. Meadows, fields, and trails were in place, allowing settlers to create towns and highways without needing to fell a single tree, because of Indian agriculture and fire, which the indigenous inhabitants used to consciously create corridors and open spaces for both human and animal movement and migration.

The converse applied as well: in every place that indigenous peoples were removed from their ancestral lands or died in droves from European diseases, the open spaces and meadows began to close up, closing off numerous herbivores' access to fresh and nutritious plants.

Trying to travel across country today is not easy in a lot of places in North America, for people or animals. Yet there was a time, people say—and some of them are still alive—when you could ride a horse over great distances without ever having to dismount, and this was because of Indian-created trails and corridors. On the other hand, I've also heard it said that a squirrel could once go from Massachusetts to Missouri without ever touching the ground. We have here two apparently different views of the forest as it was at the time of first contact. The fact is that there were large trees with large spaces between them, but overhanging branches would have allowed those squirrels to jump from one tree to another. In between, there wasn't a lot of brush or young trees coming up. This was the condition virtually everywhere in forested North America, as determined by age-class and fire-scar studies carried out by fire ecologists, as well as by the oral histories of native peoples.

Clearly the Indians were interacting closely with their environment, and in fact intervening in sophisticated ways. Let me offer a personal example. I was busted high in the Siskiyou Mountains on the Oregon-California border for harvesting osha root (*Angelica arguta*) in a botanical reserve. I understand that it's a problem for all of us when plant and butterfly collectors exploit resources. But that's not the case here. When the ranger in the fire lookout tower saw me digging and stopped me, I tried to explain that there wasn't a single young plant in the whole patch. Every plant was old and getting older, and by digging that plant, I was encouraging seeds to get established in the seedbed I had created. My actions were also recycling nutrients, something that fires, which had been outlawed in the botanical preserve, would otherwise have done.

Fire serves multiple purposes in the landscape. It stimulates germination of hard seeds; opens closed-cone conifers to release seeds that germinate following the fire; increases water retention by removing excess vegetation that sucks up groundwater and emits it into the atmosphere through evapotranspiration; breaks up the overwintering cycle of insects that prey on important wildlife and cultural plants like oaks; decreases forest soil acidity, thereby making more nutrients available to plants; and much more.

The incident in the Siskiyous highlights the whole issue of what is "natural," as well as the profound misunderstanding of Native Americans' role in shaping the landscape, which has led to a lot of mismanagement of natural resources—sometimes in the name of conservation. For instance, John Muir, for whom I generally have great respect, was mistaken about the "natural" condition of oak trees in Yosemite. Of course, the black oak (*Quercus kelloggii*) yielded acorns, an important food for the Ahwaneechee band of Miwok Indians who lived there. For at least 10,000 years the Ahwaneechee people had harvested those acorns and burned the understory almost every year to prevent brush buildup. Muir said the Indians should not be allowed to burn, and park personnel should not be allowed to cut brush under the oak trees, brush that was shading out oak seedlings, because he felt that humans have no part to play in a natural system. He believed that we need some places that are entirely shielded from human beings, in order to see the full beauty and spirit of "pristine" nature. Unfortunately for the Ahwaneechee, Muir's pristine nature was their homeland, livelihood, and church (to paraphrase Muir).

Indians had been allowed to live in Yosemite Park as long as they promoted tourism, but Muir's outlook eventually prevailed, and for a variety of reasons the Indians were removed. As a result, their major acorn-collecting places became choked with brush. The white fir *(Abies concolor)* and incense cedar *(Calocedrus decurrens)* coming up in the oak stands shaded out any healthy regeneration. There were no fires to recycle the nutrients. Acorn production declined. The open oak and conifer parkland that characterized Yosemite Valley was replaced by dense stands of conifer monocultures overtopping old dying trees.

Similarly, the Paiute in Nevada relied on osha root during the time of the Spanish influenza, when no Paiute who regularly used osha died from the flu. Osha is a very important medicinal plant that grows in the high country of the Great Basin, the Sierra Nevada, and the Klamath Mountains. It's maintained by burning. That's the only way. Fire suppression has stopped the regeneration of osha throughout the intermountain West.

This pattern has been repeated in many places. When I worked with the Klamath tribe in Klamath Falls, Oregon, with an intertribal group called the Modoc-Yahooskin Paiute Confederation, I went out to their patches of osha and mule's ears *(Wyethia angustifolia)*. In each case, there was no regeneration with these plants. They were being overtopped by Great Basin sage and conifers. These patches were on Winema National Forest land. We put a lot of pressure on the supervisor's office and finally established a traditional burning pattern in order to rejuvenate those patches. They began to proliferate and regenerate.

These are the kinds of reasons I do a lot of forest thinning, which is selective logging using a sustainable eco-forestry approach. After thinning, I burn the area and seed grasses and other native plants in the ashes.

I also work in dry tropical forest ecosystems, where I'm against using fire. Each ecosystem is different. In temperate ecosystems you need fire because these colder systems decompose ground litter very slowly compared to tropical systems. Indigenous people like the Ahwaneechee understood that. If you look at photographs of Yosemite Valley today, compared with those taken at the time of its establishment as a national park, it's unbelievable how many trees have moved into that valley. Prime wildlife habitat—the robust herbaceous understory growing in the spaces between the trees and meadows—is being taken over by conifers.

Researchers in Oregon have predicted that in about thirty years, all white oak *(Quercus garryana)* will have stopped regenerating because of overtopping by Douglas fir, the number one weed tree in the Pacific Northwest. Most white oak stands consist of small, multistemmed trees that are densely packed and stagnating; the shading-out by Douglas fir is the last nail in their coffin. What's ironic—and I've been part of it—is that we who have protested the taking of old-growth Douglas fir, or even mature second-growth Douglas fir, have tended to forget about all the other plants in the understory. Sometimes we don't see the forest for the trees.

There are many negative consequences to this kind of neglect. In many places, traditional people can no longer find ceremonial plants, ceremonial animals, or even animals for food. Modern industrial logging and fire suppression have severely impacted important traditional cultural plants and animals.

Apart from logging and fire suppression, the other major environmental problem has been the physical removal of Indians from the ancestral lands they cared for. What I'm suggesting about Indian people and their caretaking of the land is that humans are keystone species in natural ecosystems. When these caregivers are removed, certain things begin to unravel within that system. For instance, the 1988 Yellowstone fire had a catastrophic effect on forest ecosystems because people weren't limiting the fuel buildup. Lightning fires are natural, but so many fire cycles had been missed that the level of buildup was outside the range of natural or historical variability. The fire was a disturbance event with which the forest was not historically familiar. Fires had been suppressed for a very long time after the removal of the Indians. It is also true that some high-elevation forests accumulate fuel for centuries before they burn. It's the balance that's missing.

The recent floods in Yosemite—the worst in the valley's known history—provide an extreme example. The last Ahwaneechee to live in the national park (allowed to live there as long as he was employed by the park) was Jay Johnson, whose father had predicted that a natural calamity would befall Yosemite Valley when the last Indian left. The day after Jay Johnson retired on January 1, 1997, saw a rainstorm so strong that huge rocks fell from the surrounding cliffs to the valley below. The falling boulders offered a powerful and literal symbol of the unraveling that occurs when indigenous people are removed from the land.

Diversity is destroyed in many subtle ways in modern times. While flying over the British Isles from Amsterdam, I noticed that in East Anglia, the first place you see when you're coming from Europe, many farm fields were still enclosed by hedgerows. But as I got farther north and especially farther west, most of the hedgerows were gone. Traditionally, hedgerows performed a lot of important functions, among which was delineating the boundaries of fields, allowing farmers to easily tell which part of the field got too wet or too dry, which part needed additional fertilizer or manure, and which part needed a fallowing in a four-year rotation. Now, however, multinational corporations are growing monocultures of rye, corn, cereals, and vegetables from field edge to field edge, and they have begun removing all the hedgerows.

You might not think of Britain and its indigenous population as having much to do with biodiversity. This landscape has been totally humanized since pre-Roman (Celtic) times. The major change over the millennia has been the loss of old forests, which have been extremely fragmented. As a result, the beaver, wolverine, wolf, bear, otter, and virtually all wild Atlantic salmon disappeared many hundreds of years ago. Yet the greatest species loss in Britain has taken place in the past fifty years, as a result of industrial agriculture. Large-scale agriculture encouraged by huge government subsidies began to create a system that poured incredible amounts of pesticides onto these crop monocultures. This system has crowded out all the edges, all the marginal areas and places where wildlife could be.

Even an apparently small change has a devastating effect. When people used hand scythes to mow their grass, the unevenness in how this tool cut the grass allowed flowers of different heights to exist with the grasses. Just changing that alone caused a steep decline in flower populations and the extinctions of many flowering plants throughout the United Kingdom. With the consequent crash of invertebrates and pollinators came a crash of birds. In other words, ecological systems function not just top down but also bottom up. Everything is in a circle. All levels of the food web intersect, and energy flows through every level of an ecosystem.

Indigenous and local people worldwide work within that system—where they're still allowed to work that way—whether in *milpas* (gardens) in Chiapas, the Yucatan, and Guatemala, or among the manicured fields, coppiced old hardwoods, and trimmed hedgerows of Britain. British researchers found a positive correlation between the age of those hedgerows and species diversity. The older the stands are, the greater the diversity of species. Three hundred fifty years usually means a high level of species diversity. The same principle holds true with our old-growth forests in North America. (The term "old growth" is somewhat misleading: ancient forests really consist of all stages of vegetation development, which are slowly recycled by fire and other disturbances at the landscape level. "Forest integrity" is a more accurate term.)

What do British hedgerows and burning of the understory by American Indians have in common? Both are examples—models that can be multiplied globally—of indigenous humans working with natural processes to enhance the functionality of ecosystems that otherwise cannot satisfy cultural and economic needs. Some forest ecosystems are relatively resource poor, such as the redwood–mixed evergreen–conifer forest types of coastal northern California. Indian fire interrupted climate-driven forest development (succession) just enough to shift forest structure and composition in the direction of more optimal habitat for wildlife and humans. In Britain, you'd have a hard time getting forests to burn with a flamethrower. So people coppiced the wildwoods and planted hedgerows to meet their economic and cultural needs.

I participated in a conservation biology conference in Irvine, California, that focused on the California gnatcatcher, which is going extinct in Orange and San Diego counties. Yet it's thriving in nearby Northern Baja in Mexico. What's the reason? People in Mexico let fires burn (because they can't afford to put them out). As a result there is still a mosaic of vegetation of different ages. In addition, nobody really planned the towns in Mexico. Until very recently, there was usually a scattering of houses mixed with patches of weeds and gardens. But in the United States we haven't built any slack for wildlife into our development pattern, which has laid a blanket of concrete, asphalt, and petrochemical-enhanced grass over entire areas. Just locking up large areas of chaparral in southern California is not enough to restore the gnatcatcher, because this habitat is degraded due to fire suppression. Indians burned chaparral often, at least every twenty years, to create a mosaic of brush islands in a sea of grass—quality gnatcatcher habitat.

Indigenous people have recognized that you can't overly control the environment without serious repercussions. They knew this even before experiencing modern technology. As a result, they developed ethics teaching us that if we ignore the needs of our relatives in the natural world, we will suffer serious repercussions, because every animal and every tree has a spirit or soul. A forest is not just trees. A forest is a whole bunch of eyes watching you all the time.

As part of the Takelma Intertribal Project, we hold a Salmon Homecoming Ceremony in June in Oregon's Applegate Watershed. After ritually eating the salmon, we take the bones from the first cut down to the Applegate River. A couple of young Indian men go into the cold water and deposit the bones there. Those bones go downstream, and then all the fish coming upstream will see that the bones have been treated respectfully. We brought back this ceremony after an absence of over 150 years as an intertribal effort.

The indigenous approach to environmental ethics is closely tied to a practical sense of taking care of your livelihood by first taking care of the earth. As the elders say, if you take care of the plants and animals, they will take care of you. When you don't pay attention to them and don't use them, they get sad, the older people say, and go away. If you misuse them, you will suffer serious repercussions.

We have stories derived from the time when animals could talk to humans and humans could talk to animals. That special relationship has been lost. But in every ancestral land there exists a sacred geography and creation stories that weave through it. By remembering those stories and teaching them to our children, we keep alive a vision of the old relationship between humans and the natural world, and between humans and humans, that gives us ethics we can apply to daily life. The stories teach us how to live. When the stories vanish, it's over. Fortunately, we still have many stories, and creation has never stopped. The stories come to life in each new generation, and each generation has the responsibility of participating in the re-creation of the world through ceremonies and caregiving practices.

But the truth is that we have lost a great deal of knowledge, and modern science has only recently begun to explore ecological restoration. I make my living in restoration, and the more I work with the natural world, the more I realize how little control we humans have and how unpredictable everything is. On the other side of the coin, if we don't start projects, monitor and collect data, preserve and use our traditional indigenous knowledge, and make notes about what we're doing so that it enters the literature, we're never going to know in what ways humans can assist nature. At all times we have to remember that we don't heal the land by ourselves. We intervene no more than is necessary to allow natural processes to heal the land.

It's no accident that tricksters like Coyote and Raven are often creators in North American tribal stories, because it's the nature of the universe to be really iffy. There is an unpredictability to restoration. We're going to be surprised. We're talking about apparent chaos and we're talking about love. The value of indigenous knowledge is that people, just like ecosystems, have learned to be resilient through dynamic interaction with the natural world.

With this kind of awareness, people have learned to build buffers against unusual events, such as hundred-year floods and droughts. No one event can wipe you out if you have developed the capacity to bounce back. This resilient relationship with the land is the gift indigenous cultures have to offer. They teach us to work with chaos, with change, with the unpredictable, and to work with humility. Above all, we have to love the natural world, the plants and the animals, and take care of them as we would our own family.

The challenge of our time is that the scale of destruction we face today is greater than any tribal group, indigenous people, nation, or culture has ever had to deal with. This means that not only do we have to go back to traditional ecological knowledge to find out where we went off the track and how to get back on, but we also need to bring in Western ecological science as well. We need to integrate those two very different kinds of knowledge.

We can't translate worldviews across the board because the cosmologies are too different. What I'm suggesting is that we evaluate what to use, when to use it, and how to assess what we're going to restore. What standard are we going to restore to? In other words, how do we participate in an accelerated creation and re-creation process in the midst of rampant destruction?

Restoration writ large is not just a landscape restoration project. It's a community-based intergenerational endeavor. It's more a process than a product. It's about relationships. It's about our responsibility as human beings to participate every day in the re-creation of the earth.

The Green-Fire Wolf:
Saving Wildlands with a Wild Heart

Dave Foreman

Dave Foreman is one of the most illustrious figures in American conservation. An impassioned defender of our world's dwindling biodiversity, especially large carnivores, he has made a remarkable activist odyssey.

In 1973, Dave started out in the more established sector of the conservation movement, as Southwest representative of the Wilderness Society. He went on to emerge as the most visible cofounder of the radical group Earth First! which has played such an important role in reinvigorating direct-action protests to save wildlands. No stranger to controversy in those days, he had to suffer through a high-profile arrest for allegedly conspiring to monkey-wrench an Arizona nuclear reactor. Audubon Magazine named him one of the "100 Champions of Conservation" of the twentieth century.

Along with some of the nation's brilliant conservation biologists and ecological thinkers, Dave recently cofounded one of the most important conservation initiatives of our time, the Wildlands Project. He served as executive editor and publisher of its journal, Wild Earth, *until 2003. He is also the author or coeditor of several influential books, including* Ecodefense, Defending the Earth, Confessions of an Eco-Warrior, The Big Outside, *and* Rewilding North America. *He is currently director and senior fellow at the Rewilding Institute, a think tank advancing pragmatic strategies for continental conservation, and he is the lead author of the Sky Islands Wildlands Network Conservation Plan. He somehow manages to find time to backpack, run rivers, paddle canoes, fly-fish, hunt, bird-watch, and photograph the great outdoors, too.*

What powers Dave is his love of the natural world and its creatures. He has a stubborn passion for wildlands, wild things, and the wild in all of us. Dave is a great

*grizzly of conservation, and because of his efforts, some of the noblest of wild crea-
tures might just get a fighting chance at survival.*

I BELIEVE THAT EXTINCTION is the main event going on in the world
today. Since the dodo became extinct on an island in the Indian Ocean in the
1600s, we have seen dozens of species of birds and mammals disappear, and
even more insects, plants, reptiles, and fish. We are living in an age of mass
extinction.

In the five hundred million years since complex animals evolved, there
have been five great extinction events that we have carefully identified
through studying the fossil records. The last one was sixty-five million years
ago, when the dinosaurs disappeared forever because a massive comet hit earth
somewhere in the Gulf of Mexico. In the 1960s, wildlife biologists began to
compare notes from all over the world. Spotted cats like the ocelot were fast
disappearing. Reptiles like the desert tortoise were becoming endangered as
their habitats were destroyed and they were run over by dirt bikes. We passed
the Endangered Species Act to try to stem the tide of extinction, but it soon
became obvious that we were seeing not just the loss of a few beautiful species
like the ocelot and wonderful little critters like the desert tortoise. We were,
in fact, in the middle of the sixth great extinction, the Pleistocene-Holocene
event.

Leading biologists like E.O. Wilson have predicted that we could lose
up to one-third of all species in the next fifty to a hundred years. This tragedy
is a central reality of our time, and we cannot blame an asteroid for causing it.
It has one and only one cause, and that is six billion human beings breeding,
eating, manufacturing, warring, and traveling. We have become a plague of
extraterrestrial proportions on the earth, and we are causing the extinction of
many of our fellow travelers, including our closest relatives, the primates, and
many other species.

Human-caused extinction takes five main forms. One is the direct perse-
cution and killing of certain animals, such as the campaign we waged in the
mid-twentieth century to wipe out all wolves in the United States, or the mass

slaughter and poisoning of prairie dogs. Another is the introduction of exotic, invasive species, such as that of the bullfrog into southwestern streams, where it eats the native leopard frog and native fish. Disease is another major factor: exotic diseases are spread by humans, pets, rats, and domestic animals. The black-footed ferret was nearly wiped out by distemper, for example. Of course, pollution and industrial activities of all kinds pose a major threat to the survival of many species.

But the leading cause of extinction is habitat destruction through agriculture, overgrazing, development, mining, logging, and other fragmentation of the landscape. If you destroy habitat, you will lose species. A freeway is very difficult for even the wily coyote to get across.

We know from studying island ecosystems that there is a direct relationship between the size of an island and the number of species it holds. As we break up habitat in smaller and smaller pieces, we see the number of species decline. Through careful scientific research we have determined that even Yellowstone National Park is not big enough in itself to maintain viable populations of wide-ranging species like grizzly bears, wolverines, and wolves. And through research in the tropics, oceans, and temperate areas we have recently learned just how important large carnivores are. For example, if you protect enough habitat for a healthy population of wolves, you are protecting habitat for many other species as well.

Top-down regulation is the key to maintaining ecosystems. On the Pacific coast, when sea otters are present, so are healthy kelp forests. When sea otters disappear, the kelp forests do too, because the sea otter's main prey, the sea urchin, is a voracious predator of kelp forests. When you remove the otters, sea urchin populations explode, destroying the kelp forests and the hundreds of species that depend on them.

In suburban San Diego, biologist Michael Soulé has shown what happens as suburbs surround remaining patches of coastal sage scrub in the canyons. As long as coyotes are present in the canyons, all the native birds are there. As soon as the coyotes disappear, so do the native birds. Why? Because any smart house cat, like my beautiful cat Chama, knows to stay home when coyotes are about. Remove the coyotes and the house cats, foxes, skunks, and possums become emboldened and go into these habitats and eat songbirds and their eggs.

The presence of large carnivores affects not just the presence of other species but, just as important, how they interact with their habitat. We have seen how the reintroduction of wolves has entirely changed the behavior of elk in Yellowstone National Park. No longer are elk loafing around and over-grazing meadows. The elk are suddenly elk again: they're looking over their shoulders, they're running around, and the land is much healthier for it. In Isle Royal National Park in Lake Superior, when there's a healthy and balanced population of wolves, they maintain an appropriately balanced population of moose, which means that the balsam fir forest is healthy. But if we remove the wolves or there are too few wolves, the moose overpopulate and overgraze, with dire consequences for the forest.

We have known for a long time that neotropical migrant songbirds of the eastern United States—the warblers and thrushes that go south in the winter and breed in North America in the summer—are declining in numbers. Part of the reason is destruction of their habitat. But a major factor is the absence of mountain lions and wolves. Mountain lions and wolves don't eat baby songbirds. No self-respecting mountain lion is going to skulk about the forest for warbler eggs to suck. The problem is that there are no longer any mountain lions or wolves in the eastern forest, which means the smaller mesopredators multiply. Raccoons, who don't have the self-respect not to suck warbler eggs, become more abundant and act more boldly in the absence of predators. They, along with skunks and foxes, go into the forest and eat songbird eggs and baby warblers.

All over the world we are finding that when we remove large carnivores, the whole system begins to unravel. Large carnivores need big core habitats and they need connections between them. For example, a huge human-made reservoir in Venezuela created a number of islands that are too small to support populations of jaguars and harpy eagles. In the absence of these predators, leaf-eating monkeys and other small animals have become unnaturally abundant, changing the entire composition of the forest. Now only five species of trees are reproducing in a forest that once had sixty.

In the United States, we simply no longer have wild areas large enough to maintain habitat for large populations of jaguars, grizzlies, or wolves. What we need to do is to link wildlands together so that animals can disperse. All it takes to keep two geographically separated populations of mountain lions connected and to avoid inbreeding is for a horny adolescent male mountain lion to range between the two every ten years or so.

This recognition leads me to the idea of rewilding. For healthy ecosystems, we need large core areas, linkages between those core areas, and the presence of keystone species such as large carnivores. How do we achieve this? The Wildlands Project and its sister magazine *Wild Earth* are exploring how we might create such areas, link them, and reintroduce large carnivores to restore healthy landscapes.

To do our work, we have to look across national borders and across the borders between public and private land. Jaguars and thick-billed parrots are both native to New Mexico and Arizona, but they were driven south of the U.S. border a hundred years ago. If we are going to get jaguars and thick-billed parrots back in the mountains of New Mexico and Arizona, we have to protect their habitat in northern Mexico. Recently the Wildlands Project and its partners in Mexico signed a groundbreaking deal with a Mexican land grant commune to protect the largest remaining breeding area for thick-billed parrots in the Sierra Madre, a six-thousand-acre patch of old-growth forest. Because we are paying the members of the commune the value of the forest, they are not going to log it. We plan to work together to develop ecotourism, so that bird-watchers can see the parrots and the local folks can make money. We hope to show that protecting nature, protecting the thick-billed parrot and its habitat, brings more money in the long run than the one-time liquidation of that old-growth forest.

Another Wildlands project revolves around a breeding population of wild jaguars one hundred miles south of the Arizona border, where ranches sell for $15 an acre. Through a Mexican land trust, we are working to buy those ranches and hire local people as wardens. It's not gringos coming in and doing it. We're just trying to provide the money so that jaguars will be able once again to freely disperse, and we look forward to the day when a viable population of jaguars will exist in the wildlands of Arizona and New Mexico.

As well as looking beyond political borders, we have to look beyond the fragmentation of the conservation movement: some people protecting species, other people protecting land, others working on economic incentives. We have to bring it all together in a single, reasonable, coordinated effort to break down barriers and rebuild wild nature in North America, so that human civilization and society can once again begin to coexist with the wild.

I believe that's the fundamental challenge of our times. Do we have the generosity of spirit and the greatness of heart to allow some land a will of its own, where we are not dominating, controlling, and manipulating everything, where some things are beyond human control? That is the other great value of large carnivores to the human spirit: they teach us humility, a virtue in short supply. We are surrounded by human arrogance, but there is nothing like comparing your tracks to a grizzly bear's to teach you humility, to show us that we are not gods upon the planet, lords of all that we survey.

No one has explored our relationship with wild lands and self-willed animals with more understanding and humility than Aldo Leopold, who died over fifty years ago. In 1909, after graduating from Yale University with a master's degree in forestry, he caught a train to the territory of Arizona—it was not yet a state—to work for the newly created U.S. Forest Service in the White Mountains and Mogollon Rim country of eastern Arizona, at that time a vast, roadless wilderness.

Leopold's first job for the forest service was to cruise timber. He and a crew of men would go into the wilderness on horseback for two weeks at a time and count trees. The Forest Service couldn't log those trees because there were no roads, but it wanted to know what was there. On one of the trips, about a week into the wilderness, Leopold and his men had stopped for lunch on a little rimrock overlooking a rushing stream. As they ate their greasy sandwiches of biscuits and bacon, they saw a doe ford the stream below them. At least they thought it was a doe, because of her long legs. But when a bunch of wolf pups came running out of the willows on the other side of the stream, Leopold realized that it was an old mama wolf.

In those days any wolf you saw was a wolf you shot. Leopold and his men ran to their horses, pulled the thirty-thirties out of their scabbards and began to blast their way downhill at the wolves. If you hunt, as I do, you know that it's hard to aim downhill. But a lot of lead went down the hill that day. Old mama wolf crumbled, her legs shattered, and one of the pups dragged her back into the willows to die a slow death.

Leopold and his men mounted up and rode down the hill to skin the varmints and pack out their hides to sell. But something happened to Aldo Leopold that day in 1909. Decades later he wrote in *A Sand County Almanac*, "We reached the old wolf in time to watch a fierce green fire dying in her eyes. I realized then—and have known ever since—that there was something new to me in those eyes, something known only to her and to the mountain. I was young then, and full of trigger-itch; I thought that because fewer wolves meant more deer, that no wolves would mean a hunter's paradise. But after seeing the green fire die, I sensed that neither the wolf nor the mountain agreed with such a view."

Aldo Leopold helped exterminate wild wolves in the Southwest. None lived there from 1935 until a few years ago, when wild Mexican wolves were reintroduced into eastern Arizona. Looking over the map, I realized that by pure serendipity those first wolves were released only a mile from where Aldo Leopold shot the green-fire wolf. We have come full circle to be able to welcome the wild back into our hearts. Please join with me in celebrating the rewilding of the continent, the return of the wolf, of the jaguar, and of the wild in the human heart.

Have a Cow:
The Paradox of Rangeland Restoration

Dan Dagget

Dan Dagget's work with rangeland restoration is about as counterintuitive as it gets. He has shown that cows, those poster children of environmental destruction, can actually be part of the solution. He has the rare ability to solve seemingly intractable problems by questioning the assumptions that drive land management and environmental policy.

Dan knew firsthand the devastating damage caused by cattle on the fragile public lands of the West. He and a few other ecological mavericks started to mimic nature and found that, when appropriately managed, herds of hooved animals (ungulates) play an essential role in environmental restoration.

In many parts of the West, bullets have been fired at environmentalists in national forests where they have opposed grazing. Dan and his compatriots at the Quivira Coalition have brought both camps to the negotiating table, where they have discovered real mutual interests. His Pulitzer-nominated book, Beyond the Rangeland Conflict, *argues that sound ecology and profitable ranching can be compatible. This kind of conflict mediation is among the most important aspects of restoration, one not found in ecology literature.*

Dan formerly organized demonstrations for Earth First! and supported the reintroduction of the endangered Mexican wolf in the American Southwest. In 1992, the Sierra Club named him one of the most effective grassroots environmental organizers in America (though it was later critical of some of his subsequent cooperation with ranchers).

He has devised other innovative strategies, such as the website Eco Results, which visually chronicles in real time how ranchers are restoring specific ecosystems using rangeland management. The site also serves as an effective fundraising tool for the restoration projects. Dan also has helped initiate the marketing of premium "wolf-friendly" beef from ecologically managed ranches that have restored biodiversity, as a further strategy to keep the subdivision wolf from the door.

Above all, Dan has worked imaginatively and patiently to disarm environmental war zones by restoring both people and the land. In both cases, he says the real work is about restoring relationships.

IN HIS BOOK *The Web of Life*, Fritjof Capra writes that when scientists set out to discover the smallest, most basic form of matter, they encountered particles that were smaller and smaller and smaller, until finally they came to a point where there were no particles at all—no "things." There were only relationships. What that means in the most basic sense is that we don't live in a world of things. We live in a world of relationships.

As an environmentalist and activist, I experienced a cascade of awakenings when I read about that discovery. Among those awakenings, it occurred to me that if we live in a world of relationships, being an effective environmentalist must be more about creating and sustaining healthy, functional relationships than it is about dealing with things.

I also realized that the healthy, functional relationships of effective environmentalism would include relationships not just between people and nature, but between people and other people—including environmentalists and those we frequently think of as adversaries. Part of that awakening was the realization that many of the slogans, maxims, and principles I relied on as an environmental activist no longer worked. Slogans such as "No compromise" and "More for us and less for them" don't serve very well as the basis for functional relationships. Action based on such slogans might work in a world of things, where the goal is to achieve victory or establish control over ever larger collections of things (ecosystems, endangered species, public lands), but in a world of relationships, it's a liability.

If all that is true, I thought, we can learn more about being effective environmentalists from books about relationships than from books on ecology and plants, and certainly more than from books about activism.

With this in mind I started paying more attention to what has kept my wife, Trish, and me together for more than thirty years, and I began looking at that relationship as the most direct, ongoing learning experience available to me about how to live in a world of relationships and, therefore, about how to be an effective environmentalist. In fact, it occurred to me that personal relationships may provide the best continuing education course for any kind of effective work in the world.

What is the main lesson this course teaches us about being an effective environmentalist? I've been an activist for over thirty years, and for all that time I was sure that my goal was one thing: winning. Winning consisted of controlling more wilderness, gaining more protection for more endangered species, enacting more laws, electing more politicians. When I said, "No compromise," I meant it. I was like football coach Vince Lombardi, who said, "Winning isn't the best thing; it's the only thing."

In a world of relationships, that's a formula for disaster, for endless conflict and eventual breakup. Breaking up might be possible in a personal relationship, but in the environmental relationship, it isn't. We can't break up with nature, with the other components of nature, with the other humans living within nature. There's no place else to go. We have to get along or suffer the consequences of our dysfunctions.

In my marriage, it has become clear that one of the most important things Trish and I can do to keep our relationship functional is to keep agreements, fulfill responsibilities, mean what we say, and do what we say we will do. If I'm right about this relationship thing, the same can be said about our relationship with nature. Our species has plenty of responsibilities within nature that we have evolved to fulfill. We could say that we have roles to play, jobs to do for the ecos of which we all are a part. Most likely nature has come to expect us to fulfill these responsibilities—after all, evolution has shaped us to fit these jobs and the jobs to fit us. In some cases we have been fulfilling these responsibilities for millions of years, since our species and chimpanzees split off from our common ancestor. Humans have a relationship with and responsibilities to nature as predator as well as prey, as starters of fire, as slowers of water, as spreaders and cultivators of seed—to name just a few.

Ironically, just when our concern for our role in the environment is supposed to be at an all-time high, we are beginning to abandon these old relationships, even to disdain them. While we profess to know more than ever about what it is to be "native," we are beginning to act more like aliens. We live in cities that in many ways are like space stations. We extract what we need from the planet with ever more sophisticated technologies and transport it to those cities, where most of us consume without any consideration or awareness of the source of what we consume. Most of us don't have a clue where our food and clothing come from. We don't know if these products were produced in a way that kept our old agreements and responsibilities with nature, and most of us don't care. That is how an alien would act.

The most striking irony lies in the fact that many who see the problems created by our alien ways are trying to remedy them with solutions that are just as alien. To remedy the problems we have created by living like aliens, we remove ourselves more and more from what once was our home, where we once played such an important role. We create preserves and protected areas from which humans are excluded, as if we truly were aliens. We cast nature as a combination art exhibit, zoo, cathedral, and adventure park, in which we are sightseers, worshippers, caretakers, and joy-riders, but not residents, partners, or cocreators. In trying to repair our relationship with nature, we have made ourselves strangers in our own house.

We lament the fact that wolves, red-legged frogs, and California condors have become extremely rare or threatened with extinction; we say that if these species were to become extinct, there would be environmental hell to pay because the niches they fill, the jobs they do in nature, would go undone. And we go to great lengths to reintroduce these species to make sure that doesn't happen.

But no one is sounding an alarm over the fact that the niches humans once filled, the jobs we once did, are going undone. No one is studying what disasters that could cause. No one even seems aware that something is at risk here, even though scientists tell us that humans have been a keystone species—one of the most important in creating the network of relationships that exists right now. As such, if we were to become functionally extinct—if we were to completely abandon the roles we have evolved to play—most likely the results would be more disastrous than if red-legged frogs, or California condors, or even gray wolves became extinct.

I am not advocating that we dress in skins, take up spears, and begin chasing animals around the landscape. (Although I know there are some who do.) If we're going to fulfill our responsibilities to the environment, we will have to do it in a setting that involves freeways and cities and supermarkets and all that, because that's the setting that exists today.

I am advocating that we do what needs to be done when any relationship goes bad—that we start asking, "What were we doing when all this was working? What responsibilities did we fulfill then? What did nature rely on us to do? And how can we fulfill those old responsibilities in the context of a modern society?"

For me, asking those questions has meant becoming involved in rangelands, on ranches and in collaborative groups associated with ranches around the West. About ten years ago, I set out to discover places where folks were going back and restoring some of these old evolved relationships among grazing animals, grasses, soils, and human beings acting as predators, or in this case as herders, because that is what being a predator, a pack hunter, has become for humans.

Indigenous peoples tell us that predators have a coevolutionary relationship with their prey, that they put the lightning in the reflexes of the deer and the herding instinct into bison. Field biology has confirmed this wisdom, and we are now learning that by their interaction, wolves and deer and lions and wildebeest also have had a hand in creating the grasses, the watershed conditions, perhaps even the climate in which they live.

The people I wrote about in my book *Beyond the Rangeland Conflict* understood this coevolutionary dynamic, and they worked to re-create these old relationships. Trying to answer the questions "Who were we when all of this was working? What did we do? How did nature respond?" they brought cattle onto land where free-roaming animals once were. Then they interacted with those animals as human predators-become-herders would have: they herded them up and moved them on, and they waited for nature's response.

Among all the people I encountered, ranchers Tony and Jerrie Tipton of

Mina, Nevada, posed this question in its most extreme form. "If we re-create the ancient relationships among animals and grasses and soils and humans," they wondered, "can we create a functional ecosystem—a grassland—where there was none?" To make sure they got an answer that would stand up to scrutiny, they asked their question in a place that presented the greatest challenge they could find: an abandoned mine site in central Nevada. Part of the site had been reclaimed by the best that technology could offer. It had topsoil spread over it and was seeded with exotic grasses. The grasses did their best; they grew tentatively, but then began to wither and die. Subsequently, the area started to erode badly. This disaster was the best corporate America could bring to the site.

On the same site, the Tiptons first sowed seeds, the same kind that had been applied before. Then they put down hay—more hay than they knew their cows would eat, so that the hay would feed the soil as well as the animals. Finally they brought in the cows, 600 of them, more than anyone would ever graze on a piece of rangeland that size. Neighbors sat beside the road in their pickup trucks, watching and placing their bets, because after all this was Nevada.

The old mine the Tiptons tackled could be seen for miles around because it was white, glaring, and ugly. But the next spring, after the cows had left and nature had done her part of the job, the scar became lush and green. In one year, with just six inches of moisture over the winter, the Tiptons ended up producing more grass on that barren site than their neighbors did on some of their cultivated and irrigated hayfields. They accomplished this feat by acting as though they lived in a world of relationships, not of things. They did it by restoring relationships.

While the Tiptons were completing their trial, another relationship restorer, Terry Wheeler of Globe, Arizona, was tackling an even more daunting challenge: a pile of copper mine tailings 300 feet thick covering 1,100 acres. This Superfund site, visible from satellites, was a pile of rock ground into dust the consistency of talcum powder and treated with a witch's brew of chemicals, including deadly cyanide, which is used to leach out the metals. There are similar sites all over the world, including quite a few in Arizona.

You can imagine how this stuff erodes. Pour water on some talcum powder and see what happens. It erodes like crazy, and consequently it pollutes
like crazy. Dust blows off it in mare's tails that waft down into the town, where
people at a restaurant joke about eating "tailings tacos." The dust permeates
everything—what you eat, what you are. It gets into people's bodies.

Terry Wheeler also began by asking the question, "What would happen
if we tried restoring the relationships between grasses and grazers in this
place?" He put seeds and hay on this environmental disaster, and then he
turned cattle loose on it. On top of the ordinary hay he threw alfalfa, which
is sort of like chocolate ice cream to cows. The cows went charging around to
get the alfalfa, competing for it and stomping seeds, hay, and manure into the
tailings. In one season, Terry Wheeler got lush, high grass growing all the way
to the top of that 300-foot tailings pile.

In a number of places around the West, I'm working with groups of environmentalists, ranchers, government people, and just plain folks who are
trying to apply such ideas on ranches that total more than a million acres. Near
Santa Fe, an environmental group called the Quivira Coalition is helping diverse constituencies, including family ranchers and environmentalists, apply
these principles to rangelands that people want to sustain as open space. By
means of these efforts, more and more people in the rural West are realizing
that we all want many of the same things: clean air, clean water, healthy ecosystems, beautiful scenery, and plentiful wildlife. And we're realizing that the
most effective way to get those things is not through fighting, but through
healthy, functional, effective, and considerate relationships. And we've got
the results to prove it.

Think Like a Prairie:
Solving the 10,000-Year-Old
Problem of Agriculture

Wes Jackson

Wes Jackson is among the most brilliant and original researchers in agriculture, a man of penetrating vision who has deeply contemplated humanity's ancient and problematic relationship to agriculture. His goal is to reverse the radical damage caused by farming, which is arguably humanity's single most environmentally destructive activity.

Wes's credentials are prodigious: he holds degrees in biology, botany, and genetics and formerly chaired one of the nation's first environmental studies programs at California State University at Sacramento. He is the founder and president of the renowned Land Institute in Salina, Kansas, perhaps the most daring "alternative" agricultural research station in the world. He is a Pew Conservation Scholar, a MacArthur Fellow, and author of some of the most revelatory books ever written about agriculture, including the seminal New Roots for Agriculture *and* Becoming Native to This Place. *Life* magazine named him as one of the one hundred "most important Americans of the twentieth century."*

Wes has long propounded a true natural systems agriculture that mimics how nature grows food and topsoil. One can't call it "groundbreaking" because part of his thesis is precisely not to break the ground. Yet it is a symbiotic vision that encompasses a love of biomimicry as well as of farmers and community. His is systems thinking of the highest order, modeled on his beloved prairie ecosystem. If our civilization is to avoid the collapse that has befallen so many others that exhausted their ecological capital and especially their topsoil, it will be in no small part because of the seeds planted by the brilliant and formidable Wes Jackson.

I HAVE A STORY to share, related to our work at the Land Institute, about a field trip I took in Mendocino County, California, with the great soil scientist Hans Jenny of the University of California at Berkeley and his colleague in forestry, Arnold Schultz. The experience resulted in an intellectual epiphany for me.

The Pacific Plate slides under the Continental Plate in this region, lifting it up without tilting the surface. This geologic activity, in combination with the rise and fall of sea level, has created five terraces. The higher the terrace, the older it is. The youngest platform was completed at the onset of the Wisconsin glaciation, about 100,000 years ago. The first two terraces, the youngest, support redwood and Douglas fir with luxuriant growth. Terrace three is a transition zone of sorts. Terraces four and five support a non-luxuriant growth—a "pygmy forest."

If one were to harvest and weigh the total biomass from one acre of the young terraces and do the same on the old terraces, the harvest from the old would weigh much less. Why? Because many of the essential land-based nutrients that must be present for plants to capture carbon, hydrogen, nitrogen, and oxygen out of the atmosphere—calcium, phosphorus, potassium, manganese, trace minerals, and such—have leached downward and out of reach of the roots in the older terraces. These land-based elements are the ecological capital necessary for plants to capture atmospheric elements out of the global commons.

My epiphany happened as I thought about those land-based elements leaching beyond reach of the tree roots. I said to Hans and Arnold, "But this is a natural ecosystem. It ought to have the ability to recharge itself." "Yes," Hans agreed. "If you have the basic minerals there, it can be improved. But the basic minerals have to be there."

Thinking about the pygmy forest in terraces four and five and the natural leaching, I asked, "Why aren't there pygmy forests or, for that matter, pygmy prairies, pygmy whatever, all over the planet?" "Well, this is a dynamic planet," Arnold said. "It keeps recharging itself through geologic activity."

North America is a very young continent geologically. In addition, over the last 1.7 million years, we had an ice age, the Pleistocene, whose rock-grinding glaciers gave us the rich soils of the upper Midwest, where so much grain is grown. Australia, on the other hand, is in bad shape. Its last major geologic event occurred 65 million years ago, and many of its essential land-based minerals have leached beyond the reach of plants. It has poor soils, which will remain so until it gets recharged.

Soil is as much a nonrenewable resource as oil. When we perceive a need for them, we can and do bring soil or minerals from someplace else, usually at a fossil fuel cost. Agriculture is a mining operation.

Now for a little history, indeed prehistory. *Homo sapiens* has been around for about 150,000 to 200,000 years. We've had agriculture for 10,000 years or, in most places, less. During those hundred centuries, we produced and expanded our first and most important environmental problem—the problem of agriculture, with topsoil loss its main feature. It all began, probably, in western Iran, but very quickly moved around the Mediterranean. We can readily see that civilizations have been built on the ecological capital of soil, but that, except in major valley systems such as the Indus and the Nile, soils soon wear out. Plato lamented the demise of the mountains of Attica, once prosperous but later fit only for bees.

A few years ago I was in Tunis near the ruins of ancient Carthage and thought about Hannibal and that era in which the Roman Empire used all the lands along the Mediterranean for its granary. When I looked at the hillsides surrounding those ruins, I saw thin livestock, thin people, thin soils. The soils once present where I stood—the soils that once supported an empire—were now under the sea. We could develop a long list of earth abuse through agriculture in Asia, Africa, and Latin America. And in North America's upper Midwest, the largest region of the world's best land, many areas have lost half of their topsoil in just a century and a half of farming.

If it's all that bad, why is it that we have more food now than ever? The short answer is that with the Industrial Revolution we discovered and began mining lots of energy-rich carbon. If a genie would grant me just one wish, it would be that for four hours on a single day, everybody would be fitted with glasses capable of seeing only the flow of carbon through the ecosphere. We would then appreciate how dependent our lives are on fossil fuels.

Natural gas, for example, is the feedstock we use to fix atmospheric nitrogen in order to fertilize crops. We use 1.8 times as many fossil calories to sponsor nitrogen for America's fields as we use for tractors, combines, and other farm equipment. Yet we must have nitrogen fertilizer if we're going to produce the food we need. Professor Vaclav Smil of the University of Manitoba has argued that the invention around 1909 of the Haber-Bosch process—the process that uses natural gas as a feedstock to make ammonia—may well be the most important invention of the twentieth century. (In ammonia is nitrogen, which can be split off and made available for building protein.) Without Haber-Bosch, Smil contends, 40 percent of humanity would not be here because the natural fertility of the planet's soils is not good enough to support anything like the current standing crop of humans. In addition, Marty Bender of the Land Institute has estimated that there are about twice as many domestic animal pounds as there are human pounds on the planet. Humans and animals combined obviously have a major impact on the soil environment.

The story leading up to our current crisis is an old one. The experiment that began 10,000 years ago, with the greatest group of revolutionaries ever, gave us essentially all our crops and livestock. The resultant population explosion, and associated environmental devastation, was created by agriculture, aggravated by the exploitation of fossil fuels. We've yet to come to terms with it.

About twenty-five years ago, when we at the Land Institute decided to address this problem, we turned to nature. Fortunately we have, as a living model of a different way to grow food plants, about a hundred acres of native prairie that has never been plowed. We compared the prairie with fields of wheat, sorghum, or corn (all members of the grass family), and the contrast was striking: one field with plants of many different sizes and forms, the other with rank on rank of a single plant as far as the eye could see. We looked at these crops because 70 percent of the calories humans consume come from the grass family. As a species, we are grass-seed eaters, so to be serious about feeding humanity, we need to think primarily about the grass family, and secondarily about the legume family. (Trees barely make the list of the top twenty crops. Banana and coconut rank nineteenth and twentieth.)

Here's the root of the problem we confronted: Essentially all the foods that support us, at a basic level, are annual plants. They have to be planted each year, which requires that we tear the ground up every year—or if using a no-till system, apply large amounts of herbicide. And typically only one kind of plant is grown over many acres. But when we look at nature's ecosystems, almost anywhere, we find that they feature perennials grown in polycultures, not annuals grown in monocultures. Perennials regrow every year without depending on seed. We wanted to stop soil erosion because its replacement comes in geological time and our expenditure of soil has been in agricultural time. And so our question became, Is it possible to build an agriculture based on the way nature's ecosystems work? I doubt that we realized how radical our mission was. We were just trying to do what made sense.

Think about that never-plowed native prairie with its species diversity and its perennial roots. Not only are the perennial roots of that ecosystem keeping the soil from eroding, but they are also efficiently managing water and nutrients. In the process, the system is actually building ecological capital. It's efficiently recycling phosphorus, potassium, manganese, and other nutrients. That ecological capital builds and maintains itself pretty efficiently on the prairies, thanks to the Pleistocene glaciers and the Rocky Mountains, which have provided the mineral recharge. More than fertility is involved. Species diversity also means chemical diversity, so that it takes a tremendous enzyme system on the part of any insect or a pathogen to create an epidemic.

Knowing this, our agenda was clear. We set out to explore the question of whether perennialism and increased seed yield were compatible. We also wanted to determine whether a polyculture of perennials could have competitive yields with monocultures of annuals, and whether a domestic polyculture system could adequately manage insects, pathogens, and weeds. Finally, we wanted to know if such a food-producing system for humans could sponsor enough of its own nitrogen using contemporary sunlight and no petrochemical fuels or fertilizers.

Beginning in 1992, Marty Bender led the design of a ten-year side experiment at the Land Institute called the Sunshine Farm. As principal investigator, Dr. Bender set out to measure how much energy, materials, and labor would be required to maintain 50 acres of crops and 160 acres of pasture. He established a criterion that the farm had to make all the energy that it used and pay all the costs, including such energy costs as those of mining the ore in the Minnesota Iron Range to build the tractor, of processing the ore in Gary, Indiana, and of assembling the tractor in Moline, Illinois. The level of detail was exhaustive and included the embodied energy required to support draft animals—indeed, the embodied energy for every component, down to a one-pound bolt.

When the experiment compared a tractor to a draft horse, I thought the tractor would win hands-down because you can turn it off with a key and you don't have to pay the tractor to stand around and be a tractor, whereas draft horses, even at rest, have to metabolize. The problem with that way of thinking is that you don't come out some morning to find a baby tractor. A pregnant mare can work while growing her replacement. In addition, with animals you're not widening the loop away from the farm. Surprisingly, Dr. Bender learned that the draft animal and the tractor are about equal in their use of land. During a drought a tractor will "starve" faster than a horse because that tractor is "grazing" on a narrow photosynthetic base—the oil coming out of the sunflowers and soybeans—whereas the draft animal is grazing on a broader photosynthetic base. Of course, the horse has had longer to evolve. People may learn faster than nature, but nature's been at it longer.

The results of the entire experiment seemed to imply that approximately 25 percent of till acreage must be devoted to paying for the energy required for traction (whether provided by horse or machine) and about the same amount to sponsoring the nitrogen.

After some twenty-five years of research, we've concluded that it is possible to build an agriculture on the prairie model that's about as sustainable as the nature we destroy. It's possible to have polycultures of perennials. We're now perennializing some major crops—wheat, sorghum, sunflowers—as well as domesticating two wild species in the sunflower family, Illinois bundleflower and compass plant. The institute employs numerous graduate students and others who are researching and advancing this new paradigm for agriculture.

But there is more to the effort than plant breeding. Wherever there is prairie—the Canadian provinces, eastern Colorado, western Kansas, Texas, even the prairie peninsula of Ohio—there are four functional groups: warm-season grasses, cool-season grasses, legumes, and members of the sunflower family. Corn and sorghum are warm-season grasses. Wheat is a cool-season grass. Soybean is a legume. Sunflower is its own family. The idea is to mimic nature's vegetative structure in order to be granted its functions. Jack Ewel of the Institute of Pacific Island Forestry has done work in Costa Rica, where he and his group of researchers substituted vine for vine, tree for tree, and shrub for shrub, that has shown that mimicking the natural vegetative structure almost always reproduces the function. Our quest is to mimic the perennial polycultures of the prairies, substituting food plants that have the same structure as corresponding plants in the ecosystem.

I mentioned earlier that this endeavor was more radical than we had originally thought. Marrying the disciplines of ecology and evolutionary biology will be necessary to inform agronomy and agriculture, and I thought that marriage would be easy. I was wrong. Unfortunately, ecologists and agronomists form two distinct scientific cultures. An ecologist or evolutionary biologist comes from a tradition in which one has the luxury of being descriptive. An agronomist or a farmer has the burden of being prescriptive. The worldview held by ecologists and evolutionary biologists since Darwin wants to understand how the world *is.* Agronomists, on the other hand, need to know how the world *works.*

Obviously there's a lot of work ahead in reconciling these worldviews and going forward. But consider the benefits. Our staff is cheerfully at work because we know that we can have an agriculture in which the reward runs to the farmer and the landscape, rather than to the suppliers of inputs. We can have an agriculture in which this paradigm holds planetwide. Why not? Darwin's theory of evolution through natural selection holds in the Arctic just as it holds in the tropics. The new paradigm for agriculture will be universal. The industrial mind has been dictating technologies based on fossil fuel-intensive infrastructures. When we effectively parachute them into Third World agricultural economies, we set up brittle economies. That model must and will come to an end.

In the last hundred years—just 1 percent of the time in which we've had agriculture—we've seen the largest population bump in the history of humanity. We have to acknowledge that we will never have another increase like that. The soils simply aren't there to support it. About 40 percent of the soils on the planet are already in a seriously degraded condition and declining rapidly.

What we need to do is to come to terms with a new paradigm for agriculture, which is to say, to embrace the oldest paradigm for the planet. If we don't achieve sustainability in agriculture first, sustainability in a greater sense will not happen. Agriculture ultimately needs the disciplines of ecology and evolutionary biology to guide it. The industrial sector has no such disciplines to draw on and inform it. It seems fair to say that the fall of humankind began with agriculture. Should not the healing begin with agriculture? It seems possible, but it will be a long journey.

Noah's New Ark:
Conserving Seed Diversity in the Garden

Kent Whealy

In the early 1970s, Kent and Diane Whealy were given some heirloom seeds that her grandfather's parents had brought from Bavaria a century earlier. The gift began a lifelong quest to preserve the world's agricultural seed diversity. Genetic erosion of seed stocks is among the most critical dangers we face as a civilization, and Kent has been one of the most effective and far-seeing guardians of biodiversity in the garden.

In 1975 Kent and Diane launched the Seed Savers Exchange to conserve the living legacy of the plants that feed humanity. They knew that the seeds we depend on are the products of generation upon generation of sophisticated growers and backyard empiricists who have bred and selected plants with desirable adaptive characteristics of nutrition, flavor, insect resistance, and fortitude to cope with nature's challenges in the timeless game of crops and robbers.

Seed Savers Exchange makes use of a network of impassioned gardeners and farmers searching for and preserving the plethora of seed varieties that people have nurtured and saved over generations. These seeds are proven survivors indigenized to particular locales, imprinted with the cultural practices of communities, and blessed by the growers' ancestors. In the early 1990s, Kent took Seed Savers global, scouring the far reaches of the world for heirloom and traditional seeds, often just in the nick of time in remote places where these living treasures would otherwise have perished.

The gardens at Seed Savers Exchange's Heritage Farm near Decorah, Iowa, display a breathtaking bouquet of rare and endangered food plants. The 170-acre headquarters, a living museum of historic varieties, is open to the public, and each summer as many as 5,000 gardeners and orchardists come to tour the preservation gardens and historic orchard. Today this living ark faces a new threat: genetic pollution. Drift from genetically modified crops growing in nearby fields could destroy the genetic integrity of the plants raised here. This toxic trespassing is a deadly insult against which there is currently scant protection.

Periodically, Seed Savers Exchange publishes its Garden Seed Inventory. This telephone book–sized volume is a revelation in idiosyncrasy, a sacred taxonomy of nature and culture. It's also a testament to the true wealth we still have in the rich diversity of seed stocks that brilliant farmers and gardeners like Kent have cocreated in the unending dance of people and nature.

THERE IS GREAT REASON for concern about the loss of native seed strains, our irreplaceable genetic wealth. Living systems—the budding branches of apple trees or the living embryos of grains and vegetable seeds— are the only places genes can be stored. Native varieties rapidly become extinct once they're dropped in favor of the hybrid seeds that agribusiness prefers, which can be patented and designed to grow only with a profitable package of chemical inputs that the industry also sells. If native seeds are cooked and eaten rather than saved as seed stock, extinction can take place in a single year.

According to the late Jack Harlan, professor of plant genetics who founded the crop evolution lab at the University of Illinois at Urbana-Champaign, "These [native seed] resources stand between us and catastrophic starvation on a scale we cannot imagine. In a very real sense, the future of the human race rides on these materials. The line between abundance and disaster is becoming thinner and thinner and the public is unaware and unconcerned. Must we wait for disaster to be real before we are heard? Will people listen only after it's too late?"

During the past twenty-five years we've discovered that there's a tremendous heritage of heirloom varieties in North America, a heritage that's been accumulating for four centuries. Because the United States and Canada are nations of immigrants, today's gardeners are blessed with an immense cornucopia of food crops. Gardeners and farmers from literally every corner of the world invariably brought their best seeds when their families immigrated. Seeds provided living remembrances of their former lives and assured their continued enjoyment of foods from the old country.

Because the immigrants didn't know what awaited them at the end of their journey and many feared that their seeds might be confiscated, they usually smuggled them into the country. Millions of immigrants came through Ellis Island with seeds hidden under their hatbands or suitcase linings, and sewn into the hems of dresses. We are maintaining varieties in Seed Savers Exchange that supposedly came over on the Mayflower. You can bet seeds are being carried in today by refugees and immigrants from Haiti, Cuba, and Mexico. During the decade right after the Vietnam War, a tremendous amount of plant material was brought in by the boat people from Laos and Cambodia. Seeds will continue to come in this way.

A vast, almost unknown genetic treasure is quietly being maintained by elderly gardeners and farmers in isolated rural areas and ethnic enclaves all over North America. But it has never been systematically collected. When we go into pockets of rural poverty such as in the Appalachians, the Smokies, and the Ozarks, we find treasure troves of heirloom varieties among people who have never had the money to buy seeds and have always traded heirloom seeds over the garden fence.

Isolation can also be religious in origin; traditional people like the Mennonites, Amish, Dunkers, and Hutterites maintain many native crops. I'm also pleased that very slowly, some Native Americans are starting to participate in Seed Savers as they have gained trust in the organization. Most Native Americans are usually reluctant to share their seeds, believing that they are sacred. And they're right, because seeds are the sparks of life that feed us all.

Native and heirloom plants are often grown on the same farm by different generations of a family for up to 150 years. Seeds kept in the same location for that long gradually develop resistance to local diseases and insects and become well adapted to specific climates and soil conditions. But because of the continuing deterioration of rural economic conditions, young people are being forced off the land in droves, and elderly gardeners often cannot find anyone willing to maintain their seeds. Unless dedicated gardeners continue planting such unique seeds, outstanding strains become extinct as that older generation passes away. Future generations will never enjoy them, and invaluable genetic characteristics are lost forever to gardeners and plant breeders.

Diane and I founded Seed Savers in 1975 and have dedicated our lives to the conservation of genetic diversity. We immediately started trying to find other people who were keeping heirloom varieties. Our twin goals were to do everything we could to reverse genetic erosion and to dramatically increase the diversity available to gardeners and farmers who were growing healthy food for their families and others. There are 43 million families in this country that grow some of their own food, and two-thirds of the people on the planet live on what they're able to grow.

For more than two decades we've continued to locate gardeners who are keeping heirloom food crops, organizing them into an annual seed exchange. Every January, Seed Savers publishes a yearbook that lists all the seeds being maintained by our members. In 1975 that network consisted of 29 people who were offering a few dozen varieties through a 6-page newsletter. Today, the network has grown to 1,000 listed members offering 12,000 rare varieties of vegetables and fruits through a 460-page yearbook that was sent out to 8,000 gardeners.

The seed collections we're maintaining right now are huge: 24,000 varieties, including, for example, 5,600 beans, 5,200 tomatoes, 1,200 lettuces, 300 garlics, and 2,000 peppers. Excess seeds beyond our own grow-out needs are made available to Seed Savers members through the yearbook.

The collection of heirloom seeds being maintained right now at Heritage Farm is by far the best in the world. Much of this material could never be re-collected because it came from Seed Savers members who have since passed away or from areas in eastern European countries that are now mired in civil strife.

I don't think that there has been a more exciting time to be a gardener. You have access to thousands of heirloom varieties that have been rescued and maintained by excellent genetic preservation organizations. Centuries of history are available for the choosing: pre-Columbian seeds that were grown by Native American tribes throughout North America, seeds that were brought over on the Mayflower, varieties grown by Thomas Jefferson in the gardens at Monticello, seeds that were carried by the Cherokee over the Trail of Tears. These are literally the best seeds from every corner of the world, seeds that immigrants and refugees have treasured, protected, acclimated, and shared. Many remote areas in the former Communist world, where Westerners were not even allowed for over seventy years, are opening up like creaky treasure chests. Even China is starting to open up to seed collectors.

But the cruel irony is that much of this incredible genetic richness is very close to dying out. It's really up to us, and I believe that we're just now hitting our stride with the heirloom seed movement. As a movement, we have already changed the way people in America garden. We've awakened gardeners in this country to their true heritage, and that's an incredible accomplishment. Before this is over we will have created the most intense wave of horticultural interest that this country has seen since the golden age of gardening a century ago. This is true stewardship.

Weaving Community:
Restoring the Ecology of Los Angeles

Andy Lipkis

When he was fifteen Andy Lipkis began planting trees around Los Angeles to re-habilitate areas damaged by smog and fire, and he has never stopped. In 1973 he founded TreePeople, which has been a guiding light for the citizen forestry movement, and he has served as its president ever since.

Andy coined the term "citizen foresters" to describe the thousands of people TreePeople trained to plant and maintain trees on urban streets, and the term has inspired tree-planting groups throughout the United States. He was on the team that designed Los Angeles's curbside recycling program, and he cocreated the city's Urban Greening Initiative with the Forest Service after the 1992 civil unrest in order to generate desperately needed jobs.

TreePeople has airlifted fruit trees to Africa, inspired the planting of a million trees in Los Angeles before the 1984 Olympics, organized disaster relief efforts after floods and fires, and set up a wide range of initiatives to increase citizen involvement in urban tree planting and care. Andy's latest program is T.R.E.E.S.—Trans-agency Resources for Environmental and Economic Sustainability—a public-private part-nership working to encourage the coordinated management of the Los Angeles re-gion as a sustainable urban ecosystem.

Andy is also a superlative educator and communicator. Coauthor with his wife and colleague, Kate, of the very popular The Simple Act of Planting a Tree, *he coproduced an Emmy-winning series,* How Does Your Garden Grow? *with KCBS, and produced a video series to help urban forestry professionals and citi-zen tree groups market their cause to local governments. He serves on numerous boards and has received honors from groups as diverse as the Daughters of the American Revolution and the California Board of Forestry. Andy and Kate were jointly named to the United Nations Environment Programme's Global 500 Roll of Honour.*

Across the country and around the world, Andy has addressed and helped groups and agencies involved in the environment, urban forestry, sustainability, and water and energy use, including the UN, the EPA, and the United Kingdom's National Urban Forestry Unit. Only a genuine visionary could imagine Los Angeles as a living ecosystem and a coherent social ecology. Andy Lipkis has not only seen that promised land, he has been instrumental in manifesting a living model of urban sustainability and assisting many others in realizing it.

I BEGAN ORGANIZING tree planting in Los Angeles around 1970. The effort evolved from planting trees to working toward revitalizing whole ecosystems, both natural and human. We realized that just planting trees by itself doesn't work; you actually have to build communities. In that light, we created a citizen forestry movement to help people dream, design, and collaborate, to begin taking responsibility in their neighborhoods as they planted trees.

Initially we had a strong sense of what trees and forests could do. Tree planting makes people feel good. It holds the promise of sustainability, of feeding people, of preventing erosion, and of many other benefits. But after a while, we saw that the system—the government and the way society was structured—was making it inherently impossible for people to succeed in healing ecosystems and communities. When we evaluated our own work, we felt we weren't achieving our goals. We felt we were just decorating neighborhoods and schools, rearranging the deck chairs on a sinking ship.

What we decided we should try to do instead to get real results was to plant trees very strategically, aiming to replicate a natural forest ecosystem and watershed in a city. We took that notion and adjusted it to the specific realities and challenges we found in Los Angeles, and we hit on something that is now starting to work on a very large scale. In a sense, one could look at tree planting as a form of earth acupuncture, strategically placing specific trees in particular locations and involving people in order to accomplish specific healing.

Although I come from Los Angeles, I spent my college years at Sonoma State, hanging out with friends in Berkeley and Santa Cruz. They were all sure that Los Angeles was such an environmental hell that there was no hope of saving it. The city is one of the world's largest consumers of energy and producers of carbon dioxide. It also consumes much of the water in the western United States, in order to maintain the kinds of lifestyles to which its citizens have become accustomed. Yet it's ripe for change, and changing Los Angeles would have enormous benefits. If we are really going to change the world, we have to take on the biggest challenges.

Around 1990, I evaluated our twenty-year track record and realized that if we were to achieve the goal of sustainability, we needed to make still more changes, both to our own work and to how the city managed its environment and infrastructure. We saw that the city wasn't being managed right. We set out to prove that it was technologically and economically feasible to retrofit the city. We found that the city was wasting vast amounts of money day in and day out—money that could help us accomplish many of our dreams if spent right. We needed to prove our premise in demonstration projects and large-scale retrofits, and then ultimately take on the whole city.

Here's one example. We might think of schools as the human equivalents of tree nurseries in which we want to give our seedlings the best possible hope for a life that will produce good strong trees. Yet in L.A. we're raising millions of kids in hot, barren, ugly, depressing environments. The Centers for Disease Control say that skin cancer is now the fastest-growing cancer in this country, and thirteen-year-olds are the most at-risk population because we're frying them in the sun in our schoolyards. The school systems in Los Angeles and other cities say that it doesn't make economic sense to design greener school environments, and that they can't afford the gardeners. We had to prove otherwise.

In one of our projects, students in a community worked in collaboration with engineers and landscape architects to create and design a solution to this challenge. The school had a severe flooding problem and was going to spend $200,000 "fixing" it by putting in storm drains, sending precious rainfall to the ocean. Instead we created a curriculum called "Schoolyard Explorers" that turns kids into watershed managers. They go out and document where the water is going, measure air temperatures, and find places where students are exposed to too much heat and sun, or where water is being wasted or polluted. Then they dream. In this case they designed two outdoor classrooms and a stream swale to transport the floodwater to a place they really wanted, which was a grass soccer field.

We involved the kids in the design, and they in turn involved the community. Ultimately we were able to build a support base that attracted an extra $250,000 from the Los Angeles Department of Water and Power, because the agency recognized that this water, instead of becoming both a pollution and flood problem, would go back into the aquifer and recharge the city's water supply. It also recognized the positive effect the project was having on the kids and the community. Imagine that you're an inner-city kid who's been told you don't count, and you begin to see your vision and design manifest in physical form. Now the kids have the green and beautiful soccer field of their dreams, which sits on top of, and is made financially possible by, an underground stormwater cleaning machine and 100,000-gallon infiltration system.

The Los Angeles ecosystem has been so profoundly mismanaged that we're throwing away tremendous amounts of water and money, not to mention jobs and lives. The successful schoolyard demonstration project illustrates our theory that there are sufficient resources to retrofit cities if we practice integrative infrastructure management—in other words, if we begin to manage the city as if it really were a living ecosystem, which of course it is, or was, and should be.

Los Angeles isn't unlike most cities. Around 75 percent of it is covered with impermeable surfaces: the land is sealed with houses, parking lots, and freeways. In an average rainfall year, we receive enough water to meet half our needs, yet we have been throwing that water away because we can steal water from other regions. Los Angeles long ago figured out how to take water from the wider western United States. The city spends a billion dollars a year on water management, yet it doesn't seem to recognize that rainwater has value. It has been polluting that water and sending it to the ocean. This creates practically unsolvable flood and coastal pollution problems.

When we built cities, no one understood how natural systems worked. We had lost that common wisdom. Today competing, uncoordinated bureaucracies are managing the disintegrated urban ecosystem. In Los Angeles a county agency spends half a billion dollars a year to manage flood control channels and has been throwing away half a billion dollars' worth of water because its primary job is to prevent floods, not save water. A separate city water supply agency spends a billion dollars a year. These two agencies had never talked to each other. There was no integration or collaboration.

Sanitation, which is the third-largest line item in the Los Angeles budget, after police and fire, also contributes to our huge stormwater pollution problem. Forty percent of what we're sending to landfills is valuable mulch: grass, leaves, and trees. When we began this project, the sanitation folks were just throwing it all away, and of course they weren't working with any other departments.

We knew we needed to convey our vision that the city is a living system and to convince the various agencies to start collaborating, although that wouldn't be an easy task. In order to prove a new approach was viable, we brought several different agencies together, got each to contribute some money, and did a five-year study. We wanted to show that through an integrated approach we could clean up the stormwater, control floods, save energy, conserve water, improve air quality, reduce the waste stream, improve human health, and create as many as 50,000 jobs. In the process, we could save money that would otherwise be spent to purchase and import water, dispose of rainwater, and filter and decontaminate polluted stormwater to prevent pollution of the region's creeks and rivers and the beaches and bays into which they drain.

We began by bringing people from all these agencies together to do collaborative planning. They had to see themselves as comanagers of the whole ecosystem. We organized a multidisciplinary design gathering called a charrette, assembling a team of a hundred building and landscape architects, engineers, and urban foresters, in addition to agency people. That group spent four days coming up with new, integrated solutions, working in teams made up of one representative of each of the professions. Their job was to collaborate and create plans that had professional integrity for each discipline. For example, the landscape architect and engineer each had veto power over a plan that affected both their bailiwicks. Instead of regarding each other as enemies, they had to work together.

The result was a series of designs for retrofitting all the major land uses in L.A. Each land use had to cut water imports by 50 percent and have the capacity to trap and use the water from a 130-year flood event. The over-paving of the city had created a flood problem so dangerous that the county and the Army Corps of Engineers planned to spend another half billion dollars to increase the capacity of the Los Angeles River in order to hold such a flood. We said, "Let's design it so that we can keep those waters on-site and not need to expand the river channel."

We produced an incredible consensus among agencies that had never worked together before. Later we published a book called *Second Nature* describing their designs. But just having a bunch of ideas wasn't good enough; we had to test them. We installed one set of designs at a single-family home in South Los Angeles. With a water truck and fire hoses, we then simulated a flash flood or a 1,500-year storm in the middle of summer, spraying 4,000 gallons of water on the roof and property in about ten minutes. The water flowed into four main systems: from one part of the roof, it flowed through a filter and into a 3,600-gallon cistern made of recyclable plastic that fit inside the home's narrow fence line. Water from another part of the roof flowed into traditional rain gutters that were directed from the driveway onto the lawns, which had been redesigned to function as mini–retention basins. Water falling on the driveway was caught in a drain, flowing into a sand filter and then into a "dry well" under the lawn. And some of the water flowed through swales lined with mulch composed of lawn, tree, and shrub clippings, where it was filtered and absorbed into the soil. Instead of running off into the street and storm drain system as floodwater, all the water was captured, treated, absorbed, or stored for later irrigation use.

After this, some agencies that had been resisting our efforts because they believed we were promoting ideas that required unacceptable lifestyle changes saw that these changes were easy and positive enough to be accepted and implemented by normal citizens. They apologized for not having understood them earlier, and then they brought us a challenge: a massive flooding problem in part of L.A.'s San Fernando Valley. This area, an unnatural watershed formed by lack of flood control, covers 2,700 acres, is 9 miles long, and has 8,000 homes. The county was planning to put in a storm drain for $42 million. They said, "If you can prove your approach works with this watershed and will save us money, you've got our money and our backing." It took two and a half years, but working together we proved that the watershed approach was viable and feasible. The county agreed to move ahead and plan for full implementation.

By now, it wasn't just the county flood control agency at the table. We brought in people dealing with water supply, water quality, and sanitation, and did a holistic analysis. All the agencies concerned helped fund the retrofit and are working together on it. The watershed plan is complete, along with the programmatic environmental impact study, and the first-phase projects are being designed and readied for construction. In the implementation phase, we will be retrofitting much of the land for different uses: greening formerly asphalt schoolyards and putting large rainwater infiltration and storage systems under them, removing asphalt and planting more trees in parking lots, adapting gravel extraction pits into recreation areas and wildlife habitat, with stormwater treatment and groundwater recharge facilities beneath them.

Current analysis indicates that the whole project may ultimately cost around $180 million, but the value of the benefits exceeds $200 million, including the value of parks, the value of water put back in the ground, and millions in savings to the city of Los Angeles over thirty years from not having to pick up, transport, and landfill green waste.

Our most important job is to work in the community—especially in schools, so that every single kid in the watershed and every single family begins to see life very differently. They need to be empowered to know that they are literally the managers of the watershed. The implications of this project are revolutionary. City and county agencies are getting ready to spend $180 million to put in a forest instead of a cement drain. We're looking forward to seeing this approach extended around the city. The change in mind-set has been so profound that the two key agencies—which are among the largest public works agencies in the country—have changed their names and their missions. Because of what they learned from this process, the Los Angeles County Flood Control Division has become the Los Angeles County Watershed Management Division, and the city's Stormwater Management Division has become the Watershed Protection Division.

Perhaps the best news, after ten years of research and demonstration projects, is that the staffs of many agencies have begun to adopt a philosophy based on the city as ecosystem and are now working together to implement this vision. We have to remember that ecology also means social ecology.

Part III

Graffiti in the Book of Life: Genetic Engineering and the Vandalism of Nature

Ignorance Is Not Bliss:
The Perils of Genetic Engineering

David Suzuki

Iconic biologist David Suzuki has had a remarkable career spanning science, broadcasting, journalism, environmentalism, and human rights. A third-generation Canadian of Japanese origin born in Vancouver in 1936, he and his family were uprooted and incarcerated in a remote valley in British Columbia as part of the internment program during World War II. Turned loose as a child in that wild country, he bonded with nature and made a lifelong commitment against injustice and bigotry.

Destiny placed David at the birth of the genetics revolution in the early 1960s, and by the age of thirty-three he was a full professor in the Zoology Department at the University of British Columbia. He soon became the largest genetics grantee in Canada, made notable discoveries, and in 1976 cowrote An Introduction to Genetic Analysis, *still the world's most widely used genetics textbook. In 1993, he moved to the Sustainable Development Research Institute at UBC, becoming an emeritus professor in 2001.*

David has always combined his scientific work with deep social engagement. He has been at the forefront of a group of courageous scientists speaking out about the perils of genetic engineering and has been a passionate advocate for civil and human rights around the world.

As a communicator, educator, and translator of complex scientific issues into comprehensible language, David is without peer. His beguiling storytelling has instilled wonder and reverence for the natural world in the hearts of millions. In 1979, he converted the successful Canadian Broadcasting Company show Science Magazine *into the legendary series* The Nature of Things with David Suzuki, *which airs today in over thirty countries. He also created, among other programs, the series* The Secret of Life *for the BBC and PBS. David is also a syndicated colum-*

nist, and his more than thirty books, many for children, have consistently been best sellers. His work deepened through close contacts with indigenous peoples, leading to his books Wisdom of the Elders *and* The Sacred Balance *(which also became a PBS series). He created the David Suzuki Foundation in 1989 to identify and promote science-based solutions to environmental crises and communicate them globally.*

David is a world-class scientist who draws elegant connections among evolutionary biology, genetics and ecology, and the ancient empirical wisdom of indigenous peoples. His is one of the world's most important voices of warning, and his contagious love of life, people, and nature has made him a deeply beloved figure.

I AM VERY PROUD of the work I did as a geneticist and of the contributions to science made by the genetics lab I oversaw some thirty years ago. I remember those years in the lab as among the happiest, most exciting times of my life. Although I haven't carried out a scientific experiment for some time, my brain hasn't died and I still feel justified in calling myself a scientist and a geneticist. Advances in genetics research in laboratories around the world today are truly staggering. I see undergraduate students performing laboratory exercises that in 1961 I never dreamed would be possible in my lifetime. I see answers being obtained to questions that I never thought would be testable. The techniques and insights now being developed are truly amazing, and I continue to take vicarious delight in the reports of what is going on.

Nevertheless, I have publicly called for a moratorium on all field tests of transgenic organisms and a halt to the introduction into our food chain of genetically modified organisms (GMOs). For that I have been labeled by some of my fellow scientists a traitor and a heretic—but it is precisely because I love genetics and science that I am concerned about the irresponsible rush to profit without adequate testing of new products and ideas.

When I received my Ph.D. in 1961, we knew what DNA was, what genes were, how many chromosomes we had, and how genes were turned on and off. But when I go into a lab today and tell students what our hottest ideas were in 1961, they fall off their chairs laughing, because the great ideas of 1961 seem crude and naïve. Then I tell them, "You're not going to believe this, but twenty years from now, when you're hot-shot geneticists, and you tell your students what you once believed, they're going to fall off their chairs laughing at you."

My point is that it is the very nature of science at the cutting edge that most of our ideas will turn out to be wrong. This is not a derogation of science; it's just the way science progresses. You make a set of observations or collect data. You then set up a hypothesis to try to make sense of those data. You test the hypothesis and when you get your results, chances are you will find the hypothesis was far from the mark and has to be tossed out or modified and tested again. In reality, most of our current notions will eventually be discarded. That's the very essence of how science progresses.

Since we know that most of our current ideas, especially in revolutionary new fields, will turn out to be wrong, why are we in such an inordinate rush to apply every incremental insight? The answer, of course, is that now there are huge amounts of money at stake.

These days I can't stand the word "breakthrough" because it's used so often by the press to describe what are merely incremental acquisitions of knowledge. Small insights or technical manipulations are extrapolated far beyond current understandings to imply that miraculous wonders may eventually result. Since most of our current ideas are tentative and subject to being radically changed or discarded, rushing to apply these "breakthroughs," it seems to me, becomes downright dangerous, because the very rationale on which they are applied will change over time, and such change may undercut the entire premise behind what is being done.

Especially in the case of genetic engineering, it's extremely dangerous to proclaim the utility of hot new ideas when our knowledge base is so incredibly small, because the manipulative abilities in biotechnology are truly remarkable. We can isolate DNA, purify a specific segment, read the sequence, synthesize that sequence, and then insert the piece into other creatures. That is truly astonishing. You and I could never exchange genes with a carrot plant or an elephant, yet with biotechnology it's possible today. Biotech companies herald the revolutionary benefits promised by this technology, so that their stock value will go up. But when prudent scientists and concerned members of the public raise questions, the companies often reply, "There's nothing alarming or new about what we're doing. It's not really revolutionary. This type of genetic exchange goes on all the time. It's just DNA." To raise the value of their stock, they trumpet their technology as revolutionary, but when concerns are raised, they say it isn't revolutionary at all. It's just tweaking what happens in nature all the time.

Which is it, then? The fact is that biotechnology is a revolutionary area. Traditionally, breeding involved crossing a male and a female of the same species, examining their offspring, then breeding those offspring to look at their progeny. This is vertical inheritance within a species, and it is how we derived the principles of heredity. It has been a very powerful method. Biotechnology, on the other hand, allows us to take a piece of DNA of one species and move it laterally into a totally unrelated species. Such manipulation is very impressive technically, but many assume that when that hunk of DNA is transferred into a different species, it's going to follow the same ground rules that were established by the study of vertical heredity within a species. Nothing justifies that assumption.

In nature, natural selection doesn't act on individual genes. It acts on the expression of an organism's entire genome, what we call its phenotype. When you put a gene from a totally different organism into that genome, you have completely altered the context within which the transferred gene finds itself. It's comparable to taking a traditional Japanese drummer, dropping him into a Western symphony orchestra, and asking everyone to play. You'll get noise but no one can predict how it will sound. Yet biotech companies assume that they can take a gene, pop it into a totally different genome, and confidently predict what the outcome will be.

The potential benefits claimed for this kind of technology are every bit as speculative as the hypothesized dangers. But there is enough preliminary evidence (pollen drift, superweeds, health hazards) to bolster the recommendation that we proceed with far greater caution.

A very respected researcher working in the United Kingdom, Arpad Pusztai, observed that a group of rats fed genetically altered potatoes developed serious health problems. His results were published in a leading medical journal after being extensively peer-reviewed, but he was savagely attacked by many in the scientific establishment. At a press conference around that time, a Monsanto representative attacked me when I mentioned Pusztai. Pusztai's research was flawed, he said, calling it "junk science"—the favorite slur of corporate interests for research unfavorable to their products.

Pusztai himself would be the first to acknowledge the tentative nature of his work, but I would have thought that the responsible reaction when a scientist finds that rats fed genetically modified potatoes develop abnormalities would be to say, "This is worrying. What if he's right? We had better find out before feeding these potatoes to people." We can criticize his experimental technique if it had flaws, but we do preliminary studies to find out whether there are reasons to be concerned. Instead, the immediate industry response is to viciously attack the science because it may slow corporate profits. The company leading the charge, Monsanto, is the very same one that vilified Rachel Carson in 1962 when she published *Silent Spring*. After all these years, they're still doing the same thing.

North Americans are taking part in a massive experiment. We already have forty-two kinds of GMOs in the Canadian food chain. They've been slipped in without any public discussion or any labeling to indicate their presence. The testing of these foods has been totally insufficient, most of it having been conducted by the companies themselves. Europeans are saying, "If we want to find out whether eating genetically modified food is dangerous, just watch what happens in the United States and Canada." I thought we had learned in the 1960s and 1970s that before people become part of an experiment, they should be fully informed and given the choice of whether to take part or not. We don't have that choice. If it's too late to take off the shelves such foods that are already on the market, then at the very least we ought to have the right to make an informed choice. All food containing modified organisms should be labeled.

To my mind, even more significant than the human health risks of GMOs will be the ecological consequences of growing transgenic organisms in open fields where they can interact with other plants. Though biotech companies assure us of the safety of their products, history reveals that life is far more complex and interconnected than we ever imagined. One of the most ecologically destructive vectors today is the introduction of exotic species into new habitats. Transgenic organisms are comparable to exotic species—new kinds of creatures whose biological interactions in natural systems simply can't be predicted, and whose harm sometimes becomes clear only after decades. It pains me to say it, but from a scientific standpoint, the unseemly rush to exploit biotech products has been a terrible dereliction of responsibility.

Unnatural Selection:
The Bacterium That (Almost)
Ate the World

Elaine Ingham

Elaine Ingham would never treat soil like dirt. She reveres it, as we all should, since this precious substance is the thin brown line between plenty and starvation. Given the necessity of topsoil to human survival, you'd think we'd have legions of soil biologists on the case, but Elaine is one of only a handful of serious scientists delving into this microcosmos that feeds the world and helps support life on earth.

Until recently an associate research professor of forest science at Oregon State University, Elaine has twenty-five years of experience in microbiology, botany, plant pathology, and soil and ecology research. She founded Soil Foodweb Inc. and is currently president of the Soil Foodweb Institute in Australia and research director of Soil Foodweb in New York. She serves on the boards of several sustainability organizations and is an active member of numerous prestigious microbiology and ecology associations. She has done stints as president of the Soil Ecology Society and program chair of the Ecological Society of America and has penned over fifty peer-reviewed scientific papers.

Elaine speaks to groups around the world on how to grow plants without the use of toxic pesticides or synthetic fertilizers while at the same time increasing soil fertility and crop production. She has led countless workshops and training sessions at which farmers are taught highly practical techniques for building soil health, using sophisticated composting methods, and enhancing microbiological communities for crop production. Unquestionably one of the world's leading specialists in soil health, she is an exceptionally creative innovator who has made major contributions to our understanding of the soil food web (as she likes to call it) and its structure and function in terrestrial ecosystems from arctic to tropical climates. Her research spans agricultural, grassland, and forest ecologies, where she has analyzed the action of bacteria, fungi, protozoa, nematodes, and mycorrhizal fungi from over 30,000 soil samples.

When a scientist of Elaine's stature warns us about the catastrophic potential of topsoil loss and the escape of genetically modified organisms into the already compromised environment, we do well to pay close attention.

IN MY PROGRAM at Oregon State University in the early 1990s, we started testing the ecological impacts of most of the genetically engineered organisms being produced at that time. The question our lab was asked to address was, Did these engineered organisms have any impact out there in the real world?

The first fourteen species that we worked on—microorganisms, bacteria, and fungi—were organisms incapable of surviving in the natural environment. Putting them in the world would be like taking penguins from the South Pole and dropping them into the La Brea tar pits. Would there be any ecological effect if we dropped a penguin into the middle of the tar pit? Probably not; the impact would be rapidly absorbed by the system.

These first fourteen species of GMOs that we tested had a similarly negligible impact. On this basis, the USDA Animal and Plant Health Inspection Service, the regulatory agency that was determining U.S. policy on genetically engineered organisms, set a course that essentially said that a genetically engineered organism posed no greater risk to the environment than the parent organism does.

GMO number fifteen, however, was a very different story. *Klebsiella planticola*, the bacterium that is the parent organism of this new strain, lives in soils everywhere. It's one of the few truly universal species of bacteria, growing in the root systems of all plants and decomposing plant litter in every ecosystem in the world.

The genetic engineers took genetic material from another bacterium and inserted that trait in the GMO to allow *Klebsiella planticola* to produce alcohol. The aim of this genetic modification was to eliminate the burning of farm fields to rid them of plant matter after harvest. The idea was that you could, instead, rake up all that plant residue, put it in a bucket, and inoculate it with the engineered bacterium, and in about two weeks' time you would have a material that contained about 17 percent alcohol. The alcohol could be extracted and used for gasohol, for cleaning windows, or for myriad other uses: cooking with alcohol in Third World countries, for instance.

The genetic engineers thought this transformation would bring huge benefits. We would no longer have to burn fields, we would breathe better in the fall, and both the company and farmers would get a product that could be sold. There was actually a fourth win: the sludge at the bottom of the bucket is an organic fertilizer, and there are no waste products from that material.

So what's the problem? Suppose you're a farmer and you've got live, alcohol-producing *Klebsiella planticola* that you're going to spread on your fields (which might be easier than gathering up all the plant waste and putting it in buckets). Can it wash into the root systems of your plants? Most likely. Once it's there and growing in the root systems of your plants, it's producing alcohol. What level of alcohol is toxic to plants? It's one part per million. How much alcohol does this engineered organism produce? Seventeen parts per million. Very soon you will have drunk, dead plants.

We did this experiment under controlled conditions in the laboratory because I wasn't going to take this kind of risk out in the field. We constructed three kinds of microcosms of a field, filled them with normal field soil as a growing medium, and planted wheat plants in the three separate systems—each consisting of multiple units—and put them in an incubator. In the first third of the units, we added only water. We added parent, non-GMO bacterium to the second group and the engineered *Klebsiella planticola* to the third. About a week later, we walked into the laboratory, opened up the incubator, and said, "Oops, what did we do wrong?" Many of the plants were dead and were turning into slime on the surface of the soil.

In all the units with just water in the system, the plants were doing okay. In those that had been inoculated with the parent *Klebsiella planticola*, the plants were even bigger, because increased nutrient cycling in the root system makes more nitrogen available, causing the plants to grow bigger. Clearly the parent organism was a benefit to the plant. But where the engineered bacterium was growing, all the plants were dead. Later we tried this experiment using several different kinds of soils, but the result in every case was dead plants.

Take that information and extrapolate it to the real world. Given that the parent organism lives in the root systems of all plants, what's the logical outcome of releasing this organism into the natural environment? Very possibly, we would have no terrestrial plants left. Some plants, such as riparian and wetland plants, have mechanisms for dealing with alcohol production in their root systems. But the logical extrapolation of that experiment is that we would lose terrestrial plants.

I have attended some of the United Nations biosafety protocol meetings. At the 1995 meeting in Madrid, the U.S. delegation was the strongest in saying, in essence, "Don't worry, be happy. Trust us. We don't need a biosafety protocol. Why would biotech companies ever do anything to harm people?" To me, their words echoed those we've heard before from tobacco, pesticide, and fertilizer companies.

At one such meeting, I related the story of *Klebsiella planticola* as an example of the lack of adequate testing for the ecological impact of genetically engineered organisms. The biotech companies object that it costs too much to do this kind of environmental testing. In my view, that's just hype, because I pointed out that our lab spent a very insignificant amount of money to do these simple experiments, especially considering that if this bacterium were let loose in the environment, we would have some very significant problems with our food supply.

No one in his or her right mind is going to test for the kind of risk *Klebsiella planticola* represents because once you release an organism, there is no way to get it back. How far does a single-point inoculation of a genetically engineered organism spread in one year? An engineered *Rhizobium* bacterium that was released in Louisiana in the mid-1990s spread eleven miles per year and has by now dispersed across the North American continent.

At these United Nations meetings I warned that corn pollen is going to move a lot more than three feet away from the plant. "Oh no," said the biotechnology representatives present. "Corn pollen falls out of the air three feet from the plant." I would say, "Wait a minute, you've never heard of bees? How about birds? And insects? And wind?" "Oh no, it falls out of the air within three feet of the plant." Why do our bureaucrats choose to believe these scientists? Just open any plant textbook and you find that corn pollen can be found in the Antarctic and the Arctic. But if you listen to Monsanto, corn pollen can't possibly be there.

Armed with the knowledge of this peril, we need to convince members of Congress that appropriate ecological testing must be done prior to releasing GMOs into the environment. If this happens, it could help keep the problems that are already starting to occur from getting worse.

Genetic Pollution:
A Life of Its Own

Michael Pollan

Michael Pollan has the gift of being able to shift our perception those subtle few degrees that reveal the world anew. As a mainstream journalist, he has courageously bushwhacked into the thorniest briar patches of environmental affairs and made highly controversial points of view seem utterly matter-of-fact. As a passionate gardener and writer on gardening, he gravitates to the pragmatic and empirical while gleefully entertaining the farthest reaches of philosophic inquiry.

A contributing editor to the New York Times Magazine, *he has cogently covered divisive topics ranging from genetic engineering and animal agriculture to the co-optation of organic farming by agribusiness. The scope of his interests and communication skills has also led him to write for* Harper's Magazine *(where he was executive editor for many years),* Mother Jones, Vogue, Gourmet, *and* House and Garden. *His journalism has won numerous awards, including the 2000 Reuters-IUCN Global Award for Environmental Journalism for his reporting on genetic engineering and the American Humane Society's Genesis Award for his writing on animal agriculture.*

Michael is the author of several award-winning books, including the best-selling The Botany of Desire: A Plant's-Eye View of the World, *in which he deftly manages to shape-shift into a plant and look keenly at how the vegetable mind might be calling the shots in the coevolutionary dance with human culture.*

Michael grew up on Long Island and was educated at Bennington College, Oxford University, and Columbia University, all of which prepared him well for his current stint as Knight Professor at the University of California at Berkeley. There he will no doubt inspire a new crop of environmental reporters and thinkers to keep

*shifting our perceptions those few critical degrees that can help many more of us see
the world from the Earth's point of view.*

"GENETIC POLLUTION" is a term we didn't have a few years ago because
we didn't really need it. It's a very different kind of phenomenon from chemical pollution. The main difference is that it's a problem with, literally, a life of
its own. Unlike chemical spills that eventually fade or can be cleaned up, genes
that get out into the environment can multiply themselves endlessly. We can't
clean up genetic pollution or conduct a product recall.

A few years ago I grew some genetically modified potatoes as a way to
learn about them, and in doing so, I broke the organic virginity of my garden
for one season. The next season the potatoes came up on their own, feloniously,
since Monsanto, the company that developed and patented them, legally requires that you cannot regrow them yourself.

As I cultivated my garden, I explored the issue of genetic pollution. At
the time, the primary concern about GMO plants was that the genes would
escape and mix with weedy relatives of the crop plant. At that point, the promi-
nent case of migrating genes was a GMO rapeseed (canola) that had passed its
genes for herbicide resistance to a weedy relative in the mustard family. The
plant had been engineered to withstand large amounts of herbicides, which
of course would not be a desirable trait in weeds. I asked Monsanto, which
developed the technology, "Isn't this gene flow a problem for my potatoes too?"
The company's executives said, "No, because you probably don't have any
relatives of the potato near your garden. They are native to the Andes, so you
don't have to worry in North America. The corn farmers in the Midwest don't
have any wild relatives of corn growing in the Midwest either, so we don't
worry about gene flow there. To prevent that problem, we won't sell any genetically modified corn seeds in Mexico or potatoes in the Andes, where these
crops' centers of diversity lie."

Centers of diversity are very important because they are the particular
places where crops originated and evolved. It's where you find the greatest

biodiversity of these species as well as their wild progenitors. Moreover, it's where many of the landraces people have developed still grow; these are the genetic lines from which plant breeders derived our modern crop varieties.

In the fall of 2001, credible reports surfaced that the wild corn and land-races in Mexico have been genetically polluted. How did this happen? We don't know for sure. We do know that although Monsanto and the other companies weren't selling GMO corn seed there, they were selling that corn as food. Of course, corn food and corn seed are the same thing. It's likely that farmers planted some of that corn sold as food, because farmers will always try a new corn to see how it performs in their fields. They apparently planted this genetically modified corn within a year of its introduction in 1996.

We're in a situation now where this ancestral corn and these landraces now have modified genes in them. Why does that matter? One objection is that something pristine has been contaminated, but that concern is arguably a sentimental one. The more practical problem is that centers of diversity are where breeders go whenever one of our crops gets into trouble. For example, the 1845 Irish potato famine resulted from growing potatoes in a monoculture. Virtually everyone in Europe was planting just one kind of potato, called the lumper, until a blight came along and wiped out that variety, leading to a million deaths by starvation. How did we solve that problem? Breeders went to the potato's center of diversity in the Andes and, among the thousands of different potatoes there, found strains that possessed genes resistant to the blight. They incorporated these into the potatoes grown commercially and thereby saved potato farming in Europe.

In 1970 we had a corn blight in the United States and lost 10 percent of the corn crop, a staggering proportion. Again, we solved the problem by going to Mexico and finding genes for resistance among the landraces.

This diversity is a precious genetic resource. Our food security literally depends on these collections. The concern now is that the engineered genes may confer a fitness, an evolutionary advantage, on the corn plants in Mexico that have them, and those corn plants may come to dominate and drive out—which is to say, drive to extinction—some of the traditional varieties. It's a serious development, and one that was easy to foresee.

One of my larger concerns in the fight over genetic engineering is that even if opponents win this battle and keep these products off the market and out of the field, what will have been won? Removing genetically modified food from the food supply will not return us to a Golden Age. The conventional way we raise potatoes is horrifying: we grow them in giant monocultures, which is arguably as big a problem as genetic pollution. Monocultures are very brittle. Because all the plants are genetically identical, they're exquisitely vulnerable: a single virus or bacterium can wipe out all of them. Farmers have to use gargantuan quantities of the most toxic pesticides on them because they are so vulnerable to insect infestation. From a biological perspective, genetic modification is a Band-Aid on monocultural agriculture in the same way that pesticides are. The fundamental issue is really the difference between monoculture and diversity, not GMOs and conventional hybrids.

Several years ago most people assumed that they could decide whether or not they wanted to eat genetically modified foods. But I found out very quickly that it was a moot point. I'd already eaten GMOs because I'd been to McDonald's with my son, and I was eating them there. I was also eating them in potato chips. They were present throughout the food supply, which I didn't know at the time. When McDonald's started getting agitated phone calls from customers asking about the presence of GMOs in its french fries, the company had to say to itself, "Wait, we have a potential public relations problem here. And there's no benefit in these potatoes for us. They aren't any cheaper for us to buy. They don't fry up any better. So why are we selling these potatoes?" McDonald's decided to stop buying them, though without a lot of fanfare, just a little squib in the Wall Street Journal.

Frito-Lay followed suit because it also was getting calls from consumers. Farmers now saw a financial risk in planting GMO potatoes because they couldn't sell them to a significant part of the market. So the New Leaf GMO potato is no longer being planted. It has been taken off the market.

What these stories show is that the system of GMOs is itself very brittle. It threatens the very genetic reservoir to which we return when they inevitably fail—but it is also exquisitely vulnerable to consumers who are willing to say no.

Part IV

The Industrial Evolution: Biology Meets Business

Natural Capitalism:
Brother, Can You Spare a Paradigm?

Paul Hawken

Paul Hawken is perhaps the most renowned avatar of green entrepreneurship and socially responsible business. Yet he was also out getting tear-gassed in the streets of Seattle while resisting the ravages of corporate globalization. A man of profound compassion who ardently loves the natural world and comes from a generation with a deep yearning for social justice, his embrace of enlightened commerce comes from a clear-eyed analysis of the reality that industrial corporate capitalism as now practiced is the most awesomely destructive force on the planet, for both the environment and people. No task is more pressing than to transform it, and few have been as effective as Paul in catalyzing that process.

His six books have been published in over fifty-two countries and thirty languages, selling over two million copies. It would be hard to overstate the impact of The Ecology of Commerce *and* Natural Capitalism: Creating the Next Industrial Revolution, *the latter coauthored with Amory and Hunter Lovins. These landmark books make the irrefutable case that the economy is a subset of ecology, and that the only viable future for business lies in adapting to ecological principles grounded in social and economic justice.*

After a decade-long whirlwind of writing and speaking to countless people, companies, governments, and change-makers around the world, Paul has lately returned to business with multiple new companies geared toward restoring the earth. Three of the companies involve Jay Harman, the creator of PAX Scientific, and directly apply PAX's biomimetic design geometries to computers, industrial systems, and wind turbines. Another is Groxis, a super–search engine that maps the worldwide web and offers the potential to radically enhance the linkages among social-change movements everywhere.

Paul has a luminous mind, a poet's soul, an artist's eye, and a brave heart will-
ing to speak truth to power. He has consistently spotted the shifting horizon of pos-
itive possibility and lit the way for others. A true visionary of a restorative future,
he is making that dream come true.

WHEN I COINED the term "natural capitalism" in 1997, the modifier was
"ism," not "natural." Of course, many people, including the UK publisher of
my book by that title, thought I was writing about capitalism. But the book is
not an apologia for capitalism, nor is it about the care and feeding of multinational corporations, which its subtitle, *The Next Industrial Revolution*, might
imply. Essentially, natural capitalism is a metaphor for an economy that is
emerging.

The term "natural capital" was used by E. F. Schumacher in 1974 in his
book *Small Is Beautiful: Economics As If People Mattered.* At that time "natural capital" referred to natural resources, and Schumacher's concern was that
they were not being represented on balance sheets of countries or companies.
As laudable as that idea was and is, biologists and economists of Schumacher's
era largely thought of nature as things.

Today we have an expanded and different sense of what nature is. Most
important, we understand nature as a flow of services that cannot be com-
modified—services that are not bought or sold but that absolutely influence
and dictate the quality of our life on this planet, and from which all so-called
economic value is derived. These flows of services, which we mostly take for
granted, include pollination, oxygen, global climatic stability, riparian systems,
fisheries, soil fertility, topsoil, erosion control, flood catchment, and so on. What
we do know today is that in the last fifty years every living system on earth
has been in decline, and the rate of decline is speeding up. One need not know
anything about the environment except that fact in order to know what to do.

It would be convenient to see the loss of wilderness as purely an environmental issue, or even a consumption issue, and neglect its social component. Conventional wisdom tells us, "We use too much; let's cut back and
save the environment." However, it's critical to recognize that underlying the
extermination of nature is the marginalization of human beings. C. S. Lewis

wrote in *The Abolition of Man*, "What we call Man's power over Nature turns out to be a power exercised by some men over other men with Nature as its instrument." It is the power of corporations over people and place. The world's top 200 companies have twice the assets of 80 percent of the world's people. This power was never granted.

The two most complex systems in the world are living and human systems. The study of how human commercial activity is linked to living systems, characterized as "resources," is consigned primarily to economics. The practice of sustainability, as nascent and wobbly as it may be, is essentially the study of this relationship from a new perspective. Because sustainability is systemic at heart, it speaks the language of kinship and of relationships. In contrast, conventional economics speaks the language of separation, of objects, of nature as thing. The language is critical because all of us have a responsibility to enlarge the conversation the world is having about what it means to be a human at a time when every living system on earth is declining and the rate of loss is accelerating. I am too polite: actually, life is being annihilated.

Nevertheless, commerce is part of a solution, or perhaps I should say that commerce *must* be part of a solution. Imagine a world in which cars and buses become whisper-quiet, vehicles give off exhaust of only water vapor, parks and greenways have replaced unneeded urban freeways, and the very wastes of industrial society become foods for other industrial processes, in effect mimicking how nature works. In the process, landfills will close, worldwide forest cover will increase, dams will be dismantled, and the wild will be returned to our lives. Fundamental to this second industrial revolution will be the recognition that capitalism as it's currently practiced is a financially profitable, unsustainable aberration in human development. What might be called "industrial capitalism" doesn't fully conform to its own accounting principles. It liquidates its capital and calls it income. It neglects to assign any value to the largest stocks of capital it employs: the natural resources and living systems, as well as the social and cultural systems, that are the basis of human capital.

Natural capitalism as a metaphor is an attempt to describe an integrated application and program of the economics of restoration. Rather than being an approach to sustainability, natural capitalism attempts to describe a practical relationship between human beings and the biosphere that will improve the quality of life for all while dramatically reducing our impact on living systems and eventually increasing ecosystem viability and productivity. Sustainability is an insufficient goal, because there is very little that we want to sustain. Who wants to sustain Los Angeles in its present form? Furthermore, sustainability as a goal is not imaginative. It implies an end or balance point where we're taking just so much from the earth but not so much that we degrade the environment further than it already has been. It does not acknowledge nature as a dynamic flow of processes with humans in dynamic relationship. This paradigm of services, flows, and relationships is how we must address the issue.

Coupling natural capitalism with the phrase "the next industrial revolution" is an attempt to understand what economics would be if the limiting factor to human well-being were in fact perceived as the loss of living systems or life itself. Fortunately, the economic and technological trends needed to change our current unhealthy behavior are already in place.

But to understand these changes, it's first necessary to visualize how the phenomenon called the Industrial Revolution took shape. If we could back up to its beginnings, we would see a sudden, almost violent change in the means of production and distribution of goods. Brilliantly designed breakthroughs in mechanical engineering created newly complex machines. Goods in all sectors of the economy, from agriculture to industry to services, became less expensive and more widely available. Incomes rose. Canals, designed primarily to move massive amounts of coal to factories, lowered distribution costs and improved communications. Organization and management changes produced more efficient administrative systems. Production units were organized to take advantage of economies of scale. Steam and eventually electricity were harnessed to drive output. Science exploded and educational opportunities multiplied. Laissez-faire capitalism, banking, and the joint-stock corporation emerged as dominant institutions and ideologies. The final wave of the Enclosure Movement, which excluded peasants from open fields and communal grazing lands, helped increase agricultural productivity and uprooted pools of labor that crowded cities and factory towns. Mechanized, large-scale industry was an entirely new species of human endeavor that swept across the world, leaving almost nothing untouched.

A growing middle class spawned by industrialism was smitten with its newfound purchasing power. Passenger pigeons, otters, and beaver were hunted to near or actual extinction to adorn the quasi rich. Forest after forest was felled, lands cleared, mines opened, sea lanes established, indigenous peoples enslaved or hunted for bounties, military might exerted.

Industrialism was a massive substitution of manufactured capital for natural capital. It was a revolution because it allowed human beings to simultaneously produce and consume more. The more natural capital that technology sucked up, the more productive laborers became. The more work a person could do, the cheaper products became. The higher income climbed, the faster demand went up. It was a revolution because it was self-actuating.

And it has not stopped to this day. Though writers and scholars tell us that the old industrial patterns are no longer dominant, modern economic growth is just as driven by mechanization and technology today as it was during the early Industrial Revolution. Mobile phones, laptops, PDAs, and other assorted "postindustrial" technologies are no different from spinning jennies and steam engines. They require large amounts of natural capital for production and use and are designed to increase human output. Consider this one example: for every pound of electronics in your pocket or desk, approximately eight thousand pounds of waste was created somewhere in the world. This is not the information age; it is the despoliation age.

The industrial system has grown beyond its original imaginings. Since the mid-eighteenth century, more of nature has been destroyed than in all prior history. Industry is a ravenous hungry ghost stalking the world's resource systems. The marginalizations of nature and people are inextricably intertwined because we are using more of what we have less of—living systems and natural resources—in order to use less of what we have more of—human beings. The living systems that support life on earth include forests, topsoil, grasslands, savannas, wetlands, estuaries, oceans, coral reefs, the atmosphere, riparian corridors, aquifers, tundra, and biodiversity. The people are the human race. Anytime you increase the productivity of something, you use less of it.

Thus, we have a system designed to use fewer people and more nature. Un- and disemployment have been growing faster in the last twenty-five years than employment, while every living system continues its downward spiral. While what is wild shrinks and deteriorates, over one billion people who want to work cannot, and over three billion live in abject poverty.

What is it like to be a mother, a father, part of a family unit and to know that no matter what you do during the day, no matter how hard you work, no matter what efforts you make, you cannot feed your children, care for them, clothe them, or get them to school? Most of us are fortunate that we don't know. But more than a billion people do know. This is the world industrialism is creating, and it's being accelerated by e-commerce, the Internet, computerization, and telecommunications, because those phenomena are obsessively increasing the productivity of human beings but causing the worldwide polarization of income, huge information gaps, and extraordinary concentrations of wealth.

Consider the idea of road warriors rushing onto the red-eye with their Palm Pilots, their laptops, their cell phones—what's that all about? So we ask the question, Do we really want to be more productive? Do we really want to swap more productivity for the loss of our forests, our riparian systems, our resources? I don't think so.

I once met with two hundred CEOs, CFOs, CTOs, CIOs—executives of Fortune 500 companies—and I posed three questions. First I asked, "How many of you basically want to work harder five years from now than you do now? Raise your hand." No one raised a hand. Then I asked, "How many of you know somebody in your office who's a slacker, who kind of screws off?" Nobody raised a hand. I continued, "How many of you spend too much time with your children or know someone who does?" Nobody raised a hand. There was just a nervous sort of giggle from the men, which is not a pleasant sound.

So the real question is, What are we doing? We're creating a world in which we cannot spend enough time with our children. To accomplish that, we are sacking the planet.

What natural capitalism is saying is that in the developed world, the limiting factor to human well-being and development is no longer human-made capital; it is life itself. As more people place greater strain on living systems, limits to prosperity are coming to be determined by scarcities of natural systems rather than industrial prowess. Today, economic progress is becoming restricted not by the number of fishing boats but by the decreasing numbers of fish; not by the power of pumps but by the depletion of aquifers; not by the limits to which we can genetically improve cattle but by the loss of grasslands; not by the number of chainsaws but by the disappearance of our forests. Unlike traditional economic factors of production, these biological limiting factors are not fungible; in other words, they can't be replaced.

If we are to save what is wild, what is irreplaceable and majestic in nature, then ironically we will have to turn to each other and take care of all the human beings here on earth. It is not mere industry that must reform; it is our sense of each other. We have the responsibility to create a world of equals, not just a nation of equals. The first rule of ecology is that everything is connected. The first rule of earth-saving is that we are all connected as a species. The economy that destroys the tundra is the same one that creates tens of millions of refugees, that causes families to sell their daughters or compels an Asian farmer to hock his kidney. There is no boundary that will protect an environment from a suffering humanity.

By the time we reach the middle of the twenty-first century, we will need to feed, clothe, house, and employ 50 percent more people than are on earth today. We will need to provide the equivalent of half of a new world, although we aren't doing well with the one we have. To do that, I believe we need to embrace four principles that are the cornerstones of natural capitalism.

The first is *radical resource productivity*. The movement toward radical resource productivity began in the fall of 1994, when a group of sixteen scientists, economists, government officials, and businesspeople, convened and sponsored by Friedrich Schmidt-Bleek of the Wuppertal Institute for Climate, Environment and Energy in Germany, published the "Carnoules Declaration." The Factor Ten Club, as the group came to call itself, called for a leap in resource productivity to reverse the growing damage to living systems. The declaration began with these prophetic words: "Within one generation, nations can achieve a tenfold increase in the efficiency with which they use energy, natural resources and other materials."

Increasing resource productivity means obtaining the same amount of utility or work from a product or process while using less material and energy. In manufacturing, transportation, forestry, construction, energy, and other industrial sectors, mounting empirical evidence suggests that radical improvements in resource productivity are both practical and cost-effective, even in the most modern industries. Companies and designers are developing ways to make natural resources—energy, metals, cars, water, forests, and oil—work five, ten, even one hundred times harder than they do today. These efficiencies transcend the marginal gains in performance that industry constantly seeks as part of its evolution. Instead, revolutionary leaps in design and technology will alter industry itself. Investments in the productivity revolution are not only repaid over time by the saved resources, but in many cases can also reduce initial capital investments.

The world's growing population cannot attain a Western standard of living by following traditional industrial paths of development, because the resources required are too vast and too expensive and their extraction and deployment too damaging to local and global systems. On the other hand, no program of conservation can hope to succeed without addressing people's needs to live secure and satisfying lives. Only radical improvements in resource productivity can expand humanity's possibilities for growth and begin to ameliorate the polarization of wealth between rich and poor segments of the globe.

The second principle is *biomimicry*. Biomimicry, or biomimetics, is the art and science of designing processes, services, and products in a manner that both imitates life and is conducive to life. In nature, life begets life. The conditions of one living system create the means whereby other types or forms of life can flourish. Evolution itself is a long process whereby life increases in differentiation, variety, and mass. Our economy functions in almost entirely the opposite manner. Although human beings have flourished in many respects, living systems are collapsing. In any design situation, biomimicry asks, What would nature do?

Chemists, physicists, process engineers, biologists, and industrial designers are reexamining the energy, materials, and manufacturing systems required to provide specific qualities—strength, warmth, speed, tension, motion—required by products and end users. They are turning away from mechanical systems requiring heavy metals, combustion, and petroleum and seeking solutions that use minimal inputs, lower temperatures, and enzymatic reactions. Business is beginning to imitate biological and ecosystem processes, replicating natural methods of production and engineering to produce chemicals, materials, and compounds, soon perhaps even microprocessors. Some of the most exciting developments come from emulating nature's low-temperature, low-pressure, solar-powered assembly techniques, whose products rival anything human-made.

The third principle, first articulated by the Swiss economist Walter Stahel, simply says that if we're going to create an economic system that has any semblance or resemblance to biological systems, we can no longer think of ourselves as episodic manufacturers of goods but must recast ourselves as deliverers of a *flow of services.* After all, that flow of services is what we receive from nature. The materials, molecules, and compounds themselves must be carefully marshaled and monitored. Either they must be made from living systems and be capable of being biodegraded or reconstituted, or they must be technical nutrients that are returned to industrial systems in a closed loop. There are no exceptions. There is no landfill in this society.

The last principle is the *restoration of natural capital.* We cannot simply organize ourselves to be effective, efficient, or productive. We have to organize our industrial systems in such a way that our oceans, our soil, our waters, our riparian systems, and our climates are restored, step by step by step. Restoration has to be a natural outcome of what we do, not an altruistic or a legislated outcome.

At present, we have an economy that is so ingenious, so "brilliantly" designed that we tell eighteen-year-old men and women that they don't have jobs and they have no value. It's okay for you teens to buy athletic shoes or Walkmans or CDs, but don't bother us for jobs because we've created this really brilliant economy that is making people more and more redundant. That's essentially what we're saying to children: that they have no value. Then we're surprised when they hear it. They're very smart, and they feed it back to us.

MECHANICS' INSTITUTE LIBRARY
57 Post Street
San Francisco, CA 94104
(415) 393-0101

We have the highest rates of abortion, drug use, violence, gangs, and teen pregnancy of any industrial nation. The list goes on. So what does that tell us? What young people are saying to us is that they don't want to be here. At all. On earth. In the United States, besides injury, the greatest cause of mortality among teenagers between ten and fourteen years old is suicide. Not drugs, not violence, not AIDS. Suicide.

Should we be surprised at the thirty-six million people languishing in poverty in the United States? Or the thirteen million children, seven million of whom are under six years old, living in poverty in the richest country in the world? Or the twenty-seven million people who are functionally illiterate and the forty-two million who have no health insurance? Or the three hundred thousand people wandering our cities homeless, or the two million men imprisoned in the penal system? The largest penal colony in the world is the United States of America.

An industrial system that wastes its living systems and its natural resources also wastes its people, because waste is embedded in the system. It's about making people useless. Some of us may have jobs, but too many don't. If people do not feel valued, they act out their sense of "disvalue." One of the largest contributors to former California governor Gray Davis's reelection campaign was the California Correctional Peace Officers Association. That's what we're calling industry, growth, and economic development. How much more starkly can we see the wasting of our resources and our people?

In a restorative economy, we would move to systems of agriculture, forestry, transportation, construction, and communication that have the least cost to the environment. In the current economy, by contrast, we have treated the resources we have inherited, both renewable and nonrenewable, as free goods, without value until we transform them into products and services. For example, we now have cheap chemicals and cheap food, but we can't drink our water.

In a natural capitalism system, those resources constitute our capital and are valued at their true replacement cost. Instead of competing to produce the cheapest goods, we compete to produce goods and services in ways that have

the least impact on those resources, and thus the lowest cost to current and future generations. In the restorative economy, we still use the same basic mechanisms of commerce: markets, competition, and value-added innovation. But the incentives are reversed, so that instead of being rewarded for producing things at the lowest price, business is rewarded for producing at the lowest cost. The lowest-cost system is the most efficient in both industrial and biological terms, and it's better for the customer, the worker who manufactures the goods, the habitat from which it's drawn, and the generations unborn.

Restorative economies increase the productivity of our natural capital and use fewer and fewer resources to provide equivalent goods and services. When you increase the productivity of natural systems instead of the human productivity of industrial systems, you get a complete reversal of the deteriorating social and environmental conditions we see today. It takes more people to farm organically, to practice sustainable forestry, or to create closed-loop industrial systems where all materials are reused and nothing is thrown away or wasted.

In other words, the intelligent manufacturing systems of the future—those that sharply reduce our impact on the environment—also will create a resurgence of meaningful employment around the world. This shift is of critical importance, because not only are one-third of the world's workers unemployed or unable to support their families, but within the next twenty years there will be another two billion people coming into the workplace.

In the United States, more than thirty thousand nongovernmental organizations (NGOs), foundations, and citizens' groups are addressing the issue of social and ecological sustainability in the most complete sense of the word. Worldwide, the number of organizations exceeds one hundred thousand. Together they address a broad array of issues, including environmental justice, ecological literacy, public policy, conservation, women's rights and health, population, renewable energy, corporate reform, labor rights, climate change, trade rules, ethical investing, ecological tax reform, water, and much more. These groups follow Mahatma Gandhi's imperatives: some resist, while others create new structures, patterns, and means. The groups tend to be local, marginal, poorly funded, and overworked. It's hard for most not to feel palpable anxiety that they could perish in a twinkling. At the same time, a deeper pattern is emerging that is extraordinary.

If you ask all of these groups for their principles, frameworks, conventions, models, or declarations, you will find that they do not conflict. This has never happened before. In the past, powerful movements such as Christianity, Marxism, and Freudian psychology started with a unified or centralized set of ideas and then disseminated them, over time creating power struggles as the core mental model or dogma was changed, diluted, or revised. The sustainability movement did not start this way. Its proponents do not agree on everything, nor should they ever, but, remarkably, they all share a basic set of fundamental understandings about the earth, how it functions, and the necessity of fairness and equity for all people in partaking of the earth's life-giving systems.

These groups believe that self-sufficiency is a human right. They imagine a future where producing the means to kill people is not a business but a crime, where families do not starve, where parents can work, where children are never sold, and where women cannot be impoverished because they choose to be mothers. These groups believe that water and air belong to us all, not to the rich. They believe seeds and life itself cannot be owned or patented by corporations. They believe that nature is the basis of true prosperity and must be honored.

This shared understanding is arising spontaneously, from different economic sectors, cultures, regions, and cohorts. It is indisputably growing and spreading throughout this country and the world. No one started this worldview, no one is in charge of it, and no orthodoxy is restraining it. It is the fastest and most powerful movement in the world today, unrecognizable to most American media outlets because it is not centralized, based on power, or led by white, male, charismatic vertebrates. As conditions continue to worsen socially, environmentally, and politically, organizations working toward sustainability increase, deepen, and multiply.

There is a difference between blind, heady optimism and the deep conviction that no force can counter the truths we share and hold so deeply. This is the work of peace, and it is rapidly becoming the work of many. As Vaclav Havel said, "We are at the brink of a new world because the old world is no longer valid." If it is no longer valid to have one billion people dis- or unemployed, as they are today, a valid world means that in fifty years we will no longer be the only species without full employment. There will be more meaningful, dignified, living-wage jobs than there are people who can fill them. It is no longer valid for America, with 4 percent of the world's population, to consume 30 percent of the world's wealth; a new valid America would live with inspired and elegant frugality. If we are losing our legacy forests, a valid world means we will begin anew and create primary forests of the future. If the population is too large and growing, a valid world will be one wherein every single child is nurtured, cared for, and made welcome. The way to reduce population is to have all people feel honored.

We will not be able to bring back what we have lost. It will take five million years to restore the diversity of lost species. Nevertheless, we can in fifty years begin to undertake the very necessary work of restoration. We will have begun to reduce carbon in the atmosphere, recharge aquifers, bring back lands deserts have taken, create habitat corridors for buffalo, panthers, and gray wolves, and thicken our paper-thin soils.

Our children will look back fifty years from now and wonder at what they accomplished. They are avidly reading Harry Potter books, and what they know from these books is that today's world is run by Muggles. Muggles represent a hyperrational, mechanical, and authoritarian world devoid of magic. Muggles worship things, money, economic motives, and hypergrowth at all costs. What these children reflect is the reemergence of a celebratory resistance to what visionary activist Caroline Casey calls the "reality police," the angry columnists, vacant politicians, incensed economists, and others who cannot see that what is emerging now is the possibility of being fully human.

What is possible in fifty years is a world that is wonderfully messy, shockingly magical, and deliriously creative. It doesn't fit a single scenario written anywhere by anyone. It is not a world defined by technologies, tools, and products. It is not a world that can be measured by money. It is not a world that can be reduced to demographics. It will be a world defined by the acts of restoring life on earth, a world that celebrates dance, costume, song, ritual, magic, prayer, worship, and play. It will be a world that cares for its old people, its children, and its storytellers. This is the work of carefully reconstituting what has been lost by creating conditions conducive to life on earth. It is born of a culture in which no materials used in industry cause damage to anyone, now or later. It is created by a society that imitates and emulates the design brilliance of the nature that we reside within and walk upon and have never fully appreciated. Ours is a time of extraordinary work, because it is not the work of a decade or a century, but the work of a millennium.

Natural Capitalism:
Where the Rubber Meets the Road

Amory Lovins and Hunter Lovins

As Amory and Hunter Lovins point out, our industrial production systems operate at a jaw-dropping 90 percent rate of inefficiency. In other words, the Industrial Revolution moved us out of the Dark Ages and into the Dim Ages. In their roles as founders and co-CEOs (1982–2002) of Rocky Mountain Institute (RMI), the world-renowned applied research center, Amory and Hunter have dramatically helped eliminate such waste.

With his 1976 landmark Foreign Affairs *paper "Energy Strategy: The Road Not Taken" and 1977 book* Soft Energy Paths, *Amory launched a revolution in resource efficiency and energy policy oriented toward conservation and renewable energy. He has since spun off several for-profit companies, using the market as a powerful instrument with which to create environmental improvement and social change. He is currently CEO of RMI and chairman of Hypercar, Inc., whose Fiberforge process for making cost-competitive carbon-fiber auto bodies is the key to bringing hydrogen cars into wide use. Since starting out as an experimental physicist, Amory has received numerous honors and awards, including ten honorary degrees and a MacArthur Fellowship. He has written twenty-eight books and hundreds of papers. The centennial issue of the* Wall Street Journal *named him one of the thirty-nine people most likely to change the course of business in the 1990s. He did just that.*

Hunter Lovins was trained as a political scientist, sociologist, lawyer, forester, rodeo rider, and emergency medical technician. She has coauthored nine books and several hundred papers and has lectured in over fifteen countries on topics spanning sustainable development, energy and resource policy, economic development, climate change, and land management. Hunter left RMI in 2002 to become president of Nat-

ural Capitalism, Inc., a company that is making the concepts presented in this chapter the central organizing principles of business and society worldwide.

Together and separately, Amory and Hunter have consulted for scores of industries and governments worldwide, especially on advanced resource productivity in the electricity, real estate, automotive, semiconductor, chemical, and oil industries. They shared a Mitchell Prize, a Right Livelihood Award (often called the "alternative Nobel Prize"), the Nissan Prize, and the Lindbergh Award. They were named Time magazine's "Heroes for the Planet" in 2000. Amory and Hunter also teamed up with Paul Hawken to write the seminal book Natural Capitalism: Creating the Next Industrial Revolution, detailing a wealth of real-world case studies of ecological business projects that show how doing the right environmental thing actually benefits the bottom line.

It's impossible to overlook their brilliance, but these are not just gifted visionaries and theoreticians. They are savvy realists with guts, heart, and superb diplomatic skills. It's not easy to go into boardrooms in the belly of the business beast, roll up your sleeves, and conduct a respectful conversation that leads to real change. Putting their hearts on the line may be the real secret of their success.

THE LATE TWENTIETH CENTURY witnessed two great intellectual shifts. The first is the fall of communism and the apparent triumph around the world of market economics. The second, now emergent in a rapidly growing number of businesses, is the end of the war against the earth, accompanied, we believe, by the eventual competitive victory of a new form of economics we call "natural capitalism."

We use the term to emphasize that capitalism in its current manifestation is an aberration, not because it's capitalistic—certainly the greatest known form of wealth creation—but rather because it is liquidating the most important forms of capital: the natural capital whose resources and ecosystem services make possible all life.

These ecosystem services give us each year at least tens of trillions of dollars in eminently measurable economic services that are comparable in value to the entire human global economy. Because none of this value shows up on anybody's balance sheet, it's not entirely surprising that it's being liquidated.

Yet you can't correct deficient logic of this sort simply by monetizing the capital. The folks at Biosphere II in Arizona spent $200 million to prove that they couldn't keep eight people in oxygen, while our home, Biosphere I, performs this service for six billion of us every day for free.

The best technologies can't substitute for water and nutrient cycling, nor for atmospheric and ecological stability. Imagine hand-pollinating all of agriculture. Our best technologies can't substitute for natural processes of assimilating and detoxifying all of society's waste. There's no longer any scientific dispute that every living system on earth is threatened. With ten thousand more of us humans arriving every hour, what's in short supply these days isn't people. It's nature.

The limits to economic growth are coming to be set by scarcities of natural capital. Sometimes we learn the value of natural systems only when they start to break down. In 1998, in China's Yangtze Basin, deforestation caused flooding that killed 3,700 people and dislocated more than live in the United States, as well as inundating sixty million acres of cropland. It was a $30 billion disaster that forced China into a $12 billion crash program of reforestation. That's the economic price tag on the loss of an ecosystem service in just one relatively small place.

This is not to say that we're running out of commodities. You may remember the old billboards showing a gas gauge superimposed on the earth and running on empty. But we're not running out of oil. The prices of oil and copper, for example, not so long ago were about as low as they have been in history, in part because we're getting ever better at extracting the stuff. There's a lot of it, but the costs of using it are growing. This way of production entails profound ecological costs.

Natural capitalism, the alternative we propose, uses four principles that can offer business increased profits; in many cases, dramatically increased profits. At the same time, this system addresses many of the environmental problems facing us. For instance, global warming is an artifact of an economically inefficient energy policy. Just doing what's cost-effective in energy would largely abate the problem of climate change.

The four principles are:

- Harnessing advanced resource efficiency to create profits by eliminating the need to pay for extraction at one end and pollution at the other.

- Eliminating the concept of waste by redesigning industry along biological lines, closing loops in the flows of materials, and not producing persistent toxins.

- Changing the business model to encourage these two shifts by rewarding both the provider and the customer for doing more and better with less for longer.

- Reversing planetary destruction by restoring natural capital. Any good capitalist reinvests in the capital that's in short supply.

Together these principles enable companies to behave as if ecosystem services, the natural capital, were properly valued. Of course, where the rubber meets the road is in real-world case studies of successful projects actually implemented by companies, many of which we have worked with to achieve their goals.

It's pretty easy to profit by using resources much more productively because right now we use them incredibly wastefully. The stuff that drives the metabolism of industry amounts in this country to more than twenty times your body weight per person per day. That's more than a million pounds of resources per American per year. Globally, this flow is about a half trillion tons per year. Yet only about 1 percent of all the materials mobilized in the current economy ever gets embodied in a durable product and is still there six months after its sale. The difference between that 1 percent and something approaching 100 percent is obviously a large business opportunity.

Nowhere are the opportunities for savings easier to see than in energy. In this country we've already cut our energy bill by more than $300 billion a year since 1973. However, we're still wasting $300 billion worth of energy a year, and that number keeps going up. The energy we throw away at American power plants exceeds the total energy used by Japan. Our economy, like Japan's, is less than a tenth as efficient as the laws of physics permit.

Fortunately, many companies are realizing how much money they can make by correcting such waste. Southwire, an energy-intensive maker of rod, wire, and cable, cut its energy use per pound of product in half in six years, and thereby created profits at a time when many of its competitors were going under. The two engineers who achieved these savings may have saved four thousand jobs at ten plants in six states, and the company's efficiency is still improving.

In twelve years, starting in 1981, Dow Chemical's Louisiana division implemented close to a thousand energy-saving projects suggested at the shop-floor level. Its average annual return on investment exceeded 200 percent. In the later years both the savings and the returns were going up because, as often happens, the engineers were learning new tricks faster than they used up the old ones. State-of-the-shelf technologies can typically make old buildings three or four times more energy efficient. New ones can be closer to ten times more energy efficient, as well as cheaper to build.

There are many examples of this kind of improvement, such as buildings, in climates ranging from about minus 47 to plus 115 degrees Fahrenheit, that provide the same or better comfort but have lower construction costs and use no heating or cooling system. There are huge opportunities in big buildings, both new and old. Industries can achieve profitable savings in motor systems, in process designs (even condensing a giant chemical plant to the size of a watermelon, with energy and capital cost reductions to match), and of course in the next frontier of materials productivity.

The Hypercar vehicles we developed at Rocky Mountain Institute represent a design synthesis for cars and other light and medium vehicles that will use 85 percent less energy and materials to deliver superior safety and performance. It is now possible to make SUVs that emit nothing but hot water, get a hundred miles a gallon equivalent, and perform like a sports car. Over $5 billion has been committed by automakers to this line of development. That figure has been doubling every year and a half because, back in 1993, not wanting to risk the vehicle's chance of getting to market by patenting and selling the intellectual property, we put it in the public domain, where nobody can patent it. Now everyone is competing over it. It's a lot more fun that way.

On Rocky Mountain Institute's website you'll find a chronology of how quickly the elements of Hypercar vehicles are emerging in the market. This particular combination of technologies is likely to spell the end of the automotive, oil, steel, aluminum, coal, and electricity industries as we know them, and the beginning of new ones that are more benign, more profitable, and a lot more fun.

An international company was recently redesigning a standard industrial heat-transfer loop, slated for installation in a new Shanghai factory. A top European firm had supposedly optimized this system to use ninety-five horsepower for pumping, but our colleagues made two embarrassingly simple design changes that cut the pumping power from ninety-five horsepower down to seven, a 92 percent reduction that lowered the capital costs and made the system work better in every respect.

This improvement did not require any new technology, but rather two changes in the design mentality. First, the brilliant Dutch engineer Jan Schilham chose big pipes and small pumps instead of small pipes and big pumps. Normal engineering practice balances the higher capital cost of a fatter pipe against the pumping energy you save over the years from having less friction. But that textbook optimization is wrong because it ignores the capital cost of the pumping equipment—the pump, motor, inverter, and electrical parts—which all must be big enough to overcome the friction in the pipes. If you ignore that potential capital savings in equipment and optimize just one part of the system (the pipes in isolation) for a single purpose, namely saving energy, then you pessimize the system because you limit the greater capacity inherent in bringing all the components into play at once. As our work demonstrated, it's better to optimize the whole system at once. If you make the pipe somewhat bigger, the equipment can be much smaller and you save a lot of capital cost as well as operating cost.

The second innovation was even simpler, therefore more difficult. It was to lay out the pipes first, and then the equipment they connect. What's normally done is to plunk down the tanks, boilers, and so on in some arbitrary place, and then tell the pipefitter to come in and connect point A to point B. But by then those points are far apart, there's stuff in between, the equipment components are facing the wrong way or are at the wrong height, so the pipe has to go through many curlicues to get from A to B, and friction goes up roughly three- to sixfold.

The pipefitters don't mind this in the least, since they're paid by the hour and mark up the extra pipes and fittings. They don't pay for the oversized pumping equipment. They don't pay the inflated electric bill ever after. But clearly, it's smarter to use fat, short, straight pipes than skinny, long, crooked pipes. When you do that, you also get a lot of other benefits. For example, it's easier to insulate short, straight pipes, so you also save, in this case, seventy kilowatts of heat that would otherwise be lost, with a two-month payback.

The reason it's worth understanding this example is not just that pumps use a vast amount of motor energy—three-fifths of all the electricity in the world—or that every unit of flow or friction saved in the pipe conserves about ten units of fuel, cost, and global warming at the power plant. Even more important, these same design lessons for optimizing whole systems apply to practically everything that uses energy. When you take this sort of thinking seriously, you can optimize any energy-using system, from a factory process line to a whole building. The optimized system uses on the order of three to ten times less energy, works better, and costs less. We've shown this in a wide range of technical systems.

Consider real-estate development. A typical tract-home development drains stormwater away in big concrete pipes, treating it as a nuisance rather than as part of the habitat. Village Homes, an early green development in Davis, California, instead created a little natural drainage swale (a long grassy groove in the ground). After a storm it fills up with rainwater, which then soaks in or drains away one day faster than mosquito larvae can hatch. This innovation saved $800 of pipe investment per house and provided more green space.

The developers then leveraged that savings by reinvesting it in extensive edible landscaping, providing shade, nutrition, beauty, community focus, and crop revenues to support more amenities—daycare, parks maintenance, and so on. The landscaping, plus the people-centered site planning, with pedestrian and bike greenways in between the fronts of the houses, saved more land and money, and it cooled off the microclimate, producing greater comfort at lower cost. It created safe and child-friendly neighborhoods that have 90 percent less crime than nearby subdivisions. Real-estate brokers once described this development as too weird to show, but it's now the most desirable real estate in town, selling for 11 percent, or $23 per square foot, over market, in less than a third of the normal time. Many executives are realizing that protecting the climate is not costly but profitable, because saving fuel costs less than buying fuel. Using energy in a way that saves money becomes an important strategy for improving the bottom line, gaining competitive advantage, and strengthening the whole economy, while incidentally helping to solve the global warming problem.

Chemical giant DuPont announced in 2000 that over the next ten years, while growing its revenues 6 percent and earnings even more, it proposes to hold its energy use flat at worst, get a tenth of it from renewables, get a quarter of its manufacturing feedstocks from renewables, and reduce its greenhouse gas emissions by 65 percent compared to 1990—all in the name of shareholder value.

British Petroleum has rebranded its BP to Beyond Petroleum. In 2000 it announced that by 2010, it would reduce its carbon emissions 10 percent below 1990 levels. In 2002 it announced that it had achieved this goal eight years early. What it neglected to mention is that doing this saved the company $650 million a year. Company executives are saying, however, that even if the effort cost money it would be worth doing, because it makes BP the sort of company for which the best talent wants to work.

Such foresight is wise. In 2003 Swiss Re, the major European insurance company, stated that corporate failure to responsibly reduce a company's carbon emissions could well lead to shareholder suits and executive liability. The insurer said it would be reviewing corporate commitments to reduce greenhouse gas emissions and perhaps declining to insure companies and directors without such a program.

Examples like these demonstrate why the European Union has already adopted at least a fourfold, so-called factor four, gain in resource productiv-ity as the new basis for sustainable development. A number of member coun-tries have taken up that goal individually. Some are setting even more ambi-tious targets, which in general turns out to be even cheaper, because by using whole-system design you can typically tunnel through the cost barrier and make big resource savings cost less than small or zero savings.

Natural capitalism doesn't just mean reducing waste; it means eliminat-ing the whole concept of waste through better design, design that adopts bio-logical patterns, processes, and often materials. This approach implies elimi-nating any industrial output that represents a disposal cost rather than a salable product.

In their book *Cradle to Cradle*, William McDonough and Michael Braun-gart speak correctly of the need to go beyond eco-efficiency, natural capital-ism's first principle, to a world of eco-effectiveness. An example comes from their work with the DesignTex subsidiary of Steelcase Corporation to redesign the fabric for its chair backing. In Switzerland, where the current material was made, the edge trimmings were considered a hazardous waste because they contained toxins and heavy metals. They agreed to design the fabric if they could redesign the whole production process.

The company took up the challenge. Working with the chemical com-pany Ciba-Geigy, Bill and Michael went through 8,000 chemicals looking for those that weren't carcinogenic, mutagenic, teratogenic, bioaccumulative, persistently toxic, endocrine disrupting, or similarly harmful. They found only 38 chemicals that they could use, but out of those they could make all of the colors needed for the fabric. They specified organic material: ramie from the Philippines and organic wool from New Zealand.

The resulting cloth looked better. It lasted longer and felt better in the hand because it hadn't been subjected to nasty chemicals. It was also one-fifth cheaper to make and used fewer and better feedstocks. There was no need for the Swiss equivalent of the Occupational Safety and Health Adminis-tration to protect the workers, because there weren't any hazardous materi-als in the process.

When the Swiss environmental inspectors came to test the factory, they thought their equipment was broken because the output water was cleaner than the drinking-quality input water. The fabric was acting as an additional filter. The filters had been taken out of the pipes and put in the designers' heads, where they should be in the first place.

Chemistry professor Hanns Fischer at the University of Zurich realized that the university's elementary laboratory course was teaching students how to take $6,000 worth of pure, clean reagents and turn them into toxic sludge that cost the university $20,000 a year to get rid of. It occurred to him to simply reverse half the experiments and turn the waste back into the initial reagents. The students thought this was cool. They started volunteering on weekends and during vacations to come in and clean up toxic waste they had created. They eliminated 99 percent of the waste, but more important, they were learning to turn once-through, linear thinking into closed-loop, cyclic thinking. Now they can go out and save the chemical industry.

These examples represent an archetype of the kind of industry that is emerging and the kind of world we're going to live in, in which most traditional environmental regulation will become anachronistic and unnecessary. Companies that need to be regulated won't be profitable; they will spend too much time making stuff that nobody wants. This shift happens faster with feedback. After all, how clean would you make a car if you directed the exhaust into the passenger compartment? The reality is that we all live downwind, downstream. Every time we pollute, we're polluting ourselves.

Another key element of natural capitalism is to shift the structure of the economy away from a focus on matter and things to a focus on service and flow—from the episodic acquisition of goods to the continual flow of value and performance. This changing business model provides incentives for continuous improvement in the first two steps—advanced resource productivity and loop-closing to eliminate waste—because it structures the relationships so that both the provider and the customer make money in the same way: by doing more and better with much less for longer, finding more efficient solutions that benefit both parties.

This model contrasts sharply with the sale or leasing of physical goods, in which the vendor wants to sell you more stuff more often—perhaps more shoddily made stuff, certainly more wasteful and costly stuff, since you have to pay for it more than once—while you have the opposite incentive. Let's make this a little more concrete.

In Europe and Asia, Schindler, a big elevator maker, prefers not to sell you any of its elevators, but rather to lease you a "vertical transportation service." That's because it believes its elevators use less electricity and maintenance effort than competing ones. Schindler can capture that benefit by keeping the elevator, operating it, and providing you only what you want: the service of moving up and down. The resource efficiency of the elevator becomes a reduced cost for both the company and the customer.

Dow would rather not sell you a solvent. It would rather lease you a "dissolving service." Dow owns the solvent and brings it to your factory, where it does the dissolving. The company then takes it away and repurifies it. If the solvent can be reused fifty or a hundred times without much of it being lost, Dow makes more profit but can charge you less, gaining market share. Both the company and you profit from minimizing the flow of energy and materials.

An attempt to implement this "solutions economy," as Jim Womack and Dan Jones call it in *Lean Thinking*, is emerging at Atlanta carpet maker Interface. Lots of broadloom carpet is replaced every decade or so because it develops worn spots here and there. Millions of tons of it every year go to landfills and sit there for ten or twenty thousand years. To replace the carpet you must clear out your office, shut down your operations, roll up the partly worn carpet, send it to the landfill, lay down a new carpet, move back in, resume operations, and perhaps get sick from fumes in the carpet glue.

This cycle is particularly dumb because you never wanted to own the carpet in the first place. What you wanted to do was just walk on it and enjoy its cleanliness, acoustics, aesthetics, and comfort underfoot. Interface's visionary chairman, Ray Anderson, fully realized this and said, "Well, why don't I own the carpet, keep it on my balance sheet, and just lease it to customers as a tax-deductible net operating lease of a floor-covering service? Every month, my little elves will come in the night and look at where it's worn, take away just those parts (because I'll use carpet tile), and replace them with fresh carpet.

You'll always have a fresh-looking carpet, and this new business model will reduce by 80 percent or so the amount of resources flowing across your floor, because carpet consists mainly of nylon made of oil—very energy-intensive material. I may be making less carpet at the factory, because I'm replacing only the worn parts, yet I'll create more jobs in the service end of the business." Interface is moving in the right direction: substituting abundant people for scarce nature.

The latest thing Interface did was to redesign the product to go with this business model. Other manufacturers say they recycle carpet. What they actually do is downcycle it, losing the embodied energy of the nylon by putting it into PVC backing, a low-value material that shouldn't be there in the first place. Interface, on the other hand, released a product that can be completely remanufactured into identical product and even made out of renewables to start with—out of carbohydrates, not hydrocarbons. Consequently the link to the oil well is severed at the front end, and so is the link to the landfill at the back end, instead creating a continuous flow of what Michael Braungart calls a "technical nutrient" that produces value each time around.

It's also a better product. It's essentially impervious to stains and mildew. You can wash it with a garden hose. It contains no chlorine or other toxic stuff. It lasts at least four times as long as conventional carpet. It uses a third less material. In total, there's a 97 percent reduction in raw materials required when the more frugal use of nylon is combined with a service lease: a thirty-five-fold reduction in the amount of material needed to be kept in circulation in order to maintain a superior floor-covering service. All that waste gets turned into profit. And once the returned carpet tiles get remanufactured, the new materials savings will rise to 99.9 percent.

Even before this new product was created, the first four years of a systemic quest to reduce waste throughout Interface had roughly doubled revenues and tripled operating profit, and had nearly doubled employment. Its latest quarter-billion dollars of revenue were produced with no increase in energy or materials inputs—basically by mining waste.

Or consider the films division of DuPont, which was once almost broke. It's now leading its fifty-nine-firm segment because it's able to make polyester film ever thinner and stronger, so that it costs less to make. It has fewer molecules in it, but it fetches a higher price because it's more valuable to the customer. The company now also recycles it, recovering it from customers and annually remanufacturing a billion dollars' worth of polyester film at lower cost and higher margins.

The fourth principle of natural capitalism is perhaps the most important. It's also the one about which we know the least and the one we have to get a lot better at: reinvesting in natural capital. Ultimately, we believe industry will derive its feedstocks more from the grown than the mined. Making that shift means we have to get a lot better at agriculture, forestry, and farming, most of which right now are not sustainable. This kind of work is what's going to save this earth and save industry. Hints of it are already emerging—people like Alan Savory and Dan Dagget are showing how to double the carrying capacity of rangeland in ways that are restorative—but most industry still operates in ways that deplete the earth and our children's future.

One example is how the California Rice Industry Association solved a problem. Rice farmers were burning rice straw, the "waste" left in fields after harvest. It's high in silica, and there were concerns about people downwind developing silicosis. Under pressure from environmentalists, the farmers invited them to help solve the problem. Together they came up with the idea of flooding the rice fields after harvest rather than burning them, thus inviting in nature. Millions of waterfowl now flock to the fields. The birds themselves constitute a valuable crop (the farmers sell hunting licenses) and provide free fertilizer and cultivation. The straw, formerly burned or wasted, is now harvested as a valuable building material. Rice is a profitable co-product of this whole network of value creation that's now produced on a third of the state's rice acreage.

Of course, this fourth principle of restoration is the easiest one to apply, because nature does the production. All we have to do is get out of the way and allow life to flourish.

Implementing the elements of natural capitalism tends to create an extraordinary outpouring of energy, initiative, and enthusiasm at all levels of an enterprise because it removes the actual and perceived contradictions between what people do on the job and what they want for their kids when they go home. This makes natural capitalist firms the most exciting places in the world to work and the hardest to keep up with.

Civilization in the twenty-first century is imperiled by three main problems: the dissolution of civil society, weakened life-support systems, and a dwindling public purse necessary to address these problems and relieve human suffering. But all three share a common cause: waste. Problems like shortages of work, hope, security, and satisfaction are not isolated pathologies. They all flow from the interlinked wasting of resources, money, and people. The systematic correction of that waste creates a common solution that's not widely acknowledged but that is increasingly obvious.

We believe the leaders in waste reduction are going to be in the private sector, but there remains a vital role for governments and civil society. It's important to remember the purposes and limitations of markets. Markets make a great servant but a bad master and a worse religion. Markets produce value, but only communities and families produce values. And a society that tries to substitute markets for politics, ethics, or faith is seriously adrift.

It's our view that commerce has to be in the vanguard of creating a durable system of production and consumption by properly applying sound market principles. But we have to remember that not all value can be monetized. Accumulating money is not the same thing as creating wealth or improving people. Many of the best things in life are not the business of business.

Firms that conscientiously pursue the four principles of natural capitalism will gain a commanding competitive advantage because they'll be behaving as if nature and people were properly valued. They'll be making more profit even today when those values are still set essentially at zero. As Edgar Woolard remarked when he chaired DuPont, companies that take such opportunities seriously will do very well—while, he added, those that don't won't be a problem, because ultimately they won't be around.

Perhaps the real problem with capitalism—a system of wealth creation based on the productive use of and reinvestment in all four forms of capital— is that it's only just now starting to be tried.

Reinventing the Wheel:
Transportation Down the Road

Jim Motavalli

Journalist Jim Motavalli has a formidable command of a wide arc of environmental issues. Editor of E/The Environmental Magazine, *the leading U.S. independent national environmental bimonthly, he also writes the "Green Living" column for the Environmental Defense newsletter and the "Conservation Works" column for* AMC Outdoors, *freelances for a wide range of publications, hosts a biweekly public affairs and music radio show on listener-supported WPKN-FM in Bridgeport, Connecticut, and somehow finds time to teach journalism at Fairfield University.*

    One of Jim's main areas of expertise is wheels. If you want real car talk, Jim has lived under the hood of the automobile industry and is a virtual oracle as to its past sins, present impact, and future destiny. He may well be the single most authoritative source on the environmental impact of all things automotive. He writes the occasional column for the "Automobiles" section of the New York Times *and a weekly auto column that appears in the* Philadelphia Review *and five other papers, and is the "Autos and the Environment" columnist for the* Cleveland Plain Dealer. *He is the author of the essential books* Breaking Gridlock: Moving toward Transportation That Works *and* Forward Drive: The Race to Build "Clean" Cars for the Future *(both Sierra Club books). His latest book is* Feeling the Heat: Dispatches from the Frontlines of Climate Change.

    While the global car chase may seem to be dead-ending in a mangled wreck of traffic jams, sprawl, poisoned air, and global warming, Jim says we can still escape. His exit strategy is no-nonsense yet humorous, realistic but hopeful, and his exhaustive research and sensible voice explain how we can get off that endless highway without entirely giving up our love affair with the car. Fasten your safety belt for a ride with

Jim into the potentially positive future of transportation in a people-centered world. In his case, reinventing the wheel is a really smart idea.

THE REVERED AUTHOR and activist Edward Abbey is a deservedly beloved figure in the environmental movement, but in real life he drove a whole series of gas-guzzling cars, most of them in very poor condition and probably burning a lot of oil. Cars present us with many paradoxes. Many in the environmental community want the car just to go away or to see its use curtailed and mass transit encouraged. That's fine in theory, but most of us, even environmentalists, have cars. We are highly car dependent in the United States, and vehicles cause much of our pollution. Transportation is second only to industrial uses in our overall energy consumption, and highway vehicles use over three-quarters of transportation energy, 60 percent of which is attributable to cars and light trucks, which include SUVs.

To come to grips with the reality of the automobile, we have to comprehend the scope of the problem. A personal example comes from where I live in Fairfield County, Connecticut, a very congested part of a very congested region where people spend about a fifth of their time on the road, stuck in bumper-to-bumper traffic jams. The highways aren't growing, but their use climbs steadily each year, about 1.5 percent. Our main artery, I-95, is typical of highway corridors in America. Designed for 50,000 cars a day, it currently carries 150,000 a day. The same is true of another major artery, the Merritt Parkway, built much earlier, in the 1930s.

We've gotten to the point where development is so dense and land so expensive that there's no way to acquire enough land to widen highways in congested areas. Planners are thus forced to consider double- or triple-decked highways. I-95 runs along the coast; imagine the prospect of an enormous elevated highway casting its shadow on all our beaches.

The number of car trips on major Connecticut highways has increased by 96 percent since 1968. According to the 1990 census, at that time 74 percent of workers in the region drove their cars to work solo. That statistic is mirrored all over the country, and it has gotten worse since 1990. Between 1990 and 2000, the average commuter added 26 hours to his or her traffic time. In

Atlanta, where drivers added 44 hours, babies have been born in cars on the way to the hospital because mothers couldn't get there in time.

We've basically reached the limit of building new highways. Nationwide, traffic is increasing five times faster than new freeway capacity. We don't provide any meaningful subsidies or incentives for people to carpool, and nationally, carpooling has actually fallen off.

Most people consider gasoline to be a negligible expense. If you ask what criteria they use when buying a car, fuel economy is tenth on the list (though starting to move up). That's why we don't buy small cars. Today, Detroit builds almost all its small cars only because automakers don't want to get fined for exceeding the government's overall fuel efficiency mandate for manufacturers (the Corporate Average Fuel Economy, or CAFE, standards). The companies don't even think there's a small-car market, and they claim they lose money building them.

What does it really cost us to have cars on the roads when you factor in all the hidden costs? According to the International Center for Technology Assessment, a gallon of gasoline actually costs $15.14 when billions of federal and state tax breaks, subsidies, regulations, pollution cleanup costs, and other factors are added up. We are all paying a lot more for gasoline than the price at the pump. There's a reason that people in Europe or Japan pay $5 a gallon for gasoline. High prices are among the few things that actually get people off the highway. In the United States, however, one sure way to lose an election is to propose new gasoline taxes, and the highway lobby, which is one of our most powerful, will definitely work against any candidate who's not highway friendly.

A sad consequence of this is that the developing world is now looking at the United States as a model. These countries admire the American transportation system—even though it's an incredible mess—because people abroad form their images from glitzy television shows. India and China are moving very rapidly toward developing a private car–based infrastructure. The implications for global warming are immense and terrifying.

Planners originally saw highway construction as a way to modernize America and ease travel between cities. Of course, this was before people realized that automobiles caused pollution, a connection that was not commonly understood until the 1950s. It was Henry Ford and his government allies who proposed the big network of interstate roads. Their real intention was to sell more cars. They succeeded: 85 percent of all travel between cities today is by car.

The Futurama exhibit at the General Motors pavilion at the 1939 World's Fair was supposed to represent the world of 1960. Planners in 1939 thought that by 1960 we would have a great grid of fourteen-lane express motorways crisscrossing the nation. Cars would travel at a hundred miles per hour, with their spacing controlled by "radio beams." The automated highway concept is still being discussed; in fact, an automated highway system was built as a federal demonstration project in 1997. The problem was that people had a hard time going from the automated highway back to controlling the car. When people got off the automated highway, they crashed.

Yet in some ways, an automated road is an authentic approach to gridlock. You can actually move people around at a hundred miles an hour, with a small space between each bumper. Boston's "Big Dig," an enormous highway project that is one of the largest public works projects ever undertaken, has a lot of high-tech controls and devices. For instance, when you go through one of the system's tunnels, transit officials can break in on your radio station with announcements about road conditions. Such systems are now widespread in parts of Europe. Still, we're a very long way from an automated road.

On the plus side, mass transit use is way up, particularly since September 11, and ridership is rising faster than automobile use, but there's a grim little secret here. Mass transit—trains and buses—and walking and bicycling account for just a tiny share of American transportation use: about 2 to 5 percent of all travel. America's 100 million households make 1 billion trips a day. Of those, 900 million are by car, 65 million by foot or bicycle, and just 19 million by mass transit. So when we say transit ridership is up, it's true but not that significant in light of how car dependent we are. We use far more gasoline per capita than anyone else in the world.

After World War II, when soldiers came home and, through the GI Bill, were able to buy homes in the suburbs, America experienced a mass migration out of cities and into the suburbs. Cheaply available cars made that trend possible. Because auto production had stopped during World War II, there was an incredible pent-up demand for new cars. The auto industry celebrated excess in the 1950s, building enormous vehicles with huge fins. Big was better. The rush to the suburbs and the development of the drive-in were just two factors that contributed to sprawl in the United States. Another was sheer size. Public transit works much better in Europe because the distances simply aren't as great.

Until the 1960s, the auto industry claimed that its cars didn't pollute, despite growing evidence of the connection between the tailpipe and smog in Los Angeles, and it fought every environmental innovation. It threatened that factories would close, something Detroit still says quite often.

The first person to say that cars caused pollution was a scientist named Arlie Haagen-Smit, who eventually became chairman of the California Air Resources Board (CARB). He discovered that when the emission of human-made nitrogen oxides and hydrocarbons combine with ultraviolet light from the sun, the result is smog. This big revelation in 1950 was the impetus to finally do something about air pollution.

California now leads the country in clean cars. The state's emission laws led to the creation of partial zero-emission vehicles (PZEVs), which are more than 90 percent cleaner than the average 2003 car. California has the best regulations and an active resources board because it also has some of the nation's worst air pollution. CARB is important in that it drives not only the domestic car industry, but also the global industry. I've interviewed many car executives from Sweden, Germany, and Japan, and they all want to know what's happening with CARB because California is such a big market, representing 15 percent or more of U.S. sales.

Through CARB, California mandated that starting in 2004, 10 percent of cars on the road had to be "clean cars." The definition of what a clean car is has changed dramatically over the years. First it meant zero-emission electric cars. CARB favors them, but it had to backtrack somewhat because battery technology hasn't evolved fast enough. Now CARB is quite friendly to hybrid and fuel cell–powered vehicles. New York, Massachusetts, and some other northeastern states have adopted California's rules. The administration of President George W. Bush has intervened to try to stop CARB's mandates, however, because it knows California's decisions go far beyond its borders. Its efforts against the CARB mandates are headed by White House chief of staff Andrew Card, who is a former vice president of GM and former head of the Alliance of American Auto Makers.

Detroit could have made cleaner, more efficient cars long before it did. In 1933 Buckminster Fuller built a streamlined car called the Dymaxion, which got thirty miles per gallon at a time when hardly anyone had heard of automotive aerodynamics. It also could go 120 miles per hour and seat eleven people. But Detroit wasn't too interested and built only three. Another early attempt at fuel efficiency was the tiny BMW Isetta, which could get up to eighty miles a gallon in the 1950s but was a complete flop in America. At that time Americans were buying Cadillacs that were five times the Isetta's length. The Isetta had some drawbacks, such as a polluting two-stroke engine, yet it was incredibly fuel efficient.

Because the American auto industry can't make enough money on its small cars, it has gone in a completely different direction. GM now sells more than 50,000 Hummer H2s a year. The military-type H2 should not be on public roads—it gets ten miles a gallon. These big vehicles, especially SUVs, are incredibly profitable. One Ford plant in Michigan that makes only SUVs produces more than half of Ford's worldwide profits. And although people buy them largely for perceived safety reasons, SUVs are actually less safe—even for their occupants—than a standard car, because of their tendency to roll over.

On the opposite side of the spectrum, there are a few very nicely designed fuel-efficient cars, but for a variety of reasons they seldom get traction in the market. The GM EV1 probably started the clean-car revolution by being the first truly zero-emission vehicle Detroit produced. (Much earlier, between 1905 and 1910, there had been quite a few electric cars on the road, mostly marketed to women because they didn't have to be cranked and because auto executives believed women's "sphere of influence" extended only about ten miles, so the smaller range of the electric car would not be a problem. But when

the electric crank was introduced for gasoline cars, it was all over for electrics.)
The company spent $100 million developing the car, which was sold only in
California and Arizona. But it didn't sell: only 500 people leased an EV1, even
though GM offered fairly good lease terms. One could argue that GM really
didn't want to sell electric cars, but the fact is that people didn't want them.
The problem was that the EV1 couldn't go more than ninety miles on a charge.
Battery electrics are like a gasoline car whose gas gauge is already on empty,
though some new battery technologies show promise.

Detroit has now concluded that we need a big vehicle that gets better fuel
efficiency. Ford is offering a forty-mile-per-gallon hybrid version of the Escape, its small SUV, beginning in the summer of 2004. Some environmentalists think that is a terrible idea, because the Escape is still an SUV. I certainly believe the whole concept of trying to make a fuel-efficient vehicle out
of something like the Chevrolet Suburban is wrong. Amory Lovins's Hypercar concept—that of a very lightweight, smaller vehicle built from very
strong carbon fiber—makes far more sense in the long run. But Detroit almost never starts out to build from scratch a car that is lightweight and fuel
efficient.

In a program started by the Clinton administration in 1992 called Partnership for a New Generation of Vehicles, each of the car companies created
a prototype hybrid car combining gas and electric features that could get eighty
miles per gallon. DaimlerChrysler presented its version at a few auto shows,
but that was the end of it, even though we put a lot of taxpayer money into
the project. The company never actually intended to put its hybrid car into
production. Chrysler's executives said, "We'll never produce it. We're not all
that enthusiastic about hybrids because we might lose money on them."

But look at what Honda and Toyota have done recently. Toyota knew it
would lose money producing the Prius in the beginning, yet it went ahead
and launched it in the Japanese market in 1997 and in the United States in
2000. Though the company initially lost perhaps $5,000 on each one, it is
now close to breaking even. Toyota was willing to do that to create a market
for a hybrid vehicle, while Detroit has been very reluctant to follow suit.

The 2004 Prius gets sixty miles per gallon, and I believe that one of the best things we can do environmentally is to buy one. Having an alternative to driving is great, but if you're going to drive, the Prius is an incredible car. Toyota's goal is to build 300,000 hybrids a year.

The Honda Civic Hybrid has both an electric engine and a gasoline engine, a package that is fairly complicated and expensive to engineer. It sells for $20,000, the same price as the Prius. The Japanese companies, by building a lot of hybrids, have gotten the cost down rather dramatically. Hybrids are a hit in Japan, where hybrid minivans and other models are available.

Hollywood celebrities are big on hybrids. Ed Begley Jr. has long been an enthusiastic proponent of clean cars and electric vehicles. Other celebrities who drive and tout hybrids include Cameron Diaz, Leonardo DiCaprio, Danny DeVito, Ted Danson, Robin Williams, and Alexandra Paul. At least 50,000 hybrids have been sold in America so far. It's not a huge number, but contrast that with only 500 GM EV1s, 300 Honda EV Pluses, and 1,000 battery-electrics sold here over the last twenty years.

I see hybrids, however, as a great transitional technology to fuel-cell vehicles, which I believe are the cars of the future. The hydrogen fuel cell has the potential to replace the internal-combustion engine. Fuel-cell research in the United States and Europe is quite advanced; the fuel cell is not a new invention. Back in 1839, a British barrister who moonlighted as a scientist discovered that you could get electricity from hydrogen, and that the by-product would be water—drinkable water at that. This clean efficiency is the reason that our space program used the fuel cell: it could deliver electric power as well as drinking water for the astronauts, at least in theory. In practice, the water wasn't all that drinkable, but those were very early cells.

Hydrogen can be burned in an internal-combustion engine and is fairly clean, but it's even better to produce electricity from hydrogen through a chemical reaction that also produces water. The fuel cell is essentially a solid-state device without any moving parts: it's just a box called a fuel-cell "stack" because you can stack the cells up to get more power. This makes it scalable; the device can be really small or huge, to supply a tiny watch battery or a big power plant.

GM has built a fuel-cell car, the Hy-Wire, from scratch instead of stuffing a fuel cell into an existing SUV design. The vehicle is essentially an electric car that instead of batteries has a fuel cell that produces electricity from another fuel. Fuel cells are a hot area for other companies as well.

A few test fuel-cell cars are now on the road, mostly in California because the California Fuel Cell Partnership is the magnet for manufactured electric vehicle prototypes. For now it's only hundreds of cars, not hundreds of thousands. But what the latest research shows is that a fuel-cell car running on hydrogen provides almost a 300-mile range, which is comparable to the range of a gasoline-powered car today, and therefore practical. Amory Lovins predicts that eventually we'll be able to drive a car across the country on one tank of hydrogen. Hydrogen is a gas that can be liquefied at very cold temperatures, and it can also be carried in a tank in compressed gaseous form like natural gas. An ideal scenario would involve producing hydrogen locally so we could use the existing infrastructure of gas stations.

There is a growing consensus among environmentalists as well as in the auto companies that we are moving toward a hydrogen energy economy in the United States. I've interviewed many people at high levels of government and industry who concur that eventually a hydrogen economy will take us completely out of internal combustion and fossil fuels. It will mean not only replacing cars with fuel-cell vehicles, but also eventually replacing the electric grid to your house with an electricity-generating cell running on natural gas. Your computer battery will be replaced with a very small fuel cell.

Of course, the big question is how to produce the hydrogen. We can produce totally clean hydrogen energy from completely renewable sources such as wind and solar energy and biomass and geothermal sources. But we can also produce hydrogen from coal or nuclear power. The Bush administration tried to hijack hydrogen and use it as a justification for building a new generation of nuclear plants. Nuclear power was the centerpiece of the plan created by the notorious energy task force headed by Vice President Dick Cheney. That plan even looked at using nuclear fusion to produce hydrogen, although nuclear fusion has not been successfully demonstrated.

Meanwhile fuel-cell cars are progressing and the research is accelerating rapidly. A few years ago, the prototypes I drove were barely able to make it around a test track, but automakers have made dramatic improvements since then. DaimlerChrysler is putting fuel-cell buses on the road. The bus is a great way to test fuel cells because it has a nice flat floor and large roof for hydrogen storage and fuel-cell equipment.

Also in development are residential fuel cells that will allow you to get your house off the electrical grid. One jointly developed by General Electric and a New York company called Plug Power produces electricity from an available natural gas line. The power would not be interrupted by a storm, and trees wouldn't knock down the power lines. Perhaps the biggest advantage to fuel cells is that they are incredibly reliable, much more so than the grid, which is why hospitals use them for backup power. For the moment, though, these cells still produce electricity at a higher cost than the grid. Many experts thought residential fuel cells would take hold before cars, but that may not happen due to the cost factor.

Another idea for the fuel cell is to use it as a replacement for generators. One on the market now costs $8,000; you could run about half your house on it, and it's small enough to sit in your kitchen. It doesn't pollute like a gasoline generator, and it provides uninterrupted backup power. Coleman, which makes a fuel-cell generator, wants to put this type of power into portable electric products, including cell phones and computers. Theoretically, a fuel cell–powered laptop would go twenty to thirty hours before needing refueling, a big advantage over batteries. Battery technology is simply not moving as quickly as fuel-cell technology.

Public transportation is also making progress. The Acela train, which goes from Boston to Washington at 150 miles per hour (still not nearly as fast as trains go in Europe), is Amtrak's one major success story, the only profitable part of the system. Amtrak has lost about $25 billion since it was created in 1971, which sounds like a lot of money, but we spend $40 billion on highways *every year*. The Acela is attracting lots of new ridership, and it's competitive with airplanes in terms of getting from Boston to Washington.

There's a California initiative to try to connect all of that state's major cities by high-speed rail. Florida has also been pushing high-speed rail and had actually funded it until Governor Jeb Bush came into office. One of his first acts was to ax the funding, but in a heartening development, the citizens of Florida voted the funding back.

High-speed rail—especially the French TGV system—is very successful in Europe and is by far the most common way of getting from city to city there. Europeans have the advantage that their cities are generally not as distant from each other as ours. The aspect of Amtrak that really doesn't work is the long-distance cross-country routes. It's much cheaper and quicker to fly. Those routes probably aren't economical and may have to be ended, but regional high-speed rail corridors have great potential.

Light rail systems can provide important alternatives to highways for commute travel, but they can be very expensive to build. Still, an encouraging number of cities around the country have decided to bite the light rail bullet. Raleigh, North Carolina, is constructing a light rail system using the existing railroad right-of-way. (At one time we had 300,000 miles of train track in this country, but we've ripped up half of it. In many places, however, we still have the rail corridors. The national organization Rails to Trails was originally set up to preserve the corridors not just for hiking and biking trails, but so that they could become rail corridors again.)

Portland, Oregon, offers one of the best examples of how to use light rail and get the whole community on board with it. Light rail in Portland is free for a ten-block radius in the city center, and the mayor has said she wants to make the whole system free. Various regions of the country, including the Southeast and Midwest, are looking at multistate high-speed rail alliances.

Every light rail system in the world probably loses money. Such systems will not pay for themselves out of the fare box; they have to be subsidized. But if we accept that as a given, a very strong argument can be made that light rail provides a valuable social benefit to the community and is worth subsidizing.

There's a man by the name of Wendell Cox who, whenever a new light rail system is proposed, flies in from his consulting firm in Illinois and tells voters, "You're going to sink your whole city if you have this light rail system." An enemy of all transit appropriations, Cox has developed a statistical analysis to show how much money light rail loses and has helped kill systems in several places. The best ammunition against transit critics like Cox is a booklet titled "Twelve Anti-Transit Myths: A Conservative Critique," a defense of light rail written by arch-conservative Paul Weyrich and published by the Free Congress Foundation. Weyrich specifically targeted Cox and managed to pin him down on his vision of the transit future. Here is Cox's alternative to light rail for Atlanta, as reported by the *Atlanta Journal-Constitution:* "Cox believes it would be realistic to create a grid of arterial roads six to eight lanes wide, no more than one mile apart throughout metro Atlanta. There should be another grid of highways criss-crossing the region. He calls for building freeways underground in double-deck tunnels and double-decking other above-ground freeways. He advocates adding another deck exclusively for trucks. In essence, Cox is suggesting that between now and 2025, we should raze Atlanta as we know it, and replace it with Los Angeles on steroids."

Such is the alternative to building light rail and retaining existing heavy rail. Cities like Portland have dramatically reduced highway use by building light rail instead of new highways. But even Portland is still very car dependent. The only non-car-dependent city in the United States is New York City, in which about 50 percent of households do not own cars. But delivery trucks, suburban commuters, and cabs can still turn Manhattan into gridlock on any given day.

Another transportation resource we don't optimize is the use of our waterways. I recently traveled on a high-speed ferry that goes between Long Island and New London, Connecticut. It was built by the Pequot tribe as an adjunct to its casino business, to ferry in gamblers. This amazing ferry goes so fast that you can't sit on the deck when it's moving. Rapid-transit ferries can compete with cars in commute times. Sydney, Australia, is largely a commuting-by-ferry city. Ferries entail some environmental problems and cost issues, but when water routes are feasible, it's a great mode of transport. For instance, I-95 parallels the Long Island Sound for almost its entire length, yet there is very little traffic on the water. There could be economically viable ferry service in such places.

We don't really have an anti-car movement in the United States that's comparable to those in Europe. The English anti-roads movement actually halted construction of some highway bypasses after activists sat on the highway and stopped traffic. In the United States, anti-car activism is largely the result of bicycle activism. Groups such as Critical Mass in San Francisco hold protests and block traffic. In New York, there's Transportation Alternatives, which is working to make Central Park and Prospect Park car free. But they're not on the same scale as European groups.

European car-free zones have become very successful. Sixty cities have declared that they will make their centers car free. Britain has instituted the car-free day, and 75 percent of the British public say they support it. Similar ideas have spread to Central and South America. In places with huge pollution problems, such as Athens and Singapore, people can drive only every other day (license plates ending in an odd number one day, even the next), and London is now charging cars a hefty fee to enter the city center. In Denmark, 30 to 40 percent of Copenhagen commuters travel by bicycle.

China, on the other hand is heading in the opposite direction. The bicycle is seen as old hat and embarrassingly primitive. Instead, the country is building highways and adding private cars. The poignant irony is that China has no infrastructure for internal-combustion vehicles. The country could leapfrog the whole mess and build a hydrogen economy instead, and indeed there are hopeful signs that this may happen. My friend Jim Cannon, who has been to China four or five times working on sustainable transportation, felt very disillusioned when he visited there a few years ago. Then he went back recently and found that in Beijing, which may have the world's worst air pollution, there's now a fleet of 3,000 to 4,000 natural gas buses and hydrogen prototypes. There's now a lot of interest in hydrogen there, and the country has enacted strict auto emission laws. We really have to hope that China makes the right choices, because its decisions have monumental impacts on the entire planet.

To build a viable system of transportation, we will have to put two main elements together: a hydrogen energy economy to clean up vehicle exhaust, and effective, affordable public transit to get people off the highways, because even a fuel-cell car is going to create gridlock and expend resources in building highways.

Here in the United States, if we could increase our use of public transit even slightly and create the fuel-cell revolution, that combination would bring very positive benefits. Nobody likes the status quo. I find it amazing that in polls people frequently cite gridlock as one of the major problems they're concerned about, yet politicians hardly ever talk about the issue. The subtext is that most elected officials take money from the highway lobby, and they aren't listening to the will of the people on this issue. It's up to us to make sure they do.

Ecological Design:
The Architecture of Democracy

David Orr

David Orr, one of the great visionary educators of our era, has made it his mission to remind educators and the larger world that no education worthy of the name can ignore the central fact that human beings are a part of nature. Professor and chair of the Environmental Studies Program at Oberlin College in Ohio and an award-winning scholar, he has almost single-handedly put the concept of environmental literacy on the map. He has reframed the role of the university and other educational institutions in addressing the environmental crisis.

David is also a leading light in the sustainability movement, where he is renowned for his work in ecological design. At his impetus and with his guidance, Oberlin designed and built its famous state-of-the-art environmental studies center, whose architecture physically embodies the principles of ecological design as a learning environment. He has published over 120 articles in scientific and professional journals and serves as a contributing editor to the journal Conservation Biology, *the flagship of the field. He serves on several boards, including those of the renowned Rocky Mountain Institute, the Center for Ecoliteracy, and Second Nature, which works to bring a curriculum on sustainability to higher education. His landmark books* The Nature of Design, Earth in Mind, *and* Ecological Literacy *have laid the groundwork for an emerging revolution in environmental education and ecological design.*

David Orr is a true revolutionary who is awakening educators to their most crucial imperative: equipping the young with the tools they will need to heal and protect our ecosystems.

I PROPOSE A MARRIAGE among design, politics, and spirit. If design is going to be a robust concept, it has to be about much more than making things. It has to deal with systems and context.

In this larger sense, design was very much on the minds of the founders of the American republic. The Federalist Papers are a design manifesto. Toward the end of his life, James Madison, one of its chief authors, thought that the founders had figured things out for the new nation for about a century, after which, he thought, it would come undone. In large measure, it has.

Nineteenth-century European socialists were also designers of sorts. They were trying to design a better world. Unfortunately they divided themselves into factions with bitterly competing viewpoints and all kinds of little movements inside the big movement. David Brower quipped about them, "Their strategy was to draw the wagons into a circle and shoot inward." To some extent, this failure paved the way for the disastrous triumph and later collapse of bolshevism.

By our time the world is finally ready for a better approach to organizing human affairs in a mass technological industrial society, and undoubtedly there is a new, multifaceted, more benign design revolution under way. What Janine Benyus has called "biomimicry"—remaking the way we make things based on how nature works—has inspired a new generation of designers. John Todd's work of ecological engineering has flourished. There's definitely a heartening design revolution under way, but unfortunately, as of now, we're not winning the revolution. We're losing, and losing badly. We will lose the war despite being right if we don't begin to combine our concepts of design with savvy politics and a deeper sense of spirit.

The design questions we need to pose are these: What's the organization of a society that is capable of doing ecological design? What does such a society look like? How could we design institutions, whether colleges or corporations, that would be capable of doing ecological design? And what's the point, the ultimate object, of ecological design? It's not just about houses or water or any particular system. It has to be about how we think. The ultimate object of ecological design is the human mind. The object is to overcome those parts of the human mind in the culture that give rise to illusion, greed, and ill will.

This recognition brings us to a crucial juncture, a fork in the road at which serious matters need to be thought out and discussed before we choose a path. Wendell Berry tells us we have two broad approaches to the way we make the human presence in the world. One is industrialism. That's the world we live in. We've been shaped by that world, its dependence on cheap fossil fuels and its extractive economy, much of which we take for granted and don't think about critically.

Some believe that industrialization done more cleverly would be sufficient to solve our problems. I don't believe that way will work. I don't think there's any way we can take a reformed industrial society, run the film fast-forward, and wind up with anything like a sustainable or spiritually sustaining society. I can't prove that proposition, but I think that if ecological design is to mean anything at all, it has to go deeper. If we leave the presuppositions of the industrial world in place, we leave greed in place. Simply to be smarter about our greed leaves greed and illusion in the center of our world. It leaves corporations in control. I don't trust a world designed for the convenience of corporations. I don't trust a world in which we leave self-interest so firmly in place. I don't think that world can be made to work, not with six to nine billion of us on the planet.

But that choice leads us to a real conundrum because, as Berry says, "The only alternative is agrarianism." When I say the word "agrarian," I suspect most of us—those who have never farmed—get a warm, fuzzy feeling and picture a white, crinkly-eyed farmer with a white picket fence, a red barn, a silo, and cows grazing in the pasture—an image of something cute, quaint, rustic, and long gone.

Can we bring some sort of agrarian world back? Can the reality of being connected to the natural world become a basis for a design revolution? Perhaps, but it will take some stretching and a redefinition of what we consider agrarian. It means, for one thing, beginning to understand how the city, reclaimed as authentic community, can also be part of a neo-agrarian world. Can we make real cities part of an agrarian vision? We may have to rethink the dichotomies of rural and urban. We may have to contemplate ruralized cities and urbanized countrysides. Maybe we will have to find ways to coalesce the sustainable agricultural movement with the urban sustainability movement, the slow food movement, urban gardening, the environmental justice movement, and so on. Maybe that way we'll get to a world in which the pieces begin to fit together.

If we don't achieve something like this synthesis, I fear that ecological design will be easily co-opted. Greener Wal-Marts don't do it for me. Greener Nike corporate headquarters don't do it for me. Greener buildings in which we still do brown things don't do it for me. In the 1970s, some of the founders of modern computer science saw how it was likely to be pressed into service supporting the most entrenched and militaristic elements of the current society. My fear is that ecological design might end up the same way.

True ecological design requires not just a change in our conceptual capabilities, but also a change in our language capabilities. As humans, what makes us so distinctive is our remarkable facility with complex language. I propose that we must begin to reclaim words, to understand how important they are and how they're used politically. Today we have "resources," not "nature," which is very convenient if you're an economist of the neoclassical mode. We have "human resources," not "people." We talk about "producing" energy, rather than using the more accurate "extracting." And the word "patriot" seems to describe someone who drives an SUV festooned in American flags with a "God Bless America" bumper sticker. I find it hard to understand why God would want to bless this country at this moment, and even harder to understand how the word "conservative" came to apply to people willing to run risks with the entire earth. Education ought to begin with the power of language, appropriately and carefully used.

The problem we face is a problem of mind, which makes it particularly important to places that purport to improve minds. Educational institutions are good places to begin. We can begin to change minds and the world not only abstractly, through what we teach students, but by embodying what we teach through how we design, how we actually build and run campuses as microcosms of the larger society.

Ultimately I see no way out of our predicament unless design and spirit and politics are merged. We must learn to become effective politically in ways we haven't yet dreamed of. In contrast to the nineteenth-century European socialists, we need to merge around a vision and a worldview. I don't know whether the word "sustainability" captures the notion, but the idea of ecological design in its largest sense is a good place to start. If we can figure out how to blend design and spirit and politics and a renewed connection to the earth in a lasting form, future generations will look back and see this as our finest hour.

Part V

Natural Magic:
Spirit, Mystery, and Wonder

Whaaa!? How the Dragonfly Turned My Head

Steven Foster

Steven Foster is one of the preeminent figures in American herbalism. His career got off to a precocious start: at the tender age of seventeen, he was managing 1,700 acres of herbs at Maine's Sabbathday Lake Shaker Community, the country's oldest herb business (established in 1799). He has gone on to be recognized worldwide as a premier specialist in medicinal and aromatic plants.

A master consultant to scholarly researchers and commercial growers alike, Steven serves as associate editor of the journal HerbalGram, *the peer-reviewed gold standard of the herbal field. He's a wildly prolific writer, with over 700 articles and 14 books published, including such classics as* The Field Guide to Medicinal Plants and Herbs, *coauthored with the iconic James Duke, and* Herbal Renaissance.

Steven is also among the top botanical photographers in the world. His stunning images have appeared in myriad publications and his stock of over 120,000 plant photographs is one of the world's primary resources for plant identification.

Herbalism has been at the forefront of the recent rebirth of alternative medicine, part of a larger impulse that seeks to reconnect us to the garden and heal our severed links with the natural world. Steven has been one of the most accomplished, credible, and responsible leaders of this renaissance. But the plant-person kinship is a bewitching siren song, and Steven Foster always begins by restoring our sense of wonder.

ONE OF THE THINGS I encourage all of us to do is find a way to question our assumptions about our own thought processes.

Around 1980, a little event happened to me in the woods. I had moved to Arkansas at the age of twenty-two and was stuck with no job, no money, and no car. For two years, I lived alone in a cabin a mile out in the woods. It turned out to be one of the most valuable experiences of my life.

I would spend half the day writing and half the day walking in the woods. I had a favorite spot: a small permanent pool of water that had snail darters, a nice little waterfall when it was raining, and a lovely dogwood hanging over it. I would go sit there, and after doing this for a couple of years, I believed I was in touch with nature. Beneath that remained an unconscious human assumption that we have dominion over the plants and the earth, though I didn't believe that I thought this way.

But one day I was sitting there communing with nature when a dragonfly landed on a branch in front of me. When I looked at the cute dragonfly, we started staring into each other's eyes. This went on for several minutes. Then the dragonfly took its two front legs, put them on either side of its head, turned its head 180 degrees, came back to center, and turned it around the other way.

That single experience made me realize that I had to question every assumption in my mind.

From Miracle to Magic:
Spirituality as Political Consciousness

John Mohawk

You'd need an entire coatroom to house all the hats John Mohawk wears. From scholar to farmer to citizen diplomat on behalf of indigenous rights, he bridges the postmodern Western world and the traditional one of native peoples. He does so with exceptional grace and a dry sense of humor that can unleash uproarious laughter at even the most somber gatherings.

A Seneca from the Iroquois Six Nations, John is professor of American studies at the Center for the Americas at SUNY Buffalo, where he currently serves as director of indigenous studies. He is the author of scores of newspaper and magazine articles and received the Native American Journalism Association's Best Historical Perspective of Indigenous People Award in 2000 and 2001. He cut his teeth in journalism as editor from 1967 to 1983 of the legendary Indian country periodical Akwesasne Notes, *which, as possibly the most influential Native American newspaper in history, was a beacon to the movement of Indian peoples fighting for human rights at a critical historical juncture. He has also written several classic books, including, most recently,* Utopian Legacies: A History of Conquest and Oppression in the Western World.

As a citizen diplomat, John has served as a delegate for the Iroquois Six Nations Confederacy in conflict situations and has negotiated for the Mohawk Nation under similar circumstances. He is a founding board member of the Indian Law Resource Center and the Seventh Generation Fund, a seminal grant-making organization that funds indigenous projects.

John is also a passionate farmer, carrying on the family tradition. When he joined the board of Bioneers in 1995, he helped found the Iroquois White Corn Project, designed to revive traditional native agriculture and reintroduce this heirloom vegetable into the food web. Iroquois white corn, which saved George Washington's troops from starvation at Valley Forge, has been served in more than fifty top U.S. restaurants and was chosen for the prestigious Slow Food Ark of endangered traditional foods. John also opened the Pinewoods Café on the Cattaraugus Reservation in New York to bring Iroquois white corn and other traditional foods back home to the Seneca Nation.

Scholar, author, journalist, activist, diplomat, farmer, entrepreneur, raconteur, and restaurateur, John Mohawk is an American original.

IF ASKED WHETHER I AM some sort of spiritual leader, I answer that I'm not, because that has implications I don't want to embrace. But on some level, I guess, I can be a spiritual interpreter.

A long time ago, on a planet far, far away, I was connected with an utterance, which was that spirituality is the highest form of political consciousness. I haven't talked about it much in the twenty-five years since.

Spirituality is different from religion. To have a religion, you need a committee, preferably of people with some sort of political bent. The purpose of the committee is to whip up a creed that tells us what we all believe in. Then you need people to evaluate how well you formed the creed. It can get really hierarchical and quite nasty.

But spirituality is different. I propose that spirituality is a form of consciousness, and in that light I want to explore the idea of natural world spirituality. Imagine that we can fly at many billions of times the speed of light. That we can rise out of our seats and go in a straight line through the ceiling, and in a second our solar system is behind us and we're racing toward the Milky Way. In a minute, the Milky Way breaks up and we're racing toward places where we can see other galaxies. We're speeding along on this journey, seeing galaxies—not dozens, not hundreds, not thousands, but hundreds of thousands of them, in clusters. If we're going fast enough, we'll notice that we leave one cluster of galaxies only to enter another.

We're told that eventually, if we go far enough, we'll get to the end of all the clusters. Imagine: we're going on and on at almost infinite speed and now

have passed all those galaxies and can't see them anymore. When are we going to get to the end? We're not. Maybe there are other clusters. Maybe there
are even other universes out there. We can't know, can we? We can't know
because we can't get to the end. If we came to another one, we wouldn't know
where the end is because the one thing we do know is it doesn't end. It goes
on and on and on. Can I suggest that our minds are not capable of truly grasping the infinite? We can imagine it, but we can't really grasp it because we
don't have any way to measure that. That's the universe.

Imagine for a moment, with eyes closed, that we want to go back in time,
as far as we can go. We're sailing through time in a time machine that clips off
a billion years per second. They tell us that if we go further back there is nothing. Yet we don't know if there was nothing or not, because no matter how
far back we go in time, we can't get to the beginning. We can't get to the beginning because there was no beginning. There was never a beginning in time,
and there's never an end in space. We know that intellectually, but it's very
hard to grasp.

Consider for a moment what happens when a human being becomes sick.
Ever since creatures lived on the earth, all those creatures have roamed its surfaces, and sometimes its subterranean places, seeking food. When you become
ill, you and every other creature seek medicine. In the English language, those
two things are different; they're separate.

But there's another way to look at it. A plant has to protect itself in order
to survive. A plant has to develop some sort of strategy so that creatures won't
eat it. What it does is produce chemical compounds that make it inedible to
most things. Every plant living in the wild has survived because it has a strategy that makes it inedible to all or most of the creatures that live nearby. Obviously, some parts of some plants can be eaten, but most of the time the plant
wants that to be the case. Most of the time, a plant is eaten because it is using
the eater as a way of spreading its own seeds around, but when that's not the
case, the chemical compounds a plant produces are often poisonous or at least
very unpleasant to us. In other cases, though, we'll find that chemical compounds in the plant actually help us when we're sick. Our purpose of seek-

ing plants, just like that of some birds and animals, is to look for properties that we call medicinal. We say the plant is a medicine.

Western medicine approaches the plant trying to find the active ingredient inside the plant, because Western medicine thinks that way. But if you had a different mind, you would approach the plant differently. You would approach it knowing that, somehow, something created a set of chemical compounds in the plant, maybe a hundred compounds. If you are a native person of almost any indigenous culture, and you're looking for a medicinal plant, when you come to the plant, you're going to address it. You say to the plant something about how you've come here looking for some help, and you ask for help. When you're standing there with your ceremonial corn flour or tobacco, or in some cultures, your money, what are you going to offer to the plant? And what are you offering sacrifice to? Is it the plant? Is it the hundred chemicals? What is it you're looking at?

In the indigenous cultures I know, people are not exactly addressing the plant. They're not addressing the hundred chemicals. They're addressing the intelligence in the universe that put it all together. They're addressing that which put us together. They're addressing that which created the complexity of life. In some cultures, what they're addressing is called "the creator of life." They're addressing something as infinite as the universe, as mysterious. They're addressing something really sacred—something that created not DNA, not chemical compounds, but the relationships between that plant and our lives. They're addressing something of a profound essence.

In English, we really don't have words to conceive and address exactly what they're calling upon because they're calling upon the power that created life to heal. Some people might say, "They're calling on God." Well, that's interesting, because "God" has many, many forms. Form enough to be that plant at that moment. Form enough to be the person addressing the plant at that moment.

"Spirit" is a word that has a lot of complex meaning. It's very powerful. But imagine yourself being part of that—something of a spirit addressing another part of a spirit that has as its source the infinite intelligence or wisdom—as we want to call it—that is the very process of creating life on earth, the process of creating planets and stars and galaxies. This is what is addressed by many cultures as the great mystery, the great creation. They address it as something other than anthropomorphic, as something that takes our own anthropocentrism and casts it away because, spirit to spirit, it doesn't mean anything. The relation is spirit to spirit, you to plant—the essence of humankind to the essence of everything else.

All we can really do about that idea in our conscious minds is have a profound respect for it. And we should, because that which created those hundred compounds in that plant has infinite power. It has the power to create life. It has the power to change life. It has the power to transform a mouse into an elephant if you give it enough time. It has an endless amount of power, but it does not exist in isolation. It cannot be reduced to one single thing.

A plant needs water, sun, energy, the moon, the earth, the animals and other plants around it, brothers and sisters, microbes, and a million other things. Until all those things are working together, we don't have the plant, we don't have the compounds, and we don't have the magic we need.

Natural world people are people of magic. But the essence of Western culture for the last two thousand years has not been about magic; it has been about miracles. The difference between miracle and magic is that when one calls for a miracle, one is calling for a reversal of the laws of nature. If someone has died, only a miracle will bring that person back to life. But the natural world people call upon nature to produce magic. They want a certain plant to cure someone who is sick, yet they're clever enough to know it's not the plant or the compounds that are going to do the job. It's the whole thing. It's the human who calls on the magic, who believes in it, who lets it work on him or her. That's what makes it so complex, because, if all you believe in is miracles, you don't develop any language to describe these relationships. In some ways "magic" isn't really the right word. Maybe "Magic," with a capital "M." It's hard to conceive and utter what I'm trying to get at in a language that really didn't conceive of it and utter it, or hasn't for a long, long time.

Spirituality is a form of consciousness. Almost all of the world's indigenous cultures, until they become extremely damaged, perceive that they have relationships at some level with special groups of plants and animals. Almost all of them pick certain things and say, "These things signify our world and are important to us. They are special." It doesn't mean that the rest of creation isn't any good. It just means that certain things are at the center of their belief. One of the reasons they do this, I believe, is that it's mentally and physically impossible to pay attention to everything that needs paying attention to. So they pick a few main things. In some cultures, it is the buffalo; in others it might be a certain fish or tree. Then they celebrate this relationship, which I propose is a consciousness.

It's not only the human who has the consciousness; it's also the plant, the tree, the birds, and all the other things. When you address that plant, you're addressing its consciousness in time and space. How it came to be and where it came to be, you don't know. What you know is that you're part of whatever it is that brought the plant into being. You're related in this way.

The ancient Seneca thought about this stuff. They believed that creation is infinite. The creation or the creator doesn't wear a beard or walk around on a cloud, carrying a staff. The creator is the force that gave that plant consciousness, as manifested in its compounds and in its shape at that moment. When you're talking to that plant, you're talking to the essence of the spirit of life in the universe, not just on the earth. Whatever it is, is not confined to here. You can look up in the sky and see that we're not the only place that's occupied. There are other beings in the universe besides us. That's the old spirituality. Acquire that consciousness, and it becomes extremely difficult to rationalize pollution. Acquire that consciousness and it becomes very difficult to rationalize cutting down trees to make board feet worth dollars out of them.

It is true that humans also have to go to nature, to go to the tree, and say, "I have to build a house." But once you've broken the one-on-one relationship so that what appears to you is never a tree but only a board, you have separated yourself from your relationship to the spirit of things. The same is true of how to relate to your food. The first time most people I know ever see a chicken, it's wrapped in cellophane. They would say, "Well, if I had a real chicken, I'd have to kill it." Maybe. But at least you can look it in the eye, maybe even know it for a little while, and you might learn something from it.

The same thing is true about our relationships to plants and animals, food, fibers, and everything else. We have ceased to have a spiritual relationship with them, a shared spiritual consciousness. They've become commodities and we've become consumers. If there's an essence to the world's great problem, that's it. Our relation to the world is mediated by a complex system of corporations: one gets the raw material, another one processes it, another transports it to the store, and yet another markets it. Then we take it home, unwrap it, consume it, and cast it aside. One has to ask, "How many people does it take to do something like that? And how many days to take everything that is the life force of the planet and consume it?" When we say there is an absence of the sacred, or a lack of spiritual consciousness, the reality of that condition has economic implications, in that economics is in some ways very contradictory to a sense of the sacred.

People in the twenty-first century look at a thing and ask themselves how they feel about it, but I want to ask, "How do you feel about the sacred? Can you see the sacred in the other?" We live in a world where that's blurred. Things are passing by us so fast that not only are we socialized not to look for that sacred relationship, but we're actually not given the time or energy to do it. If spirituality is the highest form of consciousness, as I've proposed, it needs more of our attention.

The Phosphorescent Soul:
Swimming with Mystery

Terry Tempest Williams

At times we hear voices so authentic, heartful, and original that they bring tears to our eyes. Such is the voice of the spellbinding writer and naturalist Terry Tempest Williams. Terry stands firmly and proudly in the lineage of the great nature writers in American literature, from John Muir, Aldo Leopold, and Henry David Thoreau to Rachel Carson, Gary Snyder, Barry Lopez, and Annie Dillard. But on close reading, her luminous work defies comparison. In books such as An Unspoken Hunger, Refuge, Leap, *and* Red, *she evokes with equal eloquence an erotically charged meal in a smoky café, the cosmic meaning of Hieronymus Bosch's paintings, the secret life of desert birds on the Great Salt Lake, or the civil-disobedient redemption of a "downwinder" of nuclear testing.*

A former naturalist-in-residence at the Utah Museum of Natural History, Terry is deeply rooted in her family's Mormon traditions and Utah desert homeland, but she is no less at home in Manhattan or Tuscany. She has courageously stood in defense of the natural world she loves so fiercely and in support of social justice. She has been among the most eloquent and resolute voices on behalf of the country's wildlands, including Utah's precious Red Rock deserts. A downwinder herself, she was arrested in an act of civil disobedience to halt nuclear testing; her mother and several other relatives died from cancer almost certainly related to aboveground nuclear tests, one of which Terry witnessed as a child.

Terry is a shimmering reflection of what is best in America—a humble, gentle, compassionate, and fearless lover of life who can speak truth to power, honor tradition, and embrace change. She never forgets nor lets us forget the land that is her source of inspiration and strength.

EVERY YEAR OUR FAMILY goes to California for a vacation, usually in August. We take our nieces and the whole extended family of aunts, uncles, cousins, and grandparents. On the last night of one of these outings, my father was saying, "This younger generation—I just can't believe they have to go to the movies every minute, they have to go to the malls every minute. What is the world coming to?" Nothing will satisfy their hunger, he said. I could see his point, but I responded, "Dad, they are fourteen or sixteen. They're good kids." It was a typical family discussion that happens behind closed doors or around the dinner table.

On this last night, we built a fire on the beach. We were sitting, talking and eating, and all of a sudden the moon came up and the surf turned electric green. We all thought, "What are we drinking?! What's in our food?!" The girls exclaimed, "Wait a minute! Did you see that?" My father said, "It's nothing—you're just imagining it. It's the floodlights." As another wave broke, they cried again, "Did you see that?!" My father started rubbing his eyes, and before we could even think, we were all down at the water's edge, in the surf. The waves were breaking over us, and we were now in the water up to our shoulders, screaming with delight.

It was a beautiful phosphorescent tide. Everywhere you swept your hand, it made magic. The girls wanted to know about dinoflagellates, bioluminescence, and on and on. We could never have had this discussion if they weren't literally being baptized in those magical waves. I thought, Steven Spielberg can't touch one night of a phosphorescent tide. This sense of wonder is what makes us human.

The Eye of the World: Sex, Beauty, Fraud, and Kinship

Peter Warshall

If you crossed a zealous field biologist with a humanist anthropologist and an angel flew through the brew, you might get Peter Warshall. There are few people working in sustainability, conservation, and progressive social change who can match Peter's sheer range and effectiveness, as well as his extraordinary heart.

Peter has spent thirty years balancing conservation and development as a biologist, teacher, public official, author, and editor, most recently as the eclectic editor of Whole Earth *magazine. His grasp of natural history is as intimate as his feel for culture. His turf is the globe, but he has worked most extensively in Africa and the desert Southwest. He has served as a research scientist at the Office of Arid Land Studies at the University of Arizona, a teacher of eco-poetics at the Buddhist Naropa Institute in Colorado, and the innovative mayor of Bolinas, California.*

Peter's formal education includes a Harvard Ph.D. in biological anthropology, a Fulbright scholarship spent studying with the legendary anthropologist Claude Lévi-Strauss, and deep studies in literature, mammalogy, primatology, ornithology, natural history, resource management, biodiversity, environmental impact analysis, and conflict resolution. He is a gifted citizen diplomat who can communicate effectively with constituencies as disparate as Native American traditionalists and corporate CEOs. His ingenious efforts have helped preserve flora and fauna, including endangered jaguars living in "sky islands" in the mountains of the Southwest and Mexico. He has often acted as a negotiator and mediator, for example, between Shell Oil Company and Louisiana environmental justice groups, to reduce toxic refinery emissions and empower a neighboring community to move. Another of his specialties is water; he was a seminal figure in launching the movement for local watershed governance and protection.

Peter's passion for the natural world is matched by his love for people. He knows the great challenge of our time is to reconcile the needs of humanity and those of the wild, and he has displayed extraordinary bravery and patience in his willingness to wade into intensely polarized battles over resources and conservation, helping achieve equitable and practical solutions. And when day is done, most likely you'll find him outside, exercising his naturalist heart, trading riffs with the birds.

WE EXPERIENCE THE WORLD through the planetary lens of nature. Because our eye has the same salt concentration as the ocean, we have literally kept the ocean in our eye. Like the one-celled critter of yore, our retina and brain are looking through an ancient sea. We filter light waves from the sun in the same way bacteria did when life began. Part of what this means is that all life shares certain features of a common biological aesthetics.

Earth has been around for four billion years. The atmosphere, sounds, sunlight, rocks, oceans and rivers, mountains, and silent soils have all evolved together. It has been assumed that they evolved in a strict Darwinian "survival of the fittest" manner. Recently, however, there has been more study of how living creatures have evolved symbiotically, suggesting that commonalities may be more important to the history of the planet than antagonistic blood-and-guts conflicts. Instead of seeing only the fights, we now see that we are all on the same stage. The commonalities vision, inspired by the Gaia hypothesis (which suggests that the earth can be viewed as one integral living system) describes a biosphere nurtured everywhere by the same sun, the same light waves, the same lines and contours, and the same colors. Naturalists now can open our sense of aesthetics from a cramped worldview limited to human beings to a world shared by all terrestrial species with eyes, ears, and senses of smell and touch.

For instance, almost everyone feels that there's a relationship between art and sex. Much in art is sensual and sexy, and much about sex is beautiful. How does this relationship play out in nature? Perhaps the best-known example of coevolutionary symbiosis is the relationship between the bee and the flower. The bee desires nectar or pollen to feed its hive, and the flower needs to be fertilized by sperm from another flower, which comes in capsules called pollen. Aesthetics make it happen. The bee-seeking flower colors its landing platform yellow like a traffic sign, or presents lines in bright colors, like landing strips, to guide the bee to its nectary. When the bee enters the "painted" airport and follows the landing strip, the pollen from the flower spreads over the bee's body or onto its legs. When the bee visits the next flower, some of the pollen detaches onto specially sculpted female parts. This reciprocal aesthetic is sensual, sexy, and mutually beneficial, and it turns on a shared appreciation for knockout pigments and "painted" petals.

An ultimate example of sexy art and artful sex can be found among certain orchids. These flowers are like sex bombs, having evolved to look just like a dreamboat female insect. Two little petals resemble spread wings, and the bottom bulbous part suggests the belly of a wasp or tropical bee. In the eyes of the male insect, the orchid is transformed into a seductive Jayne Mansfield or Marilyn Monroe. Buggy guys want to mate with this insect centerfold. The design of the flower has evolved in such a way that during the "mating," the flower transfers the pollen, in a specially designed sack, onto a precise part of the male insect. When he leaves and lusts after and tries to mate with another orchid, an intricate female part of the flower catches the sack. To the insect, the colors, shapes, and high-energy emotions of the orchid compose an alluring aesthetic and an energy as moving as a Manet painting or as ridiculously delightful as a Dali.

We humans receive perks from the attraction of these living creatures to each other. A flower's design and colors create a functional attractiveness to certain bees and butterflies, but because all life shares the same four-billion-year-old biological aesthetic history, the flower also looks beautiful to us. That's the crucial leap from a constrained "That's as pretty as a picture" reaction to a more exalted sense of ourselves as graced by and united with all forms of beauty on a symbiotic planet.

Planet 'Hood:
Making the World Our Home

Luisah Teish

Luisah Teish is among the most dynamic figures in the revival of African spiritual traditions in North America. She has magnetic charisma and gives off a joy that is at once earthy and ethereal, as though she were simultaneously receiving direct current from the ground beneath and the heavens above.

Teish, as she's usually known, is a woman chief and initiated elder in the Ifa/ Orisha tradition of southwest Nigeria, one of Africa's most sophisticated spiritual, literary, and divinatory traditions. She has skillfully adapted these teachings to contemporary realities, making their ecological wisdom and respect for ancestors and the earth accessible and inspiring to audiences of all backgrounds and ethnicities. She is the director of Ile Orunmila Oshun (The House of Destiny and Love) and the School of Ancient Mysteries and Sacred Arts Center in Oakland, California. She is currently chair of the International Committee on Women's Issues for the World Orisha Congress, serves as artistic director of ASE Theater, and has authored several books, including Jambalaya: The Natural Woman's Book of Personal Charms and Rituals.

Teish is a powerful performer of African, Caribbean, and African American folktales as well as of myths celebrating women. In North and South America as well as in Europe and Australia, she has revived the ancient sacred art of storytelling as a form of social healing and community building. Drawing on the rich wisdom of the mother continent of our species, she conjures a deep appreciation of the absolute necessity for harmony between the spiritual essences of land and its human inhabitants. Just when we most need such a potion, she is reimagining a contemporary mythology of earth-honoring wisdom.

MECHANICS' INSTITUTE LIBRARY
57 Post Street
San Francisco, CA 94104
(415) 393-0101

IN CERTAIN SONGS I SING, I use the Yoruba word *Ilé*, meaning "we who are related, we who have decided we are related." It can mean a group of people who have walked into a building and who live in it. It can mean house and those of us who are in the house. Guess what else it means? Earth. Thus I am forced not to think of the earth as something I live on, but rather a house I live in. When I begin to think of the earth as a house I live in, I know that I don't want the plumbing messed up. I can't litter where I sleep.

One time a fellow in East Oakland came up to me and said, "You know, Sister Teish, you cool. You are right on, sister. I know you down with the people and everything, but what's your trip with the earth?" I told him, "In the big picture, the earth is the 'hood I live in." Then he said, "Why didn't you say that? The earth is the 'hood I live in. Okay, now I can deal with it." He understood because he's accustomed to defending his turf.

In the West African tradition, Oya, the goddess of fall, is queen of the winds of change, the boss lady of the cemetery, the mother of catastrophe. Whenever I talk about Oya, the mother of catastrophe, people shudder. But the proper definition of catastrophe is a sudden structural change. Oya doesn't move the furniture around in the house; she blows the roof off and knocks down the beams, reducing the debris to compost so that we can start over again. To some extent, I feel as if that's what happens every fall, and at this point in human history, it is what we have to do in thinking about our relationship to nature.

Somebody in my family once came in the house seething because he had heard some fundamentalist speaking on the radio, saying that the earth was here for our use, for our domination. This view is ignorant because the earth is the mother and we are the children. We are the ones that come out of her. We are the ones who are learning from her and through her, and we are the ones who are going to return to her. When I hear something like the nonsense from the radio, after I'm through being pissed off, I realize I'm talking to somebody who has been enslaved by a military-industrial-technological mind, who has lost connection with the indigenous mind that knows that we are children of this earth. We are born in the bowl of salt water in our mama's belly. We have to inhale, have to be inspired, and have to breathe in order not to expire. We have to come out and consume the sun by eating every day.

When I talk to people about African spirituality, I explain that there are many levels to the priesthood. You reach the first level when you put your hand in some dirt and can feel it. You can feel the earth and feel it as sacred. You can pick up a handful of dirt and know that it is the flesh and bones and spirit of your ancestors returned to form. You can look at a plant and understand why in my tradition we say that the lord of the plants is a man with one leg, one arm, and one eye, who still is smarter, stronger, and faster than we are. You can pick up a stone and learn how to communicate with the spirit in matter.

I believe that our alienation from indigenous mind is what allows us to poison ourselves, kill each other, and poison the environment. In this time of change, take note of the place in nature where you are regenerated and go there. If you're a child of the river, or the forest, or the mountain, or the thunder— wherever it is in nature that regenerates you—go to that place. Declare yourself one who learns from that place and is nurtured by it and is a defender of that place and that energy. Then live it.

A World Made of Stories:
Saving the Web of Cultural Life

Wade Davis

Wade Davis has led a life of far-ranging exploration on a path illuminated by curiosity and serendipity. Appointed an "explorer-in-residence" and "world culture representative" with the National Geographic Society, he is an anthropologist and ethnobotanist. A prodigy of the late, legendary Richard Evans Schultes, the towering giant of American ethnobotany who spent decades in the Amazon, Wade himself has made 6,000 or so botanical collections while living among 15 indigenous groups in 8 South American countries. He is, however, far more than a great plant investigator. As a seasoned visitor to other cultures, he has become a visionary leader in the desperate race to preserve not only our planet's vanishing biodiversity, but also its even more imperiled cultural diversity.

A celebrated writer and photographer, Wade has wandered far and wide to describe the living treasure of the cultures of traditional and indigenous peoples. His writings have awakened millions to the deep wisdom of indigenous cultures and the breathtaking beauty of the natural world. His books include The Serpent and the Rainbow, *about the Vodoun culture of Haiti,* Light at the Edge of the World, *and* One River, *which depicts the extraordinary saga of Schultes and the peoples of the Amazon basin. He has also penned countless articles in many of the world's leading publications and has played a key role in creating numerous television documentaries, including the Earthguide series for the Discovery Channel. As an activist, he is affiliated with a wide range of organizations, including the David Suzuki Foundation, Ecotrust, and Cultural Survival.*

Equally at home lecturing at the Smithsonian, sharing a mind-bending potion with an Amazonian shaman, or tracking snow leopards in the Himalayas, Wade

Davis is our greatest living mapper of the ethnosphere, that fertile living library of
diverse cultures in whose care rests the greatest remaining trove of biodiversity.

I COINED THE TERM "ethnosphere" to describe a concept suggesting
that just as there is a biosphere, a biological web of life, so too there is a cultural fabric that envelops the earth, a cultural web of life, the sum total of all
thoughts and dreams, beliefs, myths, intuitions, and inspirations brought into
being by the human imagination since the dawn of consciousness. The ethnosphere is humanity's great legacy. It is the product of our dreams, the embod-
iment of our hopes, the symbol of all that we are and all that we have created
as a wildly inquisitive and astonishingly adaptive species.

Just as the biosphere, the biological matrix of life, is today being severely
compromised, so too is the ethnosphere, only at a far greater rate. No biologist,
for example, would dare suggest that 50 percent of all species of plants and
animals are on the brink of extinction. Yet this most apocalyptic scenario in
the realm of biological diversity scarcely approaches the most optimistic assessment in the realm of cultural diversity. The key indicator is language loss.
When most of us were born, there were 6,000 languages being spoken on
earth. Today, fully half are not being taught to children, which means that,
unless something changes, these languages are effectively already dead.

A language is not merely a body of vocabulary or a set of grammatical
rules. It is a flash of the human spirit, the means by which the soul of a particular culture reaches into the material world. Every language is an old-
growth forest of the mind, a watershed of thought, an entire ecosystem of
spiritual possibilities.

There are those who suggest that communication would be facilitated and
the world would be a better place if we all spoke the same language. But what
if that language were Yoruba, Lakota Sioux, or Haida? Suddenly, as a native
speaker of English, one begins to sense what it might mean to be the last of
your people to speak your native tongue, to be enveloped in silence, to have
no way to pass on the wisdom of your elders or to anticipate the promise of

your children. Yet this tragic fate is the plight of someone, somewhere, roughly every two weeks. On average, every fortnight an elder dies and carries with him or her into the grave the last syllables of an ancient tongue. What this really means is that within a generation or two we will witness the loss of fully half of humanity's legacy. This is the hidden backdrop of our age.

There is a misconception that these indigenous cultures, quaint and colorful though they may be, are somehow fragile and delicate, destined to fade away as if by some natural law. Nothing could be further from the truth. In every instance these are dynamic living cultures and languages being driven out of existence by identifiable external threats. These threats may be industrial, as in the case of egregious forestry practices that have destroyed the subsistence base of the nomadic Penan in the rain forests of Sarawak in Borneo. In Nigeria, the Ogoni can no longer farm the once-fertile soils of the Niger delta because of toxic effluents from the petrochemical industry. Elsewhere the calamity may be caused by epidemic disease, as in the case of Brazil's Yanomami, who have suffered dreadful mortality due to exotic pathogens brought into their lives by gold miners who have recently invaded their lands. Or the agent of destruction may be ideology, as with the crude domination of Tibet by the communist Chinese. But in every case these indigenous cultures are being overwhelmed by powerful external forces. This observation is discouraging, for obvious reasons, but also encouraging, for it implies that if humans are the agents of cultural destruction, we can also be facilitators of cultural survival.

It's perhaps useful to ask what we mean when we use the term "modern world." To begin, we must recognize that all cultures are ethnocentric, fiercely loyal to their own interpretation of reality. Indeed the names of many indigenous societies translate as "the people," the implication being that every other human is a nonperson, a savage from beyond the realm of the civilized. The word "barbarian" in fact derives from the Greek *barbarus*, meaning one who babbles. In the ancient world, if you did not speak Greek you were a barbarian. The Aztec had the same notion. Anyone who could not speak Nahuatl was a nonhuman. We too are ethnocentric, often forgetting that we represent not the absolute wave of history but merely a worldview, and that modernity— whether you call it Westernization, globalization, or free trade—is but an expression of our cultural values. It is not some objective force removed from the constraints of culture. And it is certainly not the true, preordained outcome of history. It is merely a constellation of beliefs, convictions, and economic paradigms that represent one way of doing things, of going about the complex process of organizing human activities.

Indeed the Western model of development has failed in so many places largely because it has been based on the false promise that people who follow its prescriptive dictates will in time achieve the material prosperity enjoyed by a handful of Western nations. Even were this possible, it is not at all clear that it would be desirable. To raise consumption of energy and materials throughout the world to Western levels, given current population projections, would require the resources of four planet earths by the year 2100. To do so with the one world we have would so severely compromise the biosphere that the earth would be unrecognizable. In reality, development for the vast majority of the world's peoples has been a process in which the individual is torn from his past and propelled into an uncertain future, only to secure a place on the bottom rung of an economic ladder that leads nowhere.

Without doubt, images of comfort, wealth, and technological sophistication have a magnetic allure. Any job in the city may seem better than backbreaking labor in sun-scorched fields. Entranced by the promise of the new, people throughout the world have, in many instances voluntarily and in great earnest, turned their backs on the old, but the fate of the vast majority of those who sever ties with their traditions will not be to attain the prosperity of the West but to join the legions of urban poor trapped in squalor, struggling to survive. This is a very dangerous and explosive situation. Anthropology suggests that when peoples and cultures are squeezed, extreme ideologies, inspired by strange and unexpected beliefs, sometimes emerge. Al Qaeda, the Maoists in Nepal, the Shining Path in Peru, Pol Pot's Khmer Rouge in Cambodia—all of these malevolent groups have emerged out of chaotic conditions of disintegration and disenfranchisement that result when disaffected populations are cast adrift from their foundations.

Culture is not decoration or artifice; it gives meaning to lives. It is a body of knowledge that allows the individual to avoid madness, to make sense of the infinite sensations of consciousness, to find meaning and order in a universe that ultimately has neither. Culture is a body of laws and traditions, a moral and ethical code that insulates a people from the barbaric heart that, history suggests, lies just beneath the surface of all human societies and indeed all human beings. Culture alone allows us to reach, as Abraham Lincoln said, "for the better angels of our nature." To have so many individuals running around stripped raw, shadows of their former selves, free of moral or ethical constraint, is to create a very dangerous world indeed. What can possibly be more significant than the loss, in a single generation, of half of humanity's intellectual and spiritual legacy?

Just before she died, anthropologist Margaret Mead spoke of her concern that as we drift toward a more homogenous world, we are laying the foundations of a blandly amorphous and singularly generic modern culture that ultimately will have no rivals. The entire imagination of humanity, she feared, might become confined within the limits of a single intellectual and spiritual modality. Her nightmare was the possibility that we might wake up one day and not even remember what had been lost. Human beings as a recognizable social species have been around for perhaps 600,000 years. The Neolithic revolution, which gave us agriculture and with it surplus, hierarchy, specialization, and sedentary life, occurred only 10,000 years ago. Modern industrial society is but 300 years old. This shallow history does not suggest to me that our current way of life has all the answers for all the challenges that will confront us as a species in the coming millennia.

The myriad cultures of the world are not failed attempts at modernity; they are unique manifestations of the human spirit. With their dreams and prayers, their myths and memories, they teach us that there are indeed other ways of being, alternative visions of life, birth, death, and creation itself. When asked the meaning of being human, they respond with ten thousand different voices. It is within this diversity of knowledge and practice, of intuition and interpretation, of promise and hope, that we will all rediscover the enchantment of being what we are: a conscious species aware of our place on the planet and fully capable of ensuring that all peoples in every garden find a way to flourish.

This is neither a sentimental nor an academic notion. Indeed, in the wake of September 11 it has become an issue of survival. For the central challenge of our times, at least in a political sense, is to find a way to live in a truly multicultural world of pluralism. Not to freeze peoples or cultures out of the flow of history, but rather to insure that all peoples may benefit from the products of our collective genius without their participation entailing the eradication of their cultures.

Regarding language loss and the erosion of humanity's cultural and intellectual legacy, the real question is, "What do we do about it?" Obviously it is neither possible nor desirable to sequester indigenous peoples in a park like some kind of zoological specimen. You cannot make a national park of cultures or save a rain forest of the mind. Ultimately all you can do is attempt to change the way that people throughout the world view and value the contributions of these diverse cultures, these diverse manifestations of the human heart.

I have hope because major shifts in awareness have occurred over the last decades. Just forty years ago, for example, simply getting people to stop throwing garbage out of car windows was considered a great environmental victory. No one spoke of the ozone layer or of the consequences of climate change. Rachel Carson was a lone voice in the wilderness. "Biosphere" and "biodiversity" were exotic terms familiar only to a handful of scientists. Today they are part of the vernacular of schoolchildren, and environmental concerns occupy the attention of governments worldwide. Solutions may remain elusive, but no government on earth can ignore the challenge. There have been enormous changes in the roles and status of women and in attitudes toward homosexuality, and even a shift in public concern about tobacco use, to cite only a few examples.

When I was asked to join the National Geographic Society as explorer-in-residence, I was told quite boldly that my mandate was to change, in a decade, the way the world thinks about culture. One of the reasons I accepted the challenge—wildly ambitious as it is—is that I have long believed that while polemics are rarely persuasive and politicians are seldom catalysts of social change, stories and storytellers can change the world. As a storytelling platform, the National Geographic Society is difficult to beat. Every month it reaches a worldwide audience of more than 250 million people.

We decided to tell the stories of the ethnosphere, to launch a series of journeys that would take our audience to places and peoples where the cultural beliefs, practices, and rituals are so inherently wondrous that just to know of them is to be dazzled. Ideally, readers would be inspired to embrace the key revelation of anthropology, the idea that the world into which we are born does not exist in some absolute sense, but rather is just one model of reality, the consequence of one set of choices made by our particular intellectual and social lineage.

At the National Geographic Society we hope to embark over the coming years on dozens of journeys into the ethnosphere. I'd like to take people to West Africa, to Benin and Togo, to the original heartland of the Vodoun faith, to meet a people who walk in and out of their spirit realm with an ease that has always astonished ethnographic observers. In the South Pacific, I'd like to introduce the world to those great mariners, the Polynesian seafarers who read the stars and followed the ocean currents to create the largest culture sphere in history: ten million square miles, a quarter of the surface of the planet. In Mexico, the Mazatec communicate by whistling, mimicking the intonations of their tonal language to send complex messages across broad mountain valleys. It is like a vocabulary inspired by the wind. In the Amazon rain forest, Waorani hunters can smell animal urine at forty paces and identify the animal that left it. Aboriginal "dreamtime," the Naxi shamans of Yunnan who carve mystical tales into rock, the Juwasi Bushmen who for generations lived in open truce with the lions of the Kalahari—the list goes on.

Recently I went to Mali to follow the Arab merchants who for centuries have moved across this vast sea of sand to secure a precious commodity, the salt of Taoudenni. Their story intrigues me because the salt is not a mere commodity; rather, it is seen as the gold of the desert. The culture of trade and movement that has grown around its exchange has inspired a people even as it has obliged them to come to terms with the impossibly severe desert environment. The salt makes the journey necessary, but the journey makes the people, and the people in turn bring the desert alive with spirits and dreams, all the mys-

tic possibilities inherent in a land where death always lies near and life is a narrow thread woven into the fabric of destiny.

The journey is many things. It is, of course, a physical task, a necessary
element of the trade. But it is also an initiation, the measure of a man. An Arab
youth in this culture cannot marry until he has crossed the harsh sands from
Timbuktu to Taoudenni at least once. And traditionally the journey was also
a sacrifice—remembering that the word derives from the Latin "to make
sacred"—because to make the journey is to become one with the desert and
with one's fate.

There lingers a conceit that while we have been busy inventing the Internet or placing men on the moon, other societies have somehow been intellectually idle. This is simply not true. Anthropology has long taught that
whether a people's mental potential goes into technical wizardry or unraveling the complex threads of memory inherent in a myth is merely a matter of
cultural choice and orientation. In the Sahara, for example, the raw potential
of the human mind has been tapped in astonishing ways, some metaphysical,
some boldly concrete, like the very capacity to orient oneself in an endless ex-
panse of sand where there is no separation between horizon and sky, nothing
on a human scale, no point of reference save the hallucinogenic waves of delir-
ium that sweep over the unfettered imagination when the throat is scorched
with a thirst impossible to describe, impossible to bear.

Baba Oumar, the guide on my Malian trip, read the patterns of the wind
in the lee of plants and observed the direction and texture of the dunes, but
he said that orientation in the desert ultimately is a gift. Some have it; most do
not. The nature of this gift lies beyond the world of the physical. He claimed
never to have been lost. Sometimes, though, he would become momentarily
disoriented. I asked him what he did when this happened. He told me that he
simply sits still and waits for a sign from Allah. He may carry an old compass,
left over from the French, but his true compass lies within, and it is something
of the spirit that those of us not of the desert will never know.

When Europeans first went to the Arctic, they took the Inuit to be sav-
ages, failing to understand that there could be no better measure of genius than
the ability to survive in that impossible land on a technology limited to what

you could carve from bone and slate or forge with ice. It's like that in the Sahara. In Mali, we ran into a caravan that was down to its last liter of water. These six young men were a hundred kilometers from the nearest well, with a valuable herd of camels and a large consignment of salt, yet there was no sign of panic. On the contrary, just as we arrived, they were in the process of dispatching one of their mates with a camel to walk fifteen kilometers over stony ground to reach a depression in the ground that they had only heard about and that might conceivably yield water if you dug five feet beneath the surface.

While they waited for their friend to return, what did they do with their last bit of water? They kindled a twig fire and brewed us tea. A simple gesture but so pregnant with meaning. On the one hand it demonstrated the customary law of the desert, which demands that you give to any guest all that he requires. They say that should a stranger turn up at your tent, you will slaughter the last goat that provides the only milk for your children to provide a feast for your guest. The reason being, of course, that in the desert you never know when it will be you who turn up in the night, hungry or dying of thirst. The simple brewing of tea reveals a world of reciprocity that reaches back generations—bonds of loyalty and trust, never spoken about and never forgotten. As I watched one of the boys, Mohamed, pour the tea, I was amazed by his quiet confidence, his certain knowledge that he would find a way to water. That more than anything revealed to me that this searing desert was for him a home.

Even had it been summer, when temperatures reach 140 degrees and the surface of the sand becomes too hot to touch, he would have shared that water. Not to do so would have been to shame himself and deny all his social obligations, which would have implied the betrayal of his community. This is something we in the West often fail to understand. We long ago liberated the individual from the constraints of community and with such finality that we forget what an astonishing innovation it represented in human affairs. It was really the sociological equivalent of splitting the atom. We forget that in most of the world the community still dominates, for without its strength the individual cannot survive. In embracing the cult of the individual, we secure an irresistible sense of liberation and freedom, but it comes at a cost, as is evident in the alienation and isolation that characterize too many lives in the West.

I don't want to romanticize other cultures: The salt mine at Taoudenni is a brutal place to work, a harsh system of trade and labor, with many of the miners trapped in debt and dire poverty. Until relatively recently, though, the working conditions in most European and American mines were just as harsh, and certainly more perilous than those that confront the miners of Taoudenni. And around the economic activity at Taoudenni has emerged a fascinating culture, built around caravans that have moved through the desert since soon after the camel was domesticated some two thousand years ago.

The arrival of motorized transport will mean the end of the caravans; never again will trains of 50,000 animals move through the dunes. At the same time the trucks mean that the miners can sell the salt for cash, rather than having to give the camel caravans three slabs out of every four mined. Thus the min-ers will do better in a strictly economic sense. The salt will be cheaper to buy in Timbuktu and points south, simply because of increased supply. But miss-ing from such a spare economic analysis is the fact that the reason the salt of Taoudenni is so highly valued is its scarcity. People in Mali can buy sea salt from France for half the price, but they prefer the salt of the desert and pay a premium for it because of an entire range of symbolic elements and meanings. The salt of the French is said to cause diseases; that of Taoudenni is known to heal. The Taoudenni salt has a magical resonance that has less to do with its innate chemical properties—sodium chloride is sodium chloride—than with the mystique of the trade culture, the remoteness of the mine, the stories handed down over generations. Think of the gifts of the Three Wise Men: frankin-cense and myrrh. What made these so precious as to be selected as the gifts for the Christ child? Their usefulness as resins, or the value they held because of their scarcity, like diamonds or black pearls? Once the camel caravans are gone and the salt is moved by truck, the mystique will soon dissipate, and the gold of the desert will be nothing more than crude blocks of salt.

If the caravans cease to run, and if the children of the youths who gave us tea no longer know how to move through this desert, will the sky fall? No. But we're not talking about the loss of a single species or a single cultural adap-tation. We are speaking about a global waterfall of destruction unprecedented in scale. Indeed, two centuries from now this era will be remembered not for its wars or its technological innovations, but rather as the time when we either passively endorsed or actively supported the massive destruction of cultural and biological diversity on the planet.

Genocide, the physical extermination of a people, is universally condemned by civilized societies. Yet ethnocide, the destruction of a people's way of life, is often endorsed as appropriate development policy. Who is to say that American culture matters more than that of the Tuareg? At a more fundamental level, we have to ask ourselves, What kind of world do we want to live in? Most Americans will never see a painting by Monet or hear a symphony by Mozart, but does that mean that the world would not be a lesser place without these artists and their unique interpretations of reality?

Our goal at the National Geographic Society is to tell the stories of the ethnosphere, to take our audience to places of such amazing cultural wonder that they will feel viscerally the value of what these peoples offer the world. We also want to facilitate in any number of ways the ability of these peoples to tell their own stories through words, film, photography, and the Internet. We plan to turn the Internet into a virtual campfire around which we might gather to share tales from all reaches of the ethnosphere.

We don't want these accounts to be decorative. We are interested not in indulging fantasies of the exotic, but rather in celebrating the powerful depths of culture and the lessons to be learned from such deep understanding. In a sense we would like to try to do for culture what the deep ecologists and poets have done for biology.

As we attempt to understand the relationship between indigenous peoples and the natural world, we may find ourselves suggesting that indigenous people are somehow more contemplative and closer to the earth than we can ever be. Nothing could be further from the truth. Indigenous people are not nostalgic or sentimental—there is not a lot of room for either in the bitter winds of Tibet or the malarial swamps of New Guinea—but they have nevertheless forged through time and ritual a traditional mystique of the earth that is based not on a self-conscious sense of being close to the earth, but on a far subtler intuition: the idea that the earth itself is breathed into being by human consciousness.

As recently as the early decades of the twentieth century, the Australian parliament debated formally the question of whether the first people of the land were in fact human beings. Mercifully, biology has now proved that we are all brothers and sisters. All human cultures share the same raw intellectual potential, the same mental acuity. Whether that genius flows into technological wizardry or into unraveling the complex threads of memory inherent in a myth is simply a matter of choice and cultural orientation.

The Aboriginal peoples of Australia accepted life as it was, as a cosmological whole, the unchanging creation of the first dawn, when the primordial ancestors, through their thoughts, dreams, and journeys, sang the world into being. The paths taken by their ancestors have never been forgotten. They are the songlines, precise itineraries followed even today as the people travel across the template of the physical world.

As the Aborigines track the songlines and chant the stories of the first dawning, they become part of the ancestors and enter the dreamtime, which is neither a dream nor a measure of the passage of time. It is the very realm of the ancestors, a parallel universe where the ordinary laws of time, space, and motion do not apply, where past, present, and future merge into one. For them this parallel universe is every bit as real as the physical world. To walk the songlines is to become part of the ongoing creation of the world, a place that both exists and is still being formed. Thus the Aborigines view themselves as not merely attached to the earth but essential to its ongoing existence. Without the land the people would die, but without the people, the process of creation would cease and the earth would wither. Through movement and sacred rituals, the people maintain access to the dreamtime and play a dynamic, ongoing role in the world of the ancestors. The world as we know it exists even as it is still being formed, breathed into being by human consciousness. So in a world that has yet to be born, how can a people possibly embrace a cult of improvement, of change?

Whether this notion is "true" or not is hardly the point. What is interesting and consequential is how a people's conviction or belief mediates the relationship between human society and the natural world. In the high Andes, people believe that a mountain is an Apu, a sacred being that has the power to direct the destiny of all those living within the shadow of its slopes. A young child coming of age in such a place will have a profoundly different relationship to that mountain than a kid from Montana raised to believe that a mountain is a pile of inert rock ready to be mined. Is a mountain a god or a pile of ore? Ultimately, who is to say? The important point is how the belief itself mediates and defines the relationship between the human and the natural landmark.

Anthropologists are often accused of embracing an extreme relativism, as if any cultural practice can be rationalized. As if you could rationalize the heinous acts of Nazism, for example, because after all, the Nazis had an ideology, an ethnicity, and a language. In truth, no serious anthropologist calls for eliminating judgment. What anthropology encourages is the temporary suspension of judgment so that the judgments we're ethically obliged to make can be informed ones. Cultural expressions can be sublime or harsh, elegant or clumsy, inspired or foolish. But in the end the wonder lies in the fact that all are authentic expressions of the human drama.

Today there is a fire burning over the earth, taking with it plants and animals, ancient skills and visionary wisdom. At risk is a vast archive of knowledge and expertise, a catalogue of the imagination, an oral and written language composed of the memories of countless elders and healers, warriors, farmers, fishermen, midwives, poets, and saints—in short, the artistic, intellectual, and spiritual expression of the human experience in its full complexity and diversity. Quelling the flame and discovering a new appreciation for the variety of the human spirit as brought into being by culture is arguably the central challenge of our times.

Every view of the world that fades away, every culture that disappears, diminishes life's possibilities and reduces the human repertoire of adaptive responses to the problems that confront us all. Knowledge is lost, not only of the natural world but also of the spirit realms, intuitions about the meaning of the cosmos, insights into the very nature of existence. This is why it matters that we tell these stories and make these journeys.

Resources

Part I. Biomimicry: Working with Nature to Heal Nature

Organizations and Websites

Biomimicry Guild
P.O. Box 575, Helena, MT 59624
406-495-1858
www.biomimicry.net

CytoCulture Environmental Biotechnology
249 Tewksbury Ave.
Point Richmond, CA 94801
510-233-0102, fax 510-233-3777
www.cytoculture.com
cyto@cytoculture.com

Damariscotta
650 Merle St., Ste. C, Clarion, PA 16214
814-226-5792, fax 814-226-5861

Fungi Perfecti LLC
P.O. Box 7634, Olympia, WA 98507
360-426-9292, fax 360-426-9377
www.fungi.com
mycomedia@aol.com

Ocean Arks International
176 Battery St., Ste. 1, Burlington, VT 05401
802-860-0011, fax 802-860-0022
www.oceanarks.org
info@oceanarks.org

U.S. Department of Agriculture
Agricultural Research Service
Animal Manure and By-Products Laboratory
10300 Baltimore Blvd.,
Bldg. 007 Barc-West, Room 013
Beltsville, MD 20705-2350
301-504-8324 ext. 447, fax 301-504-5031
www.ars.usda.gov/pandp/people/
people.htm?personid=949

Water Stewards Network
176 Battery St., Burlington, VT 05401
802-660-8094
www.waterstewards.org
info@waterstewards.org

Books

Benyus, Janine M. *Biomimicry: Innovation Inspired by Nature.* New York: William Morrow, 1997.

Benyus, Janine M. *The Field Guide to Wildlife Habitats of the Eastern United States.* New York: Simon & Schuster, 1989.

Benyus, Janine M. *The Secret Language and Remarkable Behavior of Animals.* New York: Black Dog & Leventhal Publishers, 1998.

Stamets, Paul. *Growing Gourmet and Medicinal Mushrooms.* 3d ed. Berkeley, CA: Ten Speed Press, 2000.

Stamets, Paul, and J. S. Chilton. *The Mushroom Cultivator.* Olympia, WA: Agarikon Press, 1984.

Todd, John, with Nancy Jack Todd. *From Eco-Cities to Living Machines: Principles of Ecological Design.* Berkeley, CA: North Atlantic Books, 1994.

Journals, Periodicals, and Newsletters

Annals of Earth
Ocean Arks International
176 Battery St., Ste. 1, Burlington, VT 05401
802-860-0011, fax 802-860-0022
www.oceanarks.org/annals
info@oceanarks.org

Part II. Listening to the Land:
Ecology as the Art of Restoring Relationships

Organizations and Websites

Cultural Survival
215 Prospect St., Cambridge, MA 02139
617-441-5400, fax 617-441-5417
www.culturalsurvival.org
culturalsurvival@cs.org

Cultures on the Edge: An Open Look at
Cultural Diversity around the World
www.culturesontheedge.com

EcoResults!
P.O. Box 23713, Flagstaff, AZ 86002
928-213-5913
www.ecoresults.org
info@ecoresults.org

Heyday Books and Clapperstick Institute
2054 University Ave., Ste. 400
Berkeley, CA 94704
510-549-3564, fax 510-549-1889
www.heydaybooks.com
heyday@heydaybooks.com

Indigenous Peoples' Restoration Network
c/o Society for Ecological Restoration
International
1955 West Grant Rd., No. 150
Tucson, AZ 85745
520-622-5485, fax 520-622-5491
www.ser.org
info@ser.org

The Land Institute
2440 E. Water Well Rd., Salina, KS 67401
785-823-5376, fax 785-823-8728
www.landinstitute.org
theland@landinstitute.org

Quivira Coalition
1413 Second St., Ste. 1, Santa Fe, NM 87505
505-820-2544, fax 505-955-8922
www.quiviracoalition.org
projects@quiviracoalition.org

Seed Savers Exchange
3076 N. Winn Rd., Decorah, IA 52101
563-382-5990, fax 563-382-5872
www.seedsavers.org
arllys@seedsavers.org

TreePeople
12601 Mulholland Dr.
Beverly Hills, CA 90210
818-753-4600, fax 818-753-4635
www.treepeople.org
info@treepeople.org

The Wildlands Project
P.O. Box 455, Richmond, VT 05477
802-434-4077, fax 802-434-5980
www.wildlandsproject.org
info@wildlandsproject.org

Books

Anderson, M. Kat, and Thomas C. Blackburn, eds. *Before the Wilderness: Environmental Management by Native Californians.* Menlo Park, CA: Ballena Press, 1993.

Ashworth, Suzanne, and Kent Whealy. *Seed to Seed: Seed Saving and Growing Techniques for Vegetable Gardeners.* 2d ed. Decorah, IA: Seed Saver Publications, 2002.

Condon, Patrick, and Stacy Moriarty, eds. *Second Nature: Adapting LA's Landscape for Sustainable Living.* Beverly Hills, CA: TreePeople, 1999.

Dagget, Dan. *Beyond the Rangeland Conflict: Toward a West That Works.* 2d ed. Reno: University of Nevada Press, 2000.

Foreman, Dave. *Confessions of an Eco-Warrior.* New York: Harmony Books, 1991.

Foreman, Dave, and Bill Haywood, eds. *Ecodefense: A Field Guide to Monkeywrenching.* 3d ed. Chico, CA: Abbzug Press, 1993.

Jackson, Wes. *Becoming Native to This Place.* New York: Counterpoint Press, 1996.

Jackson, Wes, and Wendell Berry. *New Roots for Agriculture.* Lincoln: University of Nebraska Press, 1985.

Jackson, Wes, Wendell Berry, and Bruce Colman, eds. *Meeting the Expectations of the Land: Essays in Sustainable Agriculture and Stewardship.* San Francisco: North Point Press, 1984.

Lipkis, Andy, and Katie Lipkis. *The Simple Act of Planting a Tree.* Los Angeles: Jeremy P. Tarcher, 1993.

Margolin, Malcolm. *The Ohlone Way: Indian Life in the San Francisco–Monterey Bay Area.* Berkeley, CA: Heyday Books, 2002.

Margolin, Malcolm. *The Way We Lived: California Indian Stories, Songs, and Reminiscences.* Berkeley, CA: Heyday Books, 2001.

Journals, Periodicals, and Newsletters

Acres U.S.A.—A Voice for Eco-Agriculture
P.O. Box 91299, Austin, TX 78709
512-892-4400, fax 512-892-4448
www.acresusa.com
editor@acresusa.com

News from Native California
P.O. Box 9145, Berkeley, CA 94610
510-549-2802, fax 510-549-1889
www.heydaybooks.com/news/
nnc@heydaybooks.com

Quivira Coalition Newsletter
1413 Second St., Ste. 1, Santa Fe, NM 87505
505-820-2544, fax 505-955-8922
www.quiviracoalition.org/documents/
newsletter.html

Part III. Graffiti in the Book of Life:
Genetic Engineering and the Vandalism of Nature

Organizations and Websites

David Suzuki Foundation
2211 West 4th Ave., Ste. 219
Vancouver, BC, Canada V6K 4S2
604-732-4228, fax 604-732-0752
www.davidsuzuki.org
solutions@davidsuzuki.org

Genetic Engineering Archive,
Greenpeace USA
702 H St. NW, Ste. 300
Washington, DC 20001
800-326-0959, fax 202-462-4507
www.greenpeaceusa.org/bin/view/fpl/
4794/cms_category/82.html

Norfolk Genetic Information Network
http://ngin.tripod.com
ngin@gmwatch.org

Organic Consumers Association
6101 Cliff Estate Rd., Little Marais, MN 55614
218-226-4164, fax 218-353-7652
www.organicconsumers.org

Soil Ecology Society
Ralph Boerner, Membership Information
Department of Evolution, Ecology, and
Organismal Biology
Ohio State University
104 Botany and Zoology Bldg.,
1735 Neil Ave.,
Columbus, OH 43210-1293
www.wcsu.edu/ses/ses.html
boerner.1@osu.edu

Soil Foodweb Inc.
1128 NE Second St., Ste. 120
Corvalis, OR 97330
541-752-5066, fax 541-752-5142
www.soilfoodweb.com

Soil Foodweb Inc. New York
555 Hallock Ave., Ste. 7
Port Jefferson Station, NY 11776
631-474-8848, fax 631-474-8847
www.soilfoodweb.com
soilfoodwebny@aol.com

Books

Pollan, Michael. *The Botany of Desire: A Plant's-Eye View of the World.* New York: Random House, 2001.

Pollan, Michael. *Second Nature.* London: Bloomsbury, 1999.

Suzuki, David T. *The Sacred Balance: Rediscovering Our Place in Nature.* Vancouver: Allen & Unwin, 1997.

Suzuki, David T. *Wisdom of the Elders: Honoring Sacred Native Visions of Nature.* 2d ed. New York: Bantam Books, 1993.

Journals, Periodicals, and Newsletters

GeneWatch
Council for Responsible Genetics
5 Upland Rd., Ste. 3, Cambridge, MA 02140
617-868-0870, fax 617-491-5344
www.gene-watch.org
crg@gene-watch.org

GM Watch and *Weekly Watch*
Norfolk Genetic Information Network
www.gmwatch.org
list@gmwatch.org

Organic Bytes, BioDemocracy News, and *Organic View*
Organic Consumers Association
6101 Cliff Estate Rd.,
Little Marais, MN 55614
218-226-4164, fax 218-353-7652
www.organicconsumers.org/publications.cfm

Part IV. The Industrial Evolution:
Biology Meets Business

Organizations and Websites

Adam Joseph Lewis Center for
Environmental Studies
Oberlin College
122 Elm St., Oberlin, OH 44074
440-775-8312, fax 440-775-8946
www.oberlin.edu/envs/ajlc
David.Orr@oberlin.edu

Center for Ecoliteracy
2522 San Pablo Ave., Berkeley, CA 94702
fax 510-845-1439
www.ecoliteracy.org
info@ecoliteracy.org

The Global Academy
1526 Stickney Point Rd., Sarasota, FL 34231
941-954-4456, fax 941-927-6887
www.theglobalacademy.org
info@theglobalacademy.org

Groxis Inc.
80 Liberty Ship Way, Ste. 1
Sausalito, CA 94965
415-331-0550
www.groxis.com
info@groxis.com

Hypercar, Inc.
220 East Cody Ln., Basalt, CO 81621
970-927-4556, fax 970-927-4593
www.hypercar.com
info@hypercar.com
open-source chronology:
www.rmi.org/sitepages/pid414.php

Natural Capital Institute
3B Gate Five Rd., Sausalito, CA 94965
415-331-6241, fax 415-331-6242
www.naturalcapital.org
info@naturalcapital.org

Rocky Mountain Institute
1739 Snowmass Creek Rd.
Snowmass, CO 81654-9199
970-927-3851
www.rmi.org

Books

Hawken, Paul. *The Ecology of Commerce.* New York: HarperCollins, 1993.

Hawken, Paul. *The Next Economy.* New York: Ballantine Books, 1984.

Hawken, Paul, Hunter L. Lovins, and Amory Lovins. *Natural Capitalism: Creating the Next Industrial Revolution.* New York: Little, Brown, 2000.

Lovins, Amory B. *Soft Energy Paths: Toward a Durable Peace.* San Francisco: Friends of the Earth International, 1977.

Lovins, Amory B., and Hunter L. Lovins. *Brittle Power: Energy Strategy for National Security.* Andover, MA: Brick House Publishing Company, 1982.

Motavalli, Jim. *Breaking Gridlock: Moving toward Transportation That Works.* San Francisco: Sierra Club Books, 2001.

Motavalli, Jim, ed. *Feeling the Heat: Dispatches from the Frontlines of Climate Change.* New York: Routledge, 2004.

Motavalli, Jim. *Forward Drive: The Race to Build "Clean" Cars for the Future.* San Francisco: Sierra Club Books, 2000.

Orr, David W. *Earth in Mind: On Education, Environment, and the Human Prospect.* Washington, DC: Island Press, 1994.

Orr, David W. *Ecological Literacy: Education and the Transition to a Postmodern World.* Albany: State University of New York Press, 1992.

Orr, David W. *The Nature of Design: Ecology, Culture, and Human Intention.* New York: Oxford University Press, 2002.

Womack, James P., and Daniel T. Jones. *Lean Thinking: Banish Waste and Create Wealth in Your Corporation.* Rev. ed. New York: Free Press, 2003.

Journals, Periodicals, and Newsletters

Conservation Biology
4245 N. Fairfax Dr., Ste. 400
Arlington, VA 22203
703-276-2384, fax 703-995-4633
www.conbio.org
info@conbio.org

E/The Environmental Magazine
28 Knight St., Norwalk, CT 06851
203-854-5559, fax 203-866-0602
www.emagazine.com
info@emagazine.com

Environmental Defense Newsletter
257 Park Ave. S., New York, NY 10010
212-505-2100, fax 212-505-2375
www.environmentaldefense.org/library.cfm
www.environmentaldefense.org

Hypercar, Inc.—Quarterly Newsletter
220 East Cody Ln., Basalt, CO 81621
970-927-4556, fax 970-927-4593
www.hypercar.com/pages/newsletter.php

RMI Solutions
1739 Snowmass Creek Rd.
Snowmass, CO 81654-9199
970-927-3851
www.rmi.org/sitepages/pid97.php

Part V. Natural Magic:
Spirit, Mystery, and Wonder

Organizations and Websites

All Species Foundation
P.O. Box 29462, San Francisco, CA 94129
415-561-585
www.all-species.org
info@all-species.org

Center for the Americas
College of Arts and Sciences
University at Buffalo, North Campus
1010 Clemens Hall, Buffalo, NY 14260-4630
716-645-2546, fax 716-645-5977
http://wings.buffalo.edu/cas/centers/cfta/
ydb@acsu.buffalo.edu

Cultures on the Edge
www.culturesontheedge.com

Ile Orunmila Oshun
3871 Piedmont Ave., No. 52
Oakland, CA 94611
www.ileorunmilaoshun.org
info@ileorunmilaoshun.org

Indigenous Environmental Network
P.O. Box 485, Bemidji, MN 56619
218-751-4967, fax 218-751-0561
www.ienearth.org
ien@igc.org

National Geographic Society
Explorer-in-Residence Program
P.O. Box 98199,
Washington, DC 20090-8199
800-647-5463
news.nationalgeographic.com/news/2002/
06/0627_020628_wadedavis.html
ngsforum@nationalgeographic.com

Rainforest Action Network
221 Pine St., Ste. 500
San Francisco, CA 94104
415-398-4404, fax 415-398-2732
www.ran.org
rainforest@ran.org

United Plant Savers
P.O. Box 400, East Barre, VT 05649
802-479-9825, fax 802-476-3722
www.unitedplantsavers.org
info@unitedplantsavers.org

Books

Davis, Wade. *Light at the Edge of the World: A Journey through the Realm of Vanishing Cultures.* Washington, DC: National Geographic Society, 2002.

Davis, Wade. *One River: Explorations and Discoveries in the Amazon Rain Forest.* Reprint. New York: Touchstone Books, 1997.

Davis, Wade. *The Serpent and the Rainbow.* 2d ed. New York: Touchstone Books, 1997.

Duke, James A., and Steven Foster. *Field Guide to Medicinal Plants and Herbs of Eastern and Central North America.* 2d ed. Boston: Houghton Mifflin, 1999.

Foster, Steven. *Herbal Renaissance.* Layton, UT: Gibbs Smith Publishers, 1993.

Mohawk, John. *Utopian Legacies: A History of Conquest and Oppression in the Western World.* Santa Fe: Clear Light Books, 2000.

Teish, Luisah. *Carnival of the Spirit: Seasonal Celebrations and Rites of Passage.* San Francisco: HarperCollins, 1994.

Teish, Luisah. *Jambalaya: The Natural Woman's Book of Personal Charms and Rituals.* San Francisco: HarperSanFrancisco, 1988.

Teish, Luisah. *Jump Up: Seasonal Celebrations from the World's Deep Traditions.* Berkeley, CA: Conari Press, 2000.

Williams, Terry Tempest. *Red: Passion and Patience in the Desert.* New York: Vintage Books, 2002.

Williams, Terry Tempest. *Refuge: An Unnatural History of Family and Place.* New York: Vintage Books, 1991.

Williams, Terry Tempest. *An Unspoken Hunger: Stories from the Field.* New York: Vintage Books, 1994.

Journals and Periodicals

Akwesasne Notes
Kahniakehaka Nation
Akwesasne Mohawk Territory
P.O. Box 366, Rooseveltown, NY 13683-0196
518-358-3326, fax 518-358-3488
www.ratical.org/AkwesasneNs.html

HerbalGram
American Botanical Council
6200 Manor Rd., Austin, TX 78723
512-926-4900, fax 512-926-2345
www.herbalgram.org
abc@herbalgram.org

Indian Country Today
3059 Seneca Turnpike, Canastota, NY 13032
888-327-1013
www.indiancountry.com

About Bioneers

Since 1990, Kenny Ausubel and Nina Simons have been assembling bioneers for an annual conference, a gathering of scientific and social innovators who have demonstrated visionary and practical models for restoring the earth and people.

Bioneers are biological pioneers who are working with nature to heal nature and to heal ourselves. They have peered deep into the heart of living systems to devise strategies for restoration based on nature's own operating instructions. They come from many diverse cultures and perspectives and from all walks of life.

Bioneers are scientists and artists, gardeners and economists, activists and public servants, architects and ecologists, farmers and journalists, priests and shamans, policymakers and everyday people committed to preserving and supporting the future of life on earth. They herald a dawning Age of Restoration founded in natural principles of kinship, interdependence, cooperation, reciprocity, and community.

Uniting nature, culture, and spirit, bioneers embody a change of heart, a spiritual connection with the living world that is also grounded in social justice. Their pragmatic strategies effectively address many of our most pressing ecological and societal challenges.

Above all, bioneers represent a culture of solutions. Their stories demonstrate that just as people have created the environmental and social problems we face, people can also solve them, through a reciprocal partnership with nature. Over and over, they show how great a difference the actions of one individual can make.

The Bioneers Conference is a "big tent" where people from many disparate yet related fields come together. The gathering cross-pollinates both issues and networks and serves as a fulcrum for cutting-edge ideas, resources, and connections. The conference has spawned several other projects that convey the inspiring bioneer culture to the greater public:

- *Beaming Bioneers* broadcasts live portions of the Bioneers Conference to partner sites as a focal point around which they organize their own conferences that address local issues and enhance community organizing efforts.

- The radio series *Bioneers: Revolution from the Heart of Nature* features personal interviews and dynamic presentations from the Bioneers Conferences. Each year, Bioneers provides thirteen half-hour programs free to public radio stations across the country and around the world. In 2003, the series won a prestigious Silver WorldMedal for excellence in environmental programming from the New York Festivals International Radio Programming Competition. In 2002, the series received a Bronze WorldMedal and was a finalist for the United Nations Department of Public Information Award. Each series is available for purchase in CD format from Bioneers.

- The Bioneers website (www.bioneers.org) offers a rich source of accessible information and connections to numerous other key groups and individuals working for ecological restoration and social justice.

- *Bioneers Buzz* is a monthly electronic newsletter that features news and updates on the activities of the Bioneers network. It is available by subscription through the website.

- *Bioneers Letter*, a biannual newsletter for members of Bioneers, features articles, program updates, and a calendar and networking section.

- The Bioneers Youth Initiative integrates young people into the Bioneers network and helps build connectivity among young activists year-round.

SEP 3 0 2004

Bioneers actively fosters the development of a vibrant network that supports and expands opportunities for young people who are seeking to create a restorative future.

- Bioneers presents "Wisdom at the End of a Hoe" training workshops led by top practitioners of sustainable agriculture and ecological restoration to equip farmers and gardeners with state-of-the-art knowledge on advanced ecological growing methods.

For more information about Bioneers, or to become a member, please visit www.bioneers.org or call toll-free 1-877-BIONEER.